TAX JUSTICE

Edited by Joseph J. Thorndike
and Dennis J. Ventry Jr.

Also of interest from the Urban Institute Press:

Property-Tax Exemption for Charities, edited by Evelyn Brody

State Tax Policy: A Political Perspective, by David Brunori

The Encyclopedia of Taxation and Tax Policy, edited by Joseph J. Cordes, Robert D. Ebel, and Jane G. Gravelle

The Future of State Taxation, edited by David Brunori

The Ongoing Debate

TAX JUSTICE

THE URBAN INSTITUTE PRESS
Washington, D.C.

THE URBAN INSTITUTE PRESS
2100 M Street, N.W.
Washington, DC 20037

Library of Congress Cataloging in Publication Data

Tax Justice: the ongoing debate / edited by Joseph J. Thorndike and Dennis J. Ventry Jr.
        p. cm.
Includes bibliographical references and index.
    ISBN 0-87766-707-1 (pbk.: alk. paper)
    1. Tax incidence—United States. 2. Taxation—United States. I. Thorndike, Joseph J. II. Ventry, Dennis J., Jr.
    HJ2322.A3 T313 2002
    336.2'9'0973—dc21

                                                        2002009712

ISBN 0-87766-707-1 (paper, alk. paper)

Printed in the United States of America

THE URBAN INSTITUTE is a nonprofit policy research and educational organization established in Washington, D.C., in 1968. Its staff investigates the social, economic, and governance problems confronting the nation and evaluates the public and private means to alleviate them. The Institute disseminates its research findings through publications, its web site, the media, seminars, and forums.

Through work that ranges from broad conceptual studies to administrative and technical assistance, Institute researchers contribute to the stock of knowledge available to guide decisionmaking in the public interest.

Conclusions or opinions expressed in Institute publications are those of the authors and do not necessarily reflect the views of officers or trustees of the Institute, advisory groups, or any organizations that provide financial support to the Institute.

Contents

Acknowledgments

W e are indebted to the many people who made this volume possible. We were privileged to work with many of the finest scholars in public finance. Richard Musgrave deserves special thanks, his work having inspired several generations of tax scholarship. David Brunori provided the initial encouragement for the collections, and we benefited from the sage advice of W. Elliot Brownlee during the formative stages of this project. Tom Field and Chris Bergin, both of Tax Analysts, have always understood the importance of tax justice, and they lent both institutional and intellectual support to this project. In fact, we owe a debt of gratitude to Tax Analysts in general, an organization that encourages vibrant debate about equity, fairness, and a host of other tax issues. The editors of the Urban Institute Press have been unfailingly helpful and patient in seeing this project through to its completion. Finally, our spouses, Frances Thorndike and Suzan Ventry, endured endless discussions of tax justice, but remained supportive and tolerant throughout.

Introduction

Tax Justice—The Uneasy Debate

Joseph J. Thorndike and Dennis J. Ventry Jr.

In 1953, Walter J. Blum and Harry Kalven Jr. published *The Uneasy Case for Progressive Taxation,* a short but influential essay on the politics and theory of vertical equity. Their work contributed to a vigorous debate over federal taxation that had been growing in the wake of World War II. A new Republican president was making the case for broad tax cuts, and a proposal to constitutionally cap income tax rates at 25 percent had attracted considerable support among both voters and elected officials.

Despite the clamor for tax cuts, a broad though somewhat vague political consensus supported progressivity. As Blum and Kalven acknowledged, "Progressive taxation is now regarded as one of the central ideas of modern democratic capitalism and is widely accepted as a secure policy commitment which does not require serious examination." They attributed this security to the idea's intrinsic—albeit nebulous—appeal: "Like most people today," they confessed, "we found the notion of progression immediately congenial" (2).

Blum and Kalven, however, were bent upon exploring the theoretical case for progressive taxation. After a rigorous examination, they acknowledged its weakness: "It is hard to gain much comfort," they concluded, "from the special arguments, however intricate their formulations, constructed on notions of benefit, sacrifice, ability to pay, or economic stability" (102). Ultimately, they suggested, the "stubborn but

1

uneasy" case for progressivity hinged on notions of equality and distributive justice.

Fifty Years Later

Blum and Kalven's essay breathed new life into debates over tax justice and quickly became a classic among scholars. As they pointed out, however, such debates are difficult to sustain; discussing equality raises unsettling questions about the nature of American society, inhibiting frank discussion. "The lingering fear," they suggested, "must always have been that any case for progression on these grounds proves too much" (85).

In the 50 years since the publication of *Uneasy Case*, Blum and Kalven have been proven right: The debate over tax fairness—at least among many tax experts—has often drifted from frank discussion of distributive justice toward the less "unsettling" ideas associated with horizontal equity—which holds that taxpayers with equal income should pay equal taxes. While questions of inequality have engaged the scholarly community as a whole—especially political scientists and legal scholars—tax experts have generally shied away from using the revenue system to address these concerns. Still, tax justice has remained a pillar of the *political* (if not the professional) tax debate. Progressivity retains its pride of place in popular discussions of tax reform; even proponents of the flat tax—a proposal rooted firmly in concern for horizontal equity—feel compelled to trumpet the progressivity of their ideas. Indeed, current debates over tax reduction and tax system replacement raise new questions about the meaning of tax justice and its relationship to progressivity.

The political importance of issues related to tax justice suggests the need to revisit this concept. This volume brings together perspectives on tax justice from nine leading experts. The contributions include historical evaluations of the U.S. tax system, theoretical explorations of distributive justice, and analyses of tax justice issues in contemporary policy debates. Together, they offer fresh insight into this politically potent subject.

The Musgrave "Equal-Worth" Metric

The book begins with a chapter by Richard A. Musgrave—perhaps the most influential voice in tax justice debates over the last 40 years. Musgrave first provides an overview of the two principal approaches to tax justice: benefit taxation and ability to pay. While acknowledging the contributions of both, he finds fault with each. The former, he suggests, sidesteps important issues of distributive justice, while the latter necessarily relies on problematic measurements of individual utility. Musgrave concludes that arguments for progressive taxation must find their roots in an ethical premise of equal worth. Drawing on the work of philosopher John Rawls, he argues that "there remains a presumption for progressive taxation, a case not based on a dubious behavioral assumption, but on what might be called good manners in a democratic society."

With this premise in mind, Musgrave moves on to assess several recent tax reform proposals, including the so-called flat tax and the unlimited savings allowance (USA) tax. He acknowledges the attractiveness of moving to a consumption base for the federal tax system, but suggests "it may well be the better part of wisdom to stay with the income base and push for improvement, rather than undertake a massive and untested conversion to consumption."

Three Historical Perspectives

Building on Musgrave's outline of the contemporary tax debate, chapters 2, 3, and 4 offer historical perspectives on the topic. Dennis J. Ventry Jr. begins with an overview of tax justice in the American political tradition, focusing on tax policy and politics since World War II. This period, Ventry maintains, witnessed the decline of vertical equity as a serious topic of study among tax experts, especially economists. Beginning in the 1950s, and accelerating in the 1970s, economists turned their attention away from vertical equity and toward efficiency and economic growth. To the extent that economists considered questions of tax equity, they examined how deviations from horizontal equity influenced efficiency and growth, rather than how degrees of vertical equity affected prevailing norms of social and economic justice. Ventry argues that this abandonment of progressive tax equity has left tax experts out of step with the American public—a public that continues to demonstrate a keen sensitivity to questions of fairness, justice, and progressivity. While taxpayers have endorsed reductions in marginal income tax rates, he warns, they have not demanded the elimination of progressive taxation.

In the second historical chapter, W. Elliot Brownlee examines the taxation of wealthy Americans. His chapter offers an assessment of current research on the historical effects of progressive taxation, including the impact of progressive tax structures on distributions of income and wealth, economic growth, and economic stability. A definitive history of tax justice in the United States, he asserts, must explore the *effects* of tax policy, not just its intentions. Historians, he maintains, must unravel the dynamic relationship between the development of tax policy and the economic context of such a development, a context that may be partially shaped by tax policies.

Brownlee considers how an improved understanding of the economic context of tax policy would help explain why policymakers have used various methods to advance the cause of tax justice. Specifically, Brownlee underscores the need for research on the linkages between institutional development and economic performance. A better sense of institutional history and of social learning, he argues, would help explain economic development, especially the emergence and spread of incentive systems that have promoted technological advance and investments in human capital.

Carolyn C. Jones offers a third historical perspective, providing a case study of conflicts over social justice within the Federal Council of Churches and its successor, the National Council of Churches (NCC). In the years after World War II, she notes, federated Protestantism provided a battleground for opposing visions of tax justice and Christianity. Commentators offered conflicting ideas about social justice, pitching collectivism against individualism and framing them in terms consistent with the geopolitical struggle of the Cold War. Both liberal Protestants and conservative forces seeking to influence the NCC took similar approaches to tax equity, viewing the topic as a component of more fundamental debates over the nation's economic system. While certain specific issues attracted attention—the inadequacy of depreciation allowances, the tax treatment of business losses, and the double taxation of corporate earnings—debates generally focused on larger issues of economic justice.

Jones finds that debates over tax justice among Protestant clergy and lay leaders tended to follow one of two lines. The first, which she calls the educative prototype, sought to promote economic knowledge among the clergy. Because of their perceived influence, clergy members found themselves the target of both conservative and liberal activists. As the government took a more active role in the economy, partly because of the continuation of the World War II tax regime, discussions of economics became more contentious and central to federated Protestantism.

A second, more overtly religious prototype centered on fundamental questions of the role of government and the nature of man. Libertarian and conservative Protestants supported an individualized approach to faith and salvation, assigning government only a minimal role. They cast redistributive taxation as misguided and fundamentally un-Christian, smacking of communism. For leading liberals, however, taxation was a means of coercing sinful and selfish people into doing what they knew was right. They built a case for redistributive taxation on theological arguments about justice, love, and the innate selfishness of men.

In all three of this book's historical chapters, questions of distributive justice loom large. Indeed, issues of inequality and what the government should do about it have animated political debates in almost every period of American history. Understanding distributive justice, however, is no small task; the topic has long been the focus of spirited debate among philosophers, political scientists, and legal scholars. Most of this debate touches on taxation only indirectly. This book, however, includes two contributions that seek to explore questions of distributive justice in the context of U.S. federal taxation.

Endowment As an Underlying Measure

In chapter 5, Daniel Shaviro scrutinizes the way we measure inequality—an important issue in tax justice debates that hinge on distributive justice. He suggests that traditional measures of inequality, including income, consumption, and wealth, fall short of being ideal yardsticks. Such measures, he contends, can only be justified as imperfect proxies for some underlying metric of inequality. In their place, Shaviro suggests the concept of endowment, also called "ability," "faculty," and "wage rate." He explores the relevance of endowment to distribution policy under welfarist and liberal egalitarian approaches to distributive justice.

Shaviro's chapter applies the theoretical to the practical, exploring how the concept of endowment can play a larger role in tax policymaking. "Discussions of endowment may seem far from the real-world choices we face in our tax system," he admits. But "a better understanding of one's underlying aims might encourage clearer thinking about the choices we face." His work suggests, for example, that debates about replacing the income tax with a consumption tax should focus more on how the competing tax bases might influence efficiency and distribution, and less on the ideological or philosophical arguments behind either tax base. Shaviro's analysis challenges theorists and policymakers to examine *how* we tax before we decide *what* to tax.

Demystifying the Flat Tax

Noting the widespread political support for a flat-rate tax system, Barbara Fried explores the fairness of proportional taxation. Rate structures themselves, she points out, are not the proper focus of fairness debates, because they are simply the policy incarnation of other prior moral commitments about the appropriate role of government. Consequently, Fried considers the case for proportionate taxation in the context of two prominent views of governmental power: libertarianism and social welfarism. She concludes that neither approach offers a sustainable rationale for proportionate taxation.

Fried goes on to debunk several arguments for proportionate taxation that do not, at least in theory, envision a larger role for government, including the idea that a flat-rate tax system strikes a victory for equality, minimizes distortions to individuals' choices among various activities, or curbs the expropriation of wealth by the political majority. Fried finds none of these arguments convincing, concluding that the popularity of proportionate tax schemes largely reflects their apparently simple mathematical premises as well as the political expediency they offer libertarians, who would be even more comfortable with a regressive rate system.

State and Local Debates

Reassessing the meaning and importance of tax justice requires attention to all levels of government. While federal issues dominate the national headlines, state and local taxes are the focus of at least as much voter interest. In fact, state-level antitax movements, a powerful political force for almost 30 years, have helped to engineer a realignment in

American politics. To shed light on these movements, in chapter 7 David Brunori evaluates tax justice in the U.S. states. Brunori delivers a stern indictment of state revenue systems, charging them with unnecessary regressivity. Conventional views among tax professionals, he argues, would have us believe that progressive tax systems are impossible on the state level, in large part because businesses and households are thought to be highly mobile. High taxes, state legislators fear, will promote an outflow of people, business, and money to other locales with lower tax burdens. In addition, Brunori says, potent political opposition to any sort of tax increase makes it difficult in many states to restructure revenue systems. The spread of direct democracy efforts (including initiatives and referenda) also tend to thwart efforts to shift tax burdens toward businesses or wealthy individuals.

While acknowledging the economic and political obstacles to more progressive state tax systems, Brunori rejects the idea that regressive taxes are inevitable. He urges legislators to remain skeptical about claims of capital and household mobility. Furthermore, he encourages them to avoid the use of targeted business tax incentives that worsen already unjust tax systems. In his view, many of the arguments used to justify targeted tax breaks rest on flimsy evidence. Rather, they further erode the progressive qualities of state tax systems.

Joan M. Youngman offers a view of tax justice from the local perspective, analyzing the role of property taxes in local finance. She takes an objective view of this traditionally contentious tax—the cause of numerous tax revolts since its inception, particularly during the last 30 years. Her contribution distinguishes between questions of fairness about the structure and administration of the tax and questions that relate specifically to property rights. Property tax professionals, she notes, can bolster the fairness of the tax by improving the related valuation, collection, and enforcement processes.

Putting administration issues aside, Youngman emphasizes that the property tax's very essence—its continuing public claim on privately owned real property—accounts for both its enduring strengths and its enduring unpopularity. The levy's visibility, she contends, is valuable, promoting accountability in government. In addition, its independence from other tax systems (both federal and state) makes it a solid, dependable foundation for local finance. Youngman urges tax experts and policymakers not to lose sight of these merits in the debate over administration issues.

Justice by Analysis Not Aesthetics

The book concludes with a chapter by C. Eugene Steuerle, one of Washington's most prominent tax experts and the veteran of many years in the federal tax policymaking process. Steuerle makes a strong case for the importance of equity concerns in the crafting of workable tax policy. He begins with an outline of key issues, such as the definition of tax justice, its relationship to other goals (including economic efficiency), and the inherent tension between individual freedom and progressive tax structures. Steuerle acknowledges the numerous complexities involved in translating theory into practice, but he highlights ways that rigorous analysis can effectively identify workable approaches.

Steuerle notes that determining the appropriate degree of progressivity has always been a sticking point for policymakers charged with designing a tax system. Many economists faced with the same problem have thrown up their hands, relegating the answer to the realm of aesthetics, not analytical thought. Steuerle rejects this view, contending that economists in particular have an important contribution to make. Economists, he says, should reclaim "the equity ground on which policymakers instinctively move, and on which economists from Adam Smith to Richard Musgrave quite naturally walked."

Taken together, these chapters are intended to raise new questions— and to unearth old ones. Tax justice has too often been relegated to the sidelines by tax experts, especially those charged with crafting government policy. When contemplating the harsh reality of a budget deficit or the happier possibility of a budget surplus, questions of justice and equity should remain central to the public debate.

REFERENCE

Blum, Walter, and Harry Kalven Jr. 1953. *The Uneasy Case for Progressive Taxation.* Chicago: University of Chicago Press.

1

Equity and the Case for Progressive Taxation

Richard A. Musgrave

The debate over tax equity—how taxes should be distributed among the public—has a long and spirited history (Blum and Kalven 1953; Fagan 1938; Groves 1974; Seligman 1908). Economists, social philosophers, and political theorists have all had their say, and much can be learned from them. Two dimensions of tax equity, horizontal and vertical equity, are distinguished.

The principle of horizontal equity—that people in equal positions should be treated equally—is hardly debatable. A democratic society should not permit arbitrary discrimination. Questions remain about how equal positions should be defined and about how tax laws should be formulated to secure equal treatment, but the principle of equal treatment is the basic rule.

Matters are less clear-cut when it comes to the principle of vertical equity, that is, how taxation among unequals should differ. For vertical equity to be achieved, horizontal equity must also prevail. Horizontal equity, however, may coexist with various views of the vertical dimension (Musgrave 1990). Most observers agree that the tax bill should rise with income, but how fast should it rise? Choosing among the patterns of differentiation—whether tax rates should be regressive, proportional, or progressive—is controversial. This should not be surprising. Vertical equity, after all, is part of the larger problem of distributive justice, an issue that has no simple answer.

At the same time, vertical equity should not be viewed as a matter of personal taste only, a preference so subjective in nature that nothing useful can be said about it. While there may be no single answer, not all views of equity are equally good or bad. Careful analysis, past and present, yields meaningful formulations. Though equity in taxation is more complex than its economic effects, equity is not thereby rendered less important. A good tax system must allow for both.

Taxation, to begin with, is needed to pay for public services. As Adam Smith put it, the sovereign must protect his subjects against foreign invasion, and he must protect individuals against injustice from others. In addition, his duties call for "erecting and maintaining those public institutions and those public works which, though they may be in the highest degree advantageous to a great society are, however, of such a nature that the profits could never repay the expenses to any individual or small number of individuals, and which it therefore cannot be expected that any individuals or small number of individuals should erect" (Smith 1776, 185). Smith recognized that certain services, as later analysis showed, cannot be provided privately because their consumption is nonrival in nature. Consumption by any one person does not interfere with that by another. Use of these services should not be restricted. Individuals, therefore, will act as "free riders" and fail to contribute voluntarily. Assessments must be determined and people be required to pay accordingly. The question, then, is how to do this fairly.

Adam Smith provided an initial answer. "The subjects of every state," he argued, "ought to contribute towards the support of the government, as nearly as possible in proportion to their respective abilities, that is in proportion to the revenue which they respectively enjoy under the protection of the state" (1776, 310). Here, Smith combined the two distinct tracks along which later developments proceeded—benefits received and ability-to-pay views of tax equity. The benefit principle sees taxes as prices paid for public services. The ability-to-pay principle separates tax equity from the expenditure side of the budget and views equity in taxation as a problem of "fair taking." The benefit principle is distributionally neutral, while the ability-to-pay principle is not. Equity in taxation now raises issues of distributive justice.

Benefit Taxation

While the concept of "ability to pay" appeared in Smith's formulation, his was essentially a benefit perspective. Benefits are received in the form of protection given to income, income creates ability to pay, and benefits are valued in line with that ability. While focus on protection takes too narrow a view of state services, the underlying principle is clear. The rationale of equitable taxation is similar to that principle underlying consumer payments for private goods. It is fair that people should pay according to the marginal benefit that they receive.

Principle

This principle of equitable pricing holds for both public and private goods, but with an important difference. When consumers purchase private goods in the market, they will pay the same price and, in line with their preferences and incomes, they will purchase different amounts. In the case of public services, such as national defense, all enjoy the same level of service, but they will value it differently. The marginal utility of income tends to fall as income rises, so that taxpayers with higher incomes value public services more highly and should pay a higher price. Smith's suggestion that tax assessments should double as income doubles (proportional taxation) sounds appealing, but it need not hold. Depending on the slope of the income utility schedule, the benefit rule may also call for a rising ratio of tax to income as income rises (progressive taxation).[1]

Benefit taxation, by charging in line with the marginal utility which the taxpayer derives, serves as a guide to the efficient provision of public goods. In this respect, benefit taxation is similar to the competitive market pricing of private goods. But is it equitable as well? The answer again parallels that for the pricing of private goods. As seen by the philosophy of the Enlightenment and John Locke's vision of a natural order (1790, 329), divine law entitles individuals to their earnings and to the welfare they derive from the purchase of private goods. The competitive market is not only efficient but also equitable. Public goods under benefit taxation are paid for by the same rule, so that benefit taxation is equitable as well.

The view of distributive justice as entitlement to earnings has a distinguished tradition, one that retains a place in the current debate (Nozick 1974, ch. 7). Nevertheless, the need for some qualification is widely accepted. Adam Smith, while sharing Locke's basic view of a natural order and its entitlement claims, recognized that public policy should address extreme cases of poverty, and most current observers agree that provision of a social safety net is a matter of public concern. Without thereby questioning the institution of private property and its essential place in the social order, some adjustments of market outcomes are required. For the benefit rule to be just, as well as efficient, as Knut Wicksell argued, it would therefore have to be applied to a just state of pretax distribution (Wicksell 1886, 108).[2]

Implementation

The principle of benefit taxation is clear, but its implementation is difficult. Government, to charge benefit taxes, must know how individuals value the benefits they receive from public services, that is, the price they would be willing to pay to obtain them. That premise, unfortunately, is unrealistic. Public goods, as noted before, differ from private goods in an important respect. The consumption of private goods is rival and excludable. In order to obtain them, they must be purchased in the market. Consumers must reveal their preferences by deciding how much to purchase at the market price. Suppliers can respond to this information, and an efficient provision results. In the case of public goods, consumers have no such compulsion. Public services (e.g., the protection afforded by national defense or the guidance given by John Stuart Mill's lighthouse [Mill 1848, 342]), are nonrival in consumption, and exclusion may be impossible or difficult. Moreover, even if possible, limiting access to nonrival goods would be inefficient. With the benefits of public services available free of charge, some consumers, as noted, will act as "free riders," preventing the tax assessor from ascertaining the correct benefit charge. Benefit taxation—even if called for in principle— seems inapplicable in practice.

Nevertheless, the case for applying benefit taxation is not hopeless. Direct implementation becomes possible in certain settings. Expenditure benefits may attach to particular objects and locations, and may therefore be charged to those who benefit. For example, the costs of cleaning a particular street might be billed to the residents of that street, who benefit, or the costs of maintaining a highway might be charged to the road's users, although toll booths will be efficient only in hours of excess capacity, when there will be no crowding out of other users.

Where benefits from public services are spatially limited, the "free rider" problem may be overcome by the beneficiaries themselves, with citizens revealing their preferences by "voting with their feet." This is especially applicable to local finance. For example, residents of a metropolitan area may find it to their advantage to move to a location where public services, such as schools, are to their liking (Tiebout 1956). Such voting may then result in equal-preference, equal-income communities where agreed-upon services are supported by benefit taxation. "Clubs" may be formed to supply "club goods" to their members (Buchanan 1965) and thereby offer a market-like solution for the case of nonrival but excludable public goods. However, this option requires that nonmembers are excluded by zoning; it is available only where location choice, as may be the case in urban settings, can be guided by fiscal considerations and is not dominated by employment and other market factors.

More generally, voting by ballot rather than "by foot" must be relied upon to determine what is to be provided and who is to pay. Individuals, when voting on a budget proposal for specified items and their financing, know that they must comply with the outcome. Hence, they will vote according to their own preferences. The tax-expenditure vote becomes an instrument for revealing preferences, as well as for collecting revenue. This process reflects Knut Wicksell's century-old vision of a succession of budget votes (based on a unanimity or close-to-unanimity rule) that would lead to an agreed-upon, benefit tax–based budget solution (Wicksell 1886). An operational remedy to the "free rider" problem is offered, but difficulties remain. The transaction costs of successive voting cannot be overlooked, a unanimity rule is impracticable, and voting mechanisms are imperfect (Mueller 1989). Moreover, voters will intertwine distributional goals with their evaluation of public goods. Nevertheless, budget determination by voting with its link to benefit taxation is the best that can be done.

Taxation in Line with Ability to Pay

Having discussed the benefit principle, we now turn to the quite different concept of ability-to-pay taxation. Contrary to the benefit rule, which encompasses both the tax and expenditure sides of the budget, the ability-to-pay principle views equity as a one-sided problem in taking only; that is, it argues for a just distribution of the tax burden imposed by raising a given amount of revenue, regardless of benefits received. Taxation as taking thereby discards the Lockean concept of entitlement to earnings, the premise that underlies the equity case for benefit taxation, and applies a standard of fairness, or "just taking," a standard that rests on the fairness of the underlying pretax state of distribution. Such a standard grew out of the utilitarian framework of Jeremy Bentham and his successors. Equitable taxation no longer had to be distributionally neutral; instead it became part of the broader problem of how society should view income distribution.

Equal-Sacrifice Rules

The burden of taxation was then thought of as the sacrifice made when the tax is paid, and equity called for an equal sacrifice to be imposed on all people (Mill 1848). That rule, however, did not mean an equal amount of tax. The marginal utility of income is taken to fall as income rises, and the sacrifice imposed by a dollar of tax declines. Moreover, similar marginal utility of income schedules are taken to apply to all individuals. Based on these assumptions, it followed that the same tax should be paid by people with similar incomes and that tax payments should rise with income. At this stage, the concept of equal sacrifice needed closer interpretation. Some would call for the absolute level of sacrifice to be the same for taxpayers at all levels of income, as did Sidgwick (1883, 562). Under that rule, tax rates would be progressive, proportional, or regressive, depending on whether the elasticity of marginal income utility with respect to income is greater than, equal to, or short of unity. Other theorists, such as Mill (1848, 155), called for sacrifice to be proportional to the taxpayer's pretax level of welfare, requiring a more complex pattern of tax rates.

These rules, drawn from ethical perceptions of fairness, did not easily fit the economists' way of thinking, and a third concept calling for equal marginal sacrifice was proposed (Carver 1895; Edgeworth 1910; Pigou 1928). That rule would not only be equitable but would also maximize the community's aggregate welfare. What had been a search for fairness now became a rule of utilitarian efficiency. Least total or equal marginal sacrifice was enshrined (Pigou 1928, 59) as the ultimate principle of taxation. Because marginal sacrifice falls as income rises, this called for maximum progression, that is, lopping off income from the top down until the tax system cumulates the required revenue. That, however, is qualified by allowance for detrimental taxation effects, which cause the taxpayer's burden to exceed what the government gets. That loss rises with the marginal rate of tax and thereby dampens the case for progressive taxation. Concern with the efficiency effects of taxation, raised early on by Pigou, later moved to the forefront of tax analysis and came to be viewed as the central criterion for a system of "optimal taxation" (Diamond and Mirrlees 1971).

Critics soon questioned the two basic assumptions underpinning the utilitarian case for progressive taxation. They questioned whether the marginal utility of income falls with rising income and whether different individuals will derive equal utility from similar incomes (Robbins 1935). While the first premise seems plausible as a general rule, it need not always hold nor can it be tested readily. The second premise is more dubious and again does not lend itself to verification. Thus, the utilitarian case for progressive taxation was found "uneasy" (Blum and Kalven 1953), one that could not be demonstrated by scientific tests. That traditional case had been shaken by its roots, but new perspectives soon emerged.

Fair Taxation

A social welfare function was to be formulated, which would show how to best use economic resources. Set within the framework of Pareto efficiency—where arrangement "A" is preferable to arrangement "B" if one person is made better off and no one is left worse off. That rule, although a powerful tool for securing the efficient use of resources under a given state of distribution, does not permit outcomes to be ranked across different states of distribution. As a result, it did not permit choosing between alternative ways of raising a given revenue, a choice in which one party is bound to lose while another gains. A social welfare function capable to address that problem was needed.

Social Welfare Function

Attempts to define that function without involving comparison of cardinal utility levels across individuals did not succeed, yet such comparisons are necessary for aggregate welfare to be measured and alternative states of distribution to be compared. Reaching beyond Pareto optimality, welfare must be compared across individuals, and their capacity to derive welfare is taken to be the same. Thereby, postulates underlying the traditional model reappear, but they are no longer viewed as a clinical finding. Rather, they rest on a social contract, reflecting the community's judgment of what constitutes distributive justice.

How can a community arrive at such a judgment? Bentham thought that rational people, acting in their self-interest, will seek to maximize not only their own happiness, but also society's as a whole, thereby calling for an egalitarian solution (Bentham 1789). But why should people with superior potential agree to surrender their advantage and divide it with others? As Hobbes suggested earlier (1651), people will find it in their self-interest to seek the protection of a civil society and to offer some cooperation to achieve it, but this rationale falls far short of supporting Bentham's vision wherein people agree to maximize the welfare of the whole. For this broader goal, a motivation other than self-interest and an ethical norm of social behavior are required. The community must choose a social contract expressing its judgment of what constitutes distributive justice in a fair society.

Rules of Fairness

More recent discussions of distributive justice have attempted to arrive at such a formulation. Differing endowments and market earnings, contrary to the Lockean premise, do not carry a claim to entitlement; nor does self-interest point to the solution. To determine a just state of distribution, a rule of fairness has to be agreed upon. In line with Western tradition, the Golden Rule and principle of equal worth offer an appealing formulation. In that spirit, inequality is to be accepted only when it serves to improve the position of the least advantaged (Rawls 1971). Individuals are to choose among alternative states of distribution in an impartial fashion, that is, from behind a veil of ignorance, without knowing their own ultimate position in the chosen distribution. Thus seen, the problem is one of choice under uncertainty, and depends on risk aversion (Harsanyi 1955). Assuming extreme risk aversion, a "maxi-min" distribution that maximizes the welfare of the lowest member will be chosen (Rawls 1971, 154). A lower degree of progression follows for reduced risk aversion. A utilitarian view of distribution as a matter of rational choice is thus retained, but only after incorporating the ethical premise that individuals will agree to choose from behind a veil of ignorance.[3]

This reasoning, directed at the overall state of distribution, also applies to the narrower issue of raising a given amount of revenue. Taxpayers now choose among alternative rate schedules that yield the required revenue. Choosing from behind a veil, they do not know what their applicable rate bracket will be. In line with the maxi-min rule, and absent detrimental taxation effects, the case would again be for maximum progression, with income lopped off from the top down. But once more, detrimental taxation effects enter and limit what can be taken from the upper end of the income scale.

The case for progressive taxation, as it emerges from this discussion, dispells the "uneasy case" objection raised against Pigou's least total sacrifice rule. The assumptions that marginal utility of income schedules, as a matter of observation, are downward sloping and similar across individuals are no longer needed. Instead, the case for progressive taxation follows from acceptance of the ethical premise of equal worth and a setting in which individuals will agree to choose impartially. Against this background, the case for progressive taxation holds up, not based on dubious clinical assumptions, but on what might be called good manners in a democratic society.

Current Issues in Tax Reform

Beginning with the Sixteenth Amendment, and reinforced three decades later by the massive expansion of federal budgets in World War II, the personal income tax came to be seen as the best way to meet the standards of equitable and fair taxation at the federal level. Based on a broad definition of taxable income—ideally measured as accretion to wealth—it would best serve the requirement of horizontal equity, and assessed at progressive rates, it would secure a fair vertical distribution of the burden across income groups. The individual income tax base was incomplete to begin with and continuous battles were needed to protect it against further erosion—a sequence last played out by the base-broadening tax reform of 1986 and the renewed backsliding since then. In particular, credits and deductions from income tax are used to implement costly policy goals by apparent tax reduction. Tax rates as well were subject to frequent changes. Modest at the outset, they rose sharply during World War II when a drastic cut of personal exemptions transformed the income tax into a mass tax. Top rates reached 92 percent, declined to 32 percent by 1982, and then rose to their current 39.6 percent.

Controversy also extended to the corporation income tax. The treatment of strategic items in its base, such as depreciation, was a matter of continuing controversy, as was the issue of "double taxation," posed by the taxation of profits at the corporate level and of dividends at the personal level. Full integration of the two taxes was proposed by purist reformers—a plan that would have included total profits (whether distributed or retained) in the shareholder's personal income tax base along with repeal of the separate corporation tax—but this found little support. Instead, the absolute corporation tax was retained, along with giving partial relief to the shareholder.

Income taxation, as this brief survey shows, had its ups and downs throughout the years. Nevertheless, until more recently, the principle of progressive and personal income taxation remained the standard around which tax reformers could rally. That standard has retained its defenders, but it has increasingly come under fire. Some critics fault the income tax as too complex and imperfect in application. Others dislike it as a vehicle of progressive taxation, and replacement by a sales or value-added tax has been a long-standing proposal.

Still others critique the income base in principle, and recently a set of new reform plans has been offered to replace it. Most prominently, these include the "flat tax" plan offered by Hall and Rabushka (1983) and the USA (unlimited savings allowance) plan submitted by Senators Nunn and Dominici (*Tax Notes* 1996). The former proposal replaces progression with a flat rate and limits the tax base to wage income only. The latter retains rate progression but replaces income with consumption as base.

Flat-Rate Tax

We begin with Hall and Rabushka's proposal for substitution of a flat rate. For revenue to remain constant and applied to the income tax base, this would call for replacing the present 15.0 to 39.6 percent schedule by a rate of close to 20 percent. As a result, bracket rates applicable at the top would be sharply reduced, while lower-bracket rates would have to be raised. The change would shift the tax burden downward. On closer consideration, however, this shift to a flat rate, in effect, retains an element of progressivity in the lower- to middle-income range. Bracket rates apply to taxable income only, that is, to adjusted gross income (AGI) minus an initial tax-free amount comprising the personal exemption and standard deduction. That allowance is equivalent to a zero-bracket rate. Thus, the flat rate in effect leaves a two-bracket system. As AGI rises, the initial tax-free amount declines in importance, resulting in a rising ratio of tax to AGI. The declining weight of the initial allowance causes the ratio of tax to AGI (the effective tax rate, the true measure of progression) to rise, a feature that dominates the effective rate curve well up to the middle of the income scale.

Due to retention of an initial allowance, the transition to a flat rate would not greatly add to the tax burden of people at the lower end of the income spectrum. The major consequence of moving to a flat rate is a downward shift in the tax burden from the upper end to the mid-upper range. With nearly 50 percent of the current tax base, and 60 percent of revenue, accounted for by the top 10 percent of returns, the resulting shift to the middle of the income spectrum would be substantial. The equity of such a shift may well be questioned, especially in view of the increase in inequality that occurred during the 1990s, with a sharp rise in the income share going to the top end of the scale.

Matters of equity aside, proponents argue that the flat rate would bring about tax simplification. With only a single rate, taxpayers would no longer need to apply successive bracket rates to compute their liability. While true, little would be gained, since liabilities under progressive rates need not be computed but are read off from readily available tax tables. In order to achieve a major simplification of personal returns, legislators would have to combine rate flattening with a drastic broadening of the tax base to disallow uncalled-for exclusions and deductions. More drastic simplification would go further, disallowing the initial tax-free amount. The tax could then be withheld at the company level, eliminating the need for personal returns. This approach, however, would greatly increase the burden at the lower end and surrender the principle of personal and ability-to-pay–based taxation. Ultimately, the income base would then be used in the same crude way as currently applies to the consumption base via retail sales and value-added taxes.

Unnecessary complication in the tax code should, of course, be avoided, but the case for simplification also has limits. It stands to reason that equitable taxation in a complex world cannot be expedited via postcard returns, especially not for the upper-income ranges. Paying taxes is a price of civilization, as Justice Oliver Wendell Holmes said, and a price worth paying.

Change to Consumption Base

Next to a change in rates, a change in tax base is proposed. The case for a consumption base, made by the USA plan, is not a new one, and it has been advanced over time for different reasons. Thomas Hobbes (1651) thought it fair to tax people on what is consumed rather than on what is set aside. Nicholas Kaldor (1955) thought that higher incomes could be reached more effectively by taxing consumption. The main case against the income tax, however, advanced by Mill (1848) and later on by Irving Fisher (1942) and economic theorists that followed, faulted the income tax base for double taxing its interest component.

Under the income tax, income from all sources is taxed upon receipt, and may then be consumed without further taxation. But if saved and set aside for future consumption, the interest on savings is taxed again, resulting in double taxation. This double taxation is unfair, the argument goes, because it violates the principle of horizontal equity. Moreover, it discriminates against future consumption compared with present consumption, creating distortion in the efficient timing of consumption. This discrimination against saving or interest income may be removed by dropping the income tax and taxing consumption when it occurs.

The case for taxing the consumption base has merit, but it is not conclusive. A good argument can be made also in support of income, or accretion, as the proper measure of taxable capacity. The very holding of wealth carries benefits prior to future consumption. Those benefits are not part of the consumption base and would require a supplementary tax on the holding of wealth. Moreover, not all income is consumed by the recipient, making a supplementary tax on bequests necessary. At the same time, the USA tax is superior to traditional consumption taxes of the retail sales or value-added type, which apply in *in rem* form and leave a regressive distribution of the tax burden. That objection no longer holds for the USA plan, which taxes at the personal level, allows for a tax-free minimum (a zero-rate bracket), and applies progressive rates to the remainder of the consumption base.

Implementation of the USA plan involves two steps. First, it eliminates the corporation profits tax, along with the many difficulties encountered in measuring corporate profits, and replaces it with a cash flow–type business tax. The base of the business tax is defined as gross receipts minus operating expenses and investment outlays. Thus, the base differs from the profits tax by permitting taxpayers to expense investments instead of deducting them over the life of the asset. In this way, taxpayers experience a gain equal to the present value of the tax, discounted at the normal rate of return. The normal return to capital is thus excluded from taxation, with only above-normal returns subject to tax. The company tax base, in effect, equals that of a consumption-type value-added tax. While referred to somewhat misleadingly as a business tax, it far from replaces the current profits tax.

The base of the personal tax component of the USA tax is similarly defined in cash flow terms. Rather than requiring taxpayers to add their grocery bills, which would be impracticable, the base is to be determined as the difference between cash receipts (including cash income, borrowing, and sale of assets) and cash uses that are not consumption related (i.e., debt repayment, acquisition of assets, and accumulation of balances). To assure compliance, cash transactions would have to be conducted with the use of certified accounts, which would require auditing and control. If successful, the elimination of special credits and deductions, which now plague the income tax, would simplify the returns. However, political pressures now supporting income tax loopholes, such as the deduction of mortgage interest and preferential treatment of capital gains, would likely reappear in some form. New problems, such as the control of certified accounts and drawing of a line between the acquisition of durables and investment, would also have to be met. In all, the simplification gained by thus replacing the income tax may prove less than promised by the proponents of the USA plan.

Change to Wage-Income Base

The flat-tax plan, like the USA plan, abandons the income tax base but replaces it with a tax on wage income only. Like the USA tax, it also replaces the corporation tax by a cash-flow tax, with investment reported as an expense when made. The plan differs, however, in that wage payments are excluded from the business base and taxed at the recipient level. With wage payments excluded, the base of the business tax by this amount falls short of a value-added tax base. At the personal level, an initial tax-free amount is allowed as under the USA tax, but then a flat rate of 17 percent is applied. The wage base is readily measured and in this respect is much preferable to the consumption base, but how do the two bases compare on grounds of horizontal equity?

As noted, both procedures avoid "double taxation," one by exemption of interest as seen from the income sources side and the other by exemption of savings from the uses side. On closer consideration, the claim of similarity holds true only under rather restrictive assumptions and at an aggregative level.[4] It need not hold at an annual level and for individual taxpayers. Taxing consumption only when seen from the income use side may appear as rewarding the prudent—at least it did in a more puritan age. However, leaving capital income tax free while taxing wage income only seems unfair when viewed from the income sources side. If anything, the traditional distinction between "earned" and "unearned" income, as used in the tax code and made in the language of the earned-income credit, seems to point in the other direction. Why should the disutility of surrendering leisure be disregarded, while allowing for the disutility of postponing consumption?

In all, the consumption base, though more complex in administration, seems preferable to the wage base. At the same time, it may well be wiser to stay with the income base and push for its improvement than to undertake a massive and untested conversion to consumption.

Devolution and Globalization

It is not surprising that progressive taxation has been the prerogative of central government finance. Income taxes at the lower levels of government, such as those imposed by the states, stop at bracket rates much below those of the federal tax, and local governments rarely use such taxation. There are two reasons for this. First, the comprehensive income base needed for progressive taxation calls for inclusion of all income, whatever its source, and this information cannot be accessed readily by lower levels of government. Second, lower-level governments' capacity to engage in progressive taxation is constrained by the risk they face of losing their tax base to other lower-tax jurisdictions. "Voting by feet" again enters the equation, but not (as noted previously) to share common likes for public goods, but to escape their common dislike of taxation. Progressive taxation is therefore impeded, especially since capital is the more mobile factor, and capital income weighs more heavily when moving up the income scale. Devolution of expenditure functions, if combined with federal grants, need not have this effect, but devolution of the taxing function inevitably retards progressive taxation. What some observers see as an unhappy by-product of devolution, others will see as a sound reason for undertaking devolution.

These considerations, applicable to all levels of taxation within a nation, also apply to central governments operating in an international setting. With increased involvement in trade and greater capital movement across national boundaries, progressive taxation, especially of capital income, becomes increasingly difficult to achieve at both the personal or corporate level. As the development of recent years has shown, the desire to attract capital or to prevent outflow leads to downward competition, uniformity, and the flattening of tax rates. International tax coordination could serve to neutralize such effects but is not in the cards. These built-in forces of globalization, rather than domestically held views of distributive justice, may well determine the future of progressive income taxation.

NOTES

1. The outcome depends on the ratio of the price elasticity of demand for public goods to its income elasticity. Depending on whether that ratio exceeds, equals, or falls short of unity, the tax rates rise, remain unchanged, or fall with income.

2. This condition cannot be met by attaching surcharges to benefit taxation, thereby destroying its efficiency claim. Rather, the solution calls for a budget system that combines an "allocation branch" of benefit tax–financed public services with a "distribution branch" designed to correct the state of distribution through a tax-transfer system (Musgrave 1959, ch. 1). Both systems are needed if benefit taxation is to be just, as well as efficient. Though benefit taxation by itself involves no redistribution, the broader problem of distributive justice nevertheless remains in sight.

3. Rawls (1974, 164) subsequently distanced himself from this somewhat awkward formulation, in which the ethical premise of impartial choice is followed by self-interested utility maximization under uncertainty (Musgrave 1992). As restated, Rawls's case for maxi-min is founded more broadly, based on the ethical premise of citizens as free and equal persons.

4. Consider a competitive, closed economy without a public sector. For this economy as a whole, total income sources or gross national income (including wages and gross return to capital) equals gross national product or total income uses (including consumption, maintenance of, and addition to capital stock). In a stationary and competitive economy, the gross return to capital will equal maintenance and no addition will be made to the capital stock, thus leaving wages to equal consumption. This condition, however, does not necessarily hold in a growing economy, and the equality applicable to the economy as a whole also does not necessarily apply to the accounts of its individual members.

REFERENCES

Bentham, Jeremy. 1789. *An Introduction to the Principles of Morals and Legislation.* Edited by James H. Burns and Herbert L. Hart. 1970. London: Hafner.

———. 1802. "Principles of the Civil Code." In *The Works of Jeremy Bentham.* Vol. 1, edited by J. Bowring. 1931. New York: Clarendon.

Blum, Walter, and Harry J. Kalven Jr. 1953. *The Uneasy Case for Progressive Taxation.* Chicago: University of Chicago Press.

Buchanan, James. 1965. "An Economic Theory of Clubs." *Economica* 32 (125): 1–14.

Carver, Thomas. 1895. "The Ethical Basis of Distribution and Its Application to Taxation." *Annals* 6: 79–99.

Diamond, Peter, and James Mirrlees. 1971. "Optimal Taxation and Public Production." *American Economic Review* 61 (1): 8–27.

Edgeworth, Francis. 1910. "The Subjective Element in the First Principles of Taxation." *Quarterly Journal of Economics* 24 (3): 459–70.

Fagan, Elmer D. 1938. "Recent and Contemporary Theories of Progressive Taxation." *Journal of Political Economy* 46 (4): 457–98.

Fisher, Irving. 1942. *Constructive Income Taxation.* New York: Harper.

Groves, Harold. 1974. *Tax Philosophers.* Edited by Donald J. Curran. Madison: University of Wisconsin Press.

Hall, Robert E., and Alvin Rabushka. 1983. *Low Tax, Simple Tax, Flat Tax.* New York: McGraw-Hill.

Harsanyi, John. 1955. "Cardinal Welfare, Individualistic Ethics, and Interpersonal Comparison of Utility." *Journal of Political Economy* 63 (4): 309–21.

Hobbes, Thomas. 1651. *Leviathan.* Edited by C. B. Macpherson. 1968. London: Pelican Classics.

Kaldor, Nicholas. 1955. *An Expenditure Tax.* London: Allen.

Locke, John. 1790. *Two Treatises of Government.* Edited by Peter Laslett. 1967. Cambridge: Cambridge University Press.

Mill, John Stuart. 1848. *Principles of Political Economy.* London: Penguin.

Mueller, Dennis C. 1989. *Public Choice II.* Cambridge: Cambridge University Press.

Musgrave, Richard A. 1959. *The Theory of Public Finance.* New York: McGraw-Hill.

———. 1990. "Horizontal Equity, Once More." *National Tax Journal* 43: 113–32.

———. 1992. "Social Contract, Taxation and the Standing of Deadweight Loss." *Journal of Public Economics* 49 (3): 369–81.

Nozick, Robert. 1974. *Anarchy, State, and Utopia.* New York: Basic Books.

Pigou, Arthur C. 1928. *A Study in Public Finance.* London: Macmillan.

Rawls, John. 1971. *A Theory of Justice.* Cambridge: Harvard University Press, Belknap Press.

———. 1974. "Concepts of Distributional Equity: Some Reasons for the Maximin Criterion." *American Economic Review* 64 (2, May): 141–46.

Robbins, Lionel. 1935. *Nature and Significance of Economic Science.* London: Macmillan.

Seligman, Edward. 1908. *Progressive Taxation.* New York: Columbia University Press.

Sidgwick, Henry. 1883. *The Principles of Political Economy.* London: Macmillan.

Smith, Adam. 1776. *The Wealth of Nations.* Edited by Edwin Cannan. 1904. New York: Putnam.

Tax Notes. 1996. "Description and Explanation of Unlimited Savings Allowance Income Tax System, Special Supplement." Arlington, Va.: Tax Analysts. February.

Tiebout, Charles. 1956. "A Pure Theory of Local Expenditures." *Journal of Political Economy* 64: 416–24.

Tobin, James. 1970. "On Limiting the Domain of Inequality." *Journal of Law and Economics* 13: 263–77.

Wicksell, Knut. 1886. *Finanztheoretische Untersuchungen nebst Darstellung des Steuerwesen Schwedens.* Jena: Fischer. Also see *Readings in the Classics of Public Finance,* translated and edited by Richard A. Musgrave and Allan Peacock. 1958. London: Macmillan.

2

Equity versus Efficiency and the U.S. Tax System in Historical Perspective

Dennis J. Ventry Jr.

The concept of tax justice in the United States has historically involved both social and economic factors. Americans have used the tax system to regulate economic privilege, and to restore equitable income and wealth distributions. Tax justice "American style" considers both horizontal equity (the equal taxation of equals) and vertical or progressive equity (the unequal taxation of unequals). It emphasizes the latter, however, measuring relative societal burdens against relative societal benefits and reflecting larger notions of social justice.

As the United States industrialized during the 19th century, and as concentrations of wealth increased, taxation's role as a social instrument became more important. "The man of great wealth," stated President Theodore Roosevelt, "owes a peculiar obligation to the State, because he derives special advantages from the mere existence of government" (1906, 27). The failure of the market economy in the 1930s prompted politicians and tax theorists to emphasize the morality of taxation. "The case for drastic progression in taxation," argued economist Henry Simons, "must be rested on the case against inequality—on the ethical or aesthetic judgment that the prevailing distribution of wealth and income reveals a degree (and/or kind) of inequality which is distinctly evil or unlovely" (1938, 18–19). By the 1940s, distributive forms of tax justice had become so intertwined with federal tax policy that President Franklin Roosevelt proposed capping after-tax incomes at $25,000.[1]

Even into the 1950s, the case for steeply progressive taxation could be defended on ethical and moral grounds (Blum and Kalven 1953; De Jouvenel 1952).

Over the last two generations, however, the tax pendulum has swung from equity to efficiency concerns. Modern-day tax discussions avoid unsettling questions of relative burdens and benefits. In particular, they avoid considering taxation's potential for mitigating income and wealth inequalities, both of which have increased steadily since the early 1970s. Theorists, politicians, and the American public share responsibility for this trend, and among theorists, economists bear special culpability. Beginning in the 1950s, and accelerating in the 1970s, economists turned their attention from equity—particularly vertical equity—to efficiency and economic growth. To the extent that economists considered equity at all, they focused on how deviations from horizontal equity influenced efficiency.[2] They ceded professional jurisdiction over distributive equity to legal theorists and philosophers.[3]

The turn of economists away from progressive equity—in combination with a sustained period of stagnant economic growth, inflation, and public cynicism toward government—prompted the American people to support tax policies that emphasized efficiency rather than equity. This environment allowed tax-cutters to push through tax reforms that excluded equity considerations. In addition, it gave credence to the conservative supply-side notion that "if equity didn't matter, and only efficiency did, then taxes should be set only as to minimize distortions" (Steuerle 1999, 1593).

This chapter suggests that the American people still care about remedying "unlovely" income inequalities through taxation. They still perceive the moral and ethical power of taxes. At a time of heightened income and wealth inequalities—the social ills that historically have motivated considerations of redistributive taxation in the United States—we would do well to reconsider tax justice and its policymaking implications.

The first part of this chapter, "Theory versus Reality," examines the history of tax justice in the United States. It describes a republican and liberal-democratic foundation to U.S. tax policies that supports progressive, ability-to-pay taxation. In addition, it evaluates how post–World War II tax theorists abandoned progressive equity in favor of efficiency. The theoretical turn from progressive tax equity precipitated the de-emphasis on redistribution as a policymaking construct. The second part,

"The Role of Economists," emphasizes the divergence of tax justice as defined by theorists, on the one hand, and average taxpayers, on the other. It draws a connection between changes within the economics profession and the triumph of efficiency policies over equity policies. Moreover, it suggests that although American taxpayers endorsed lower marginal income tax rates beginning in the 1960s (and a flat tax in the 1990s), they did not necessarily endorse less progression. The last part, "Bridging the Divide between Equity and Efficiency," bridges both the theoretical and practical gap, arguing that tax theorists have a professional as well as a civic obligation to consider the moral and ethical aspects of taxation.

Theory versus Reality: Tax Justice in the United States

"The public's perception of tax equity," Richard Musgrave has written, "can hardly be expected to coincide with . . . models as conceived by philosophers and economists" (1996a, 348). We seldom hear taxpayers clamoring for tax cuts on the basis of particular social welfare functions or the consequences of "deadweight loss" (situations where someone loses and no one gains). Neither do we hear politicians reveal that they have formulated their tax reforms from behind a Rawlsian veil of ignorance (Rawls 1971, 1974). Taxpayers and their legislators possess simpler, yet powerful, concepts of tax justice.

A historical examination of tax justice in the United States, from the founding of the republic to the present, reveals that Americans have perceived taxation as an instrument of social justice. They have favored tax policies that impose higher burdens, both absolutely and relatively, on high incomes and concentrated wealth than on low incomes.

This relatively simple conception of tax justice can result in tax policies that make little sense to economists and theorists. Consider corporate income taxes, for example. The American public perceives a direct connection between corporate income tax rates and corporate income tax payments (Sheffrin 1996). Economists, on the other hand, agree that corporations can shift the incidence of increased income tax rates toward workers (in the form of lower wages) and consumers (in the form of higher prices). The American public could be justified in arguing for higher corporate tax rates, however, if it desires improved progressivity. To the extent shareholders (a high-income cohort) bear the burden of higher corporate income taxes (in the form of decreased dividends, for example), raising corporate income tax rates might improve progressivity. The history of taxation in the United States reveals similar examples of the public's simple but powerful understanding of tax justice.

The Democratic (Small "d") and Republican (Small "r") Underpinnings of U.S. Taxation

The terms "Democratic" and "Republican" can refer to political parties. But they also reflect the founding ideals of the American republic, which permeate the history of both the nation and its tax system. These shared histories underscore a fundamental American paradox: the tension between political equality and individual liberty. The founding fathers mitigated this tension by balancing the ideal of Lockean liberalism— which emphasized private rights—with traditional republicanism or civic humanism—which emphasized public virtue.

Republican ideals helped create a tax system that taxed wealth and privilege despite a national aversion to infringements on individual liberty. From the beginning of the republic, federal and state legislators used taxation to restrict privilege (by taxing corporate charters, for example), and to "affirm communal responsibilities, deepen citizenship, and demonstrate the fiscal virtues of a republican citizenry" (Brownlee 2000, 31). The ideal of civic virtue created a unique form of ability-to-pay taxation that was hostile to excess accumulation and to citizens who asserted entitlement through birth. Republican notions of tax justice tolerated persons who created wealth, but not those who inherited it. Inherited wealth, as well as gross concentrations of wealth (inherited or not), characterized an aristocratic society, not a free and virtuous republic.

The U.S. Constitution restricted the federal government from levying direct, nonuniform taxes, thereby limiting its ability to promote a distributive form of tax justice. States faced no such restriction and actively promoted social justice through taxation. State governments taxed property at a flat, *ad valorem* rate, believing that high-income individuals spent a larger share of their income on land and property than low-income persons did. Throughout the first half of the 19th century, states expanded their use of the general property tax to include tangible property (land, equipment, and household goods) as well as intangible property (cash, credit, stocks, and mortgages). By including intangible property, states increased the percentage of taxes paid by wealthy citizens. Several states experimented with income taxes prior to the Civil War "with the avowed purpose of removing inequalities in the tax system," and raising civic contributions from wealthy residents (Blakey 1914, 25). High-income individuals owed a debt to society. Their success depended on sustained economic and political order. High-income individuals created wealth, but they also benefited from the system in which they lived.

Social Forces and Progressive Taxation: Tax Justice from 1860 to 1945

Beginning in 1860 and continuing until the end of World War II, a series of national crises caused dramatic changes in the U.S. tax system. These changes reflected the influence of a democratization of politics, as well as an expansion of the American state. In the process, notions of tax justice evolved to include a progressive federal income tax.

The Civil War prompted the Lincoln administration to locate new sources of revenue beyond tariffs and excises. Northern Republican leaders believed that increasing consumption taxes would erode confidence in the national government. The administration sought an alternative form of financing that reflected the principle of ability to pay, and the Union government settled on the nation's first federal income tax. The tax was modest by today's standards, amounting to a flat rate of 3 percent on incomes above $800. During the war, Congress lowered the exemption to $600 and created an additional rate schedule. By 1865, individuals with incomes over the exemption and under $5,000 paid a 5 percent tax, while those with incomes over $5,000 paid 10 percent. Despite low statutory rates, the Civil War income tax doubled tax liabilities for the richest Northerners (Brownlee 2000).

At the end of hostilities, wealthy Americans demanded repeal of the income tax. It was a temporary wartime measure, not an experiment in public finance. So in 1872, Congress let the income tax expire. At the same time, Congress reduced wartime excises—a political move designed to induce nonwealthy Americans to accept the termination of the income tax, which was widely perceived to be a class-based tax. The federal government went back to relying on tariff revenues. State governments, too, reverted to less progressive tax systems. Although states raised property tax rates, wealthy residents evaded their tax obligations. State and local governments did not possess the administrative capacity to identify noncompliance, much less prosecute it. They were forced to adopt a property tax they could collect easily with standardized assessment techniques and an emphasis on real estate. In the process, states reduced taxation of wealthy individuals relative to nonwealthy individuals, relying increasingly on more regressive forms of taxation.

Meanwhile, farm prices fell sharply between 1870 and the late 1890s. Farmers grew uneasy and launched a series of agrarian revolts that called for, among other things, social justice through tax reform. Republican tariff policies favored manufacturing and industrial interests over farmers and professionals. In the 1890s, the Populists in the West and South called for a progressive tax on corporate profits and high incomes to reallocate the tax burden toward corporate monopolies and wealthy shareholders. A progressive income tax, its proponents argued, could break inequitable concentrations of economic power.

When Democrats took control of Congress in 1893, Populists rushed progressive taxation onto the policy agenda. Many key Democrats, believing that taxation could realign the political parties along sectional lines, supported progressive taxation (Trilling 1980). In 1894, Congress passed the nation's second federal income tax. The new law exempted the first $4,000 of personal income, taxed gifts, and inheritances, and levied a 2 percent tax on personal and corporate incomes. In late 1894, the American economist E. R. A. Seligman reflected on the social forces that animated the new income tax. "The democratic trend towards justice in taxation cannot be prevented here, as it has been impossible to prevent it in other countries" (Seligman 1894, 648). Popular notions of tax justice, Seligman argued, demanded progressive taxation as a means to remedy social and economic inequities.

Even before Congress could collect on the second federal income tax, the Supreme Court declared it unconstitutional. The Court's 1895 decision in *Pollock v. Farmers' Loan and Trust Co.* (158 U.S. 601) incited proponents of progressive taxation. According to one commentator, "the great majority of citizens" considered the decision "a radical reversal of long standing precedents and an unwarranted overthrow of the will of the people" (Blakey 1914, 25). Politicians from the two major parties could hardly ignore the public outcry for progression. Democrats included a progressive income tax in their 1896 presidential platform. And Republicans, though largely opposed to an income tax, enacted a temporary progressive estate tax and an excise tax on the sugar and oil trusts to finance the Spanish-American War.

By the early 1900s, Republicans—from insurgent reformer Senator Bob LaFollette to party leaders Theodore Roosevelt and William Howard Taft—endorsed progressive income taxation. Previously confined to the West, Midwest, and South, the public clamor for a federal income tax crossed sectional boundaries and moved into northeastern urban centers. Middle-class and professional propertied Americans resented their rising tax burdens while wealthy individuals escaped paying their fair share. Personal and corporate income taxes as well as transfer taxes, the middle class believed, could produce a fairer tax distribution. Even high-income and conservative groups supported federal income taxation. They saw the adoption of a progressive income tax as one way to stave off more radical calls for industrial democracy (Stanley 1993). In 1909, Congress submitted the Sixteenth Amendment to the states for ratification. Many Republican leaders believed that the amendment would fail (Blakey 1914; Brownlee 2000; Hull 1948). And, in fact, it got off to a rocky start, with New York, Massachusetts, and other powerful states rejecting it immediately. However, the amendment prevailed, and in 1913, it became law.

The third federal income tax featured only a moderate degree of progression. It taxed personal and corporate incomes at a "normal" rate of 1 percent, and it included a graduated surtax up to 6 percent for individual taxpayers. It provided exemptions of $3,000 for singles and $4,000 for married couples, effectively excluding all but the very wealthiest Americans.[4] Despite its modest scope, the new law was a symbol of democracy, exemplifying the movement for greater social justice in an industrialized nation. Cordell Hull (D-TN) called the income tax a triumph, "the one great equalizer of the tax burden and therefore a tremendous agency for the improvement of social conditions" (1948, 71). Progressive income taxation complemented both the popular will and a growing consensus among tax theorists. "The tendency in all countries and among both the theorists and the masses," wrote economist Roy Blakey, "is strongly in the direction of graduated or progressive taxation, and the present income tax is distinctly in harmony with this tendency" (1914, 33). The reaction of wealthy Americans to income taxation paid tribute to its power. Henry Cabot Lodge called it "confiscation of property under the guise of taxation" and "the pillage of a class" (Witte 1985, 77). Although the federal income tax before World War I was hardly confiscatory, President Wilson's wartime revenue acts substantiated these charges.

The Wilson administration greatly expanded the federal income tax. The Revenue Act of 1916 raised income tax rates to 15 percent, and preserved the high exemptions. It created a graduated federal tax on estates over $50,000, increased the corporate income tax rate to 2 percent, and subjected munitions manufacturers to a 12.5 percent excess-profits tax. Wealthy Americans complained that the Wilson administration was explicitly pursuing a redistributive program of "soaking the rich,"[5] and they were right. By war's end, personal income tax rates ranged from 15 to 77 percent. Estate tax rates rose to 25 percent. The corporate income tax ranged from 30 to 65 percent, and the excess-profits tax accounted for nearly two-thirds of federal tax revenues during World War I. Although personal exemptions fell to $1,000 for singles and $2,000 for married people, the income tax remained a class-based tax. The richest 1 percent of Americans paid 80 percent of federal income tax revenues collected in 1918. This cohort paid effective tax rates that topped 15 percent, up from 3 percent in 1916 (Brownlee 2000).

The Wilson administration's soak-the-rich mentality was hardly in advance of public opinion. Efforts to expand the power of the income tax began immediately after its enactment. A small but growing number of politicians, theorists, and citizens recognized that income taxation could do more than supplement existing forms of revenue; it could replace them. Moreover, an expanded progressive income tax could redistribute wealth, which had grown more concentrated between 1913 and 1916 (Williamson and Lindert 1980).

Other Americans were less sanguine regarding the leveling effects of progressive taxation. Wealthy individuals and corporate America objected to the wartime tax program. When President Wilson proposed doubling existing rates in 1918, critics of the class-based tax system took to the stump during that year's congressional elections. They sold their anti-tax message through populist appeals for smaller government. Their efforts paid off, and Republicans regained control of Congress. In 1920, the White House also fell to Republicans, and Warren Harding promised a "return to normalcy."

Harding, with the help of a Republican Congress, made good on his promise. Treasury Secretary Andrew Mellon directed tax reforms that sharply reduced personal and corporate tax rates. The top marginal individual rate fell from a wartime high of 77 percent to 58 percent in 1921, and 25 percent by 1928. Congress reduced the estate tax rate to 20 percent, and increased the exclusion to $100,000, exempting all but one-half of 1 percent of decedents. Congress also eliminated the excess-profits tax, a symbol of economic justice. In addition to rate cutting, Republican Congresses undermined progressive taxation by punching loopholes in the Internal Revenue Code. The 1920s witnessed the creation of the preferential tax treatment of capital gains, the oil and gas depletion allowances, and the exclusions for employer contributions to pensions and life insurance plans. In conjunction with reduced statutory rates, these new loopholes lowered effective tax rates on wealthy taxpayers, from 15.8 percent in 1920 to 7.4 percent by 1926 (Brownlee 2000).

Andrew Mellon, despite endorsing certain tax dispensations, perceived the necessity of preserving a semblance of tax justice. He persuaded corporations and wealthy Americans to support progressive taxation, if only in principle. Mellon believed that keeping tax schedules graduated (albeit flatter) could mitigate radical demands for restructuring the capitalist system. Mellon and his fellow corporate liberals preserved progressivity in the estate tax, and retained wartime corporate income tax rates. Moreover, at Mellon's behest, Congress enacted a reduced tax rate for "earned" income. Thus, although Mellon and the Republican leadership dulled the redistributive sting of progressive income taxation, they preserved its message of social justice.

The Great Depression, especially its protracted nature, reversed the course of federal taxation. In an effort to balance the budget, Herbert Hoover endorsed higher taxes on the rich. The 1932 Revenue Act raised the top marginal rate for individuals from 25 to 63 percent, and increased exemption levels only slightly. It also increased estate taxes by reducing the exclusion to $50,000 and raising the rate from 20 to 45 percent. Although Hoover initiated the process, Franklin Roosevelt recommitted the federal government to soak-the-rich taxation.

Partly to deflect criticism from the left, but largely because he believed in progressive, ability-to-pay taxation, Roosevelt launched a series of radical tax reforms beginning in 1935 (Brownlee 1996, 2000; Lambert 1970).[6] Roosevelt went before Congress personally to rail against "accumulation[s] of wealth," which he felt should be tapped through more progressive taxation (Blum 1959). The 1935 Revenue Act looked much like Roosevelt's original proposal, which the press dubbed the "Wealth Tax." It increased the top marginal rate for individuals to 77 percent, made the estate tax more progressive, taxed intercorporate dividends, and created a graduated tax on corporations.

In 1936, Roosevelt pushed the progressive envelope further. He proposed, and Congress passed, a graduated undistributed-profits tax. In addition, between 1934 and 1937, Roosevelt and Treasury Secretary

Henry Morgenthau conducted a war against tax loopholes and evasion.[7] The most celebrated case involved former Treasury Secretary Andrew Mellon, whom the Treasury Department alleged owed over $3 million in back taxes and penalties. The Board of Tax Appeals found Mellon innocent of tax evasion in 1937, yet required him to pay $400,000. The Board made an example of Mellon and publicized the inequities of tax loopholes. The publicity gave Roosevelt the platform he needed to ask Congress to create the Joint Committee on Tax Evasion and Avoidance. Congress granted the new committee authority to name taxpayers who exploited tax avoidance techniques, and that same year, the Roosevelt administration presented Congress with a list of 67 high-income tax evaders. Consequently, Congress passed the Revenue Act of 1937, restricting the most egregious loopholes (personal holding companies, deductions for corporate yachts and secondary estates) and closing others (tax preferences for nonresident taxpayers). Together, the 1936 and 1937 Revenue Acts raised effective tax rates on the nation's wealthiest individuals to above 15 percent for the first time since World War I.

Roosevelt, bolstered by his legislative successes as well as signs of economic recovery, pursued his tax reforms for 1938. Proposals included raising the undistributed-profits tax, eliminating the exemption for federal, state, and local bonds, and creating a graduated tax on capital gains. Business leaders and wealthy taxpayers responded by lobbying Congress for tax reduction. Aided by the recession of 1937–38, these tax protestors convinced Congress that Roosevelt's tax policies had precipitated the economic downturn. The economy needed tax cuts, not tax reform. The 1938 Revenue Act weakened the undistributed-profits tax and eliminated the graduated corporate income tax. Furthermore, in 1939, Congress abolished the undistributed-profits tax. Roosevelt lamented the turn away from progressive taxation, but the reversal was hardly permanent. America's entry into World War II and subsequent wartime revenue demands meant greater reliance on progressive federal income taxation.

Growth versus Equity: The Modern Federal Income Tax, 1945 to 1964

World War II produced a mass-based income tax. In 1939, the Treasury Department collected federal income taxes from 4 million individuals. By 1945, reduced personal exemptions increased the number of income taxpayers to 43 million. The new income tax contained steeply progressive rates, ranging from 22 to 94 percent (Moody 1998), and it generated a near majority of all federal tax receipts. In 1939, the federal income tax yielded just $892 million, only 13.6 percent of federal tax receipts. By 1944, it produced $19.7 billion, or 45 percent of all federal tax revenues (Moody 1998).

The broad-based, revenue-buoyant income tax ushered in an "era of easy financing" whereby politicians could enact both tax reductions and new expenditure programs (Steuerle 1996). As an instrument of policy, the new federal income tax could help reverse recessions and curb inflation by cutting and raising taxes, respectively. "Nothing like this was possible in, say 1930 or 1938," observed the Committee for Economic Development (CED), "because there were not large amounts of taxes to cut" or raise. "Before current tax payments and withholding were introduced [two other wartime alterations] there was no way in which a tax cut could have a *quick* effect on individuals' available incomes" (CED 1954, 28, emphasis in the original). Despite a general recognition of the tax system's potential utility, neither experts nor policymakers fully understood the new fiscal instrument. What effect would it have on the widely anticipated postwar inflation? To what extent would it smooth business cycles? Without an accurate sense of how the mass-based income tax might influence the postwar economy, experts and politicians disagreed on its application. To what extent should the tax system stimulate capital investment, technological development, and entrepreneurial activity? How far should the income tax go in redistributing wealth?

To complicate matters, analysts considered these issues while the economics profession was undergoing a theoretical transformation. Fiscal theory, as much as fiscal practice, had broken from its moorings to classical economics, and both were speeding in the direction of Keynesianism. With the Great Depression a living memory, New Deal economics had avoided taxing consumption and instead taxed saving (Brinkley 1995; Hawley 1995; Stein 1990), resulting in a tax policy that emphasized progressive rates.

Macroeconomic policy in the postwar period looked very different. The Keynesian-influenced "new economics" considered saving a virtue, not a vice. It addressed postwar anxieties regarding pent-up consumer demand and inflation (CED 1946 and 1948; Shere 1948; Tobin 1949). Moreover, it pursued fiscal policies that produced full employment (Gurley 1952; Noyes 1947). Consequently, postwar tax policy de-emphasized progressive taxation and promoted capital investment for wealthy taxpayers and corporations. It met aggregate demand with increased supply.

Postwar tax programs—conservative and liberal, Republican and Democratic—emphasized economic growth through tax reduction (Groves 1944; Lutz 1947; Paul 1947). Excessive tax rates created economic inefficiencies and dried up private investment. Moreover, high marginal tax rates stifled economic growth by discouraging work effort and reducing productivity. High tax rates also prompted taxpayers (both individual and corporate) to lobby for tax preferences. Lower tax rates could promote saving and investment, stimulate the economy, and discourage tax avoidance. For many postwar tax reformers, tax cuts were inherently good, a policymaking panacea. According to Roswell Magill of the right-leaning Tax Foundation, "lower tax rates would be the most important step that could be taken to promote all of the broad objectives of tax reform. It would provide a tax climate more favorable to economic growth. It would lessen the extent of inequities that exist in the tax system. It could mean a more reasonable use of the principle of progression. It would reduce interference with the free market allocation of economic resources" (Magill 1959, 96). Tax cuts meant progress, equity, and efficiency.

The widespread appeal of lower marginal tax rates suggested that the U.S. income tax system after World War II would exhibit flatter rates. But progressive taxation proved resilient, and the top marginal income tax rate for individuals remained above 90 percent throughout the 1950s. Moreover, the top corporate rate—as high as 77 percent from 1950 to 1953—never fell below 52 percent. Calls for tax cuts to stimulate the economy were met by equally vociferous calls to preserve progressive, ability-to-pay taxation.

For 20 years after World War II, tax policies that promoted economic growth on the one hand and progressive equity on the other vied for preeminence. The contest between growth and equity involved experts, politicians, and the public. Three distinct groups of postwar tax reformers debated the trade-offs between growth and equity: conservatives or "anti-taxers," "supply-side" liberals, and "demand-side" liberals.

Conservatives advocated tax cuts. Taxes distorted the free market. They reduced private investment, threatened the capitalist system, and financed wasteful government spending. Taxes created a tax-and-spend cycle of higher tax burdens, and bigger expenditure programs. The tax-and-spend philosophy, moreover, produced deficits. "We have our highest peacetime taxes," conservative Carl Curtis (R-NE) argued. "Yet, in spite of all those tax receipts, the Fair Deal is running an annual deficit of over $5,000,000,000" (1950, 8329). A year later, the Republican National Committee warned that Democratic tax-and-spend policies would "further cheapen the dollar, rob the wage earner, impoverish the farmer, and destroy the savings, insurance and investments of millions of people" (Shafer 1951, A3987).

The conservative economic vision accomplished tax cuts alongside expenditure cuts. It preached fiscal prudence. "Be nifty and thrifty in fifty," Robert Rich (R-PA) exhorted his colleagues in the House of Representatives (Rich 1950, 8331). Taxes should raise only enough revenue to finance the most essential government services.

According to postwar conservatives, taxation—especially progressive taxation—was socialistic. Redistributive tax policies fostered class discrimination, and threatened tyrannies of the majority. Political economist F. A. Hayek wrote, "Once it is admitted that a majority has a right to impose upon minorities burdens of a kind which the majority does not bear itself, there is little reason [to doubt] that this will be used only for discrimination against the rich" (1956, 271). Progressive taxation, by jeopardizing individual liberties, contradicted the founding principles of the U.S. republic.

In the context of the Cold War, progressive taxation adumbrated communism. Like communist Russia, it challenged democratic institutions and portended revolution. The Communist Manifesto, anti-taxers were quick to point out, advocated a progressive income tax and the abolition of inheritances. The expansive reach of the postwar federal income tax would dry up private investment, as Marx had predicted, and destroy capitalism. For many postwar conservatives, the communist invasion was already underway. In 1947, Harold Knutson (R-MN) railed against the subversive influence of progressive taxation: "For years we Republicans have been warning that the short-haired women and long-haired men of alien minds in the administrative branch of government were trying to wreck the American way of life and install a hybrid oligarchy at Washington through confiscatory taxation" (Jones 1988, 294). Karl LeCompte (R-IA) issued a call to arms against excessive taxes. "Continued use of the taxing power," he warned, "will destroy the very things, the very weapons, we must use against the threat of communism" (1953, A104). For conservatives, the power to tax was the power to destroy.

Conservative forces engaged in a protracted effort during the 1950s to limit Congress' ability to levy progressive taxes. They offered constitutional amendments and congressional resolutions designed to amend, reform, and repeal the Sixteenth Amendment.[8] This decade-long effort encapsulated the conservative critique of taxation in the postwar period. "Its purpose and effect," explained Chauncy Reed (R-IL), "are merely to eliminate in large measure from our system of taxation its socialistic features" (1955, 1002). Limiting the taxing powers of Congress would safeguard "liberty" and "freedom" (Gwinn 1950, A304-5).

In their effort to reduce progression within the federal income tax and to promote private investment, conservatives supported certain tax preferences. They defended low taxes on capital gains. They supported the income-splitting joint return. And they endorsed depletion allowances and accelerated depreciation. Conservatives, like their liberal counterparts, knew that tax subsidies operated like spending subsidies. They also knew that spending from the tax side of the budget helped conservative constituents more than it helped liberal constituents. For one thing, conservative constituents generally reported more taxable income, and thus benefited to a greater degree from tax deductions. For another, conservative constituents were more likely to report unearned income on their tax returns, and thus utilized tax subsidies for unearned and investment income.

Conservatives did not endorse all loopholes. They appreciated the effect loopholes had on tax progression, but they also understood that tax preferences distorted economic activity and the free market. Tax subsidies were patently unfair; moreover, they helped some taxpayers, but not others. If only for political reasons, conservatives endorsed efforts to close particularly egregious tax apertures. Conservatives also realized that tax subsidies reduced federal revenues. Closing loopholes could raise revenue, which, in turn, could help balance the budget, pay down debt, cut federal spending, and reduce tax rates.

Like conservative tax reformers, supply-side liberals supported reduced taxes on high incomes and corporate America. Unlike the anti-taxers, however, this tax reform cohort did not seek tax reduction for the sake of shrinking the size of government or saving the country from an insidious communist invasion. Nor did it endorse tax loopholes to carve out special privileges for the rich. Rather, it believed that tax cuts stimulated the economy, enhanced employment, and induced growth. Targeted tax incentives for business and capital investment benefited the economy. Excessive tax rates on high-income individuals distorted economic behavior, reduced work effort, and discouraged entrepreneurship.

Excessive taxes on business were worrisome as well. Corporations grew slowly under the burden of heavy tax rates. Higher corporate taxes could destroy the ability of American industry to compete in world markets, and corporate America fueled these fears. In 1953, U.S. Steel told Congress that the excess-profits tax (levied from 1950 to 1953) amounted to "a destructive tax, dishonestly named. It [was] not a tax upon excessive profits. It [was] an excessive tax upon normal profits, on business efficiency, on industrial growth, and on public service" (Colmer 1953, A600–1). Tax cuts were needed to save American industry.

Supply-side liberals desired as few barriers to growth as possible. They espoused what economist Herb Stein termed "domesticated" Keynesianism, a form of Keynesianism akin to its original British formulation—that is, one less concerned with structural economic weakness than with economic stimuli and recovery (1990). While the first generation of American Keynesians (Mariner Eccles, Mordecai Ezekiel, and Alvin Hansen) concerned itself with distribution and consumption in a period of economic depression and war, the second generation worried about investment and production during a period of prosperity and peace. These supply-side liberals advocated economic policies that facilitated growth in an efficient manner. Spreading the tax burden throughout the income distribution and carefully using targeted tax incentives could provide the least distortive fiscal policy stimulus. "A broadly based income tax with as few special provisions as possible," tax scholar Walter Blum suggested, "is most compatible with the kind of economic growth most people desire, and the kind in which we will have the least wastage of investment" (1955, 246). Cutting tax rates could also lead to fewer tax inequities by reducing the incentive to punch loopholes in the tax code.

Supply-side liberals did not advocate tax cuts simply for the sake of economic growth.[9] They perceived social and economic benefits flowing from tax reduction. An enlarged economic pie could benefit all income levels. "An ever-expanding economy could produce undreamed-of abundance and material gain for all classes," argued Leon Keyserling, chairman of President Truman's Council of Economic Advisers. "Business could expect higher profits, labor better wages, farmers larger incomes, and, above all, those at the bottom of the economic scale could experience a truly decent life" (Hamby 1973, 300). To the extent tax cuts served up more generous helpings of the economic pie, supply-side liberals pursued them aggressively.

Tax cuts were also in the interest of national security. In the context of the Cold War, they were essential if America was to meet and exceed Soviet economic growth. The strength of the U.S. economy reflected the strength of capitalism and of democracy. Determining who was "winning" the Cold War was measured as much by aggregate rates of economic growth as by the number of nuclear warheads. Fears over the Soviet economic juggernaut peaked in the latter half of the 1950s. Important economic indices suggested the Soviets were about to declare victory on the economic battlefield. Between 1953 and 1958, the Soviet economy grew between 7 and 8 percent annually, eclipsing the growth rate of the U.S. economy, which averaged a comparatively sluggish 1.5 percent over the same period.

The strong Soviet economy, in turn, financed military and technological advances. In 1957, the Soviets successfully launched *Sputnik*, a scientific space satellite. Some Americans feared that if the Soviets could thrust an object beyond the earth's atmosphere, they might also be able to launch an intercontinental nuclear missile to the United States. The specter of raining nuclear bombs prompted a national debate on "catching up" to the Soviets. Meeting the Soviet threat required a strong economy. According to supply-siders (and conservatives, too), the most efficient way to enhance economic growth was to reduce taxes on capital and investment income.

"Sputnik complexes" fueled the postwar preoccupation with economic growth and influenced the supply-side position on tax reform. For supply-side liberals, "reform" meant abolishing economically distorting tax preferences, but preserving, and even creating, tax subsidies that stimulated the economy. On the one hand, tax preferences could be economically inefficient, threaten the revenue viability of the new tax regime, and undermine taxpayer morale. On the other hand, supply-side tax reformers perceived far-reaching benefits to tax subsidies that enhanced economic growth.

Supply-side liberals perceived tax cuts and tax reform as linked, especially when tax cuts and reduced loopholes spurred the economy. Following the lead of their "more liberal" brethren—the demand-side liberals—supply-siders recognized that closing tax loopholes could pay for rate reduction. Strategically, they believed they could enact tax cuts if they compromised on tax reform. That is, they believed that demand-side liberals would be more inclined to support supply-side tax cuts alongside fewer tax loopholes.

The supply-side group of liberal tax reformers included Wilbur Mills (chairman of the House Ways and Means Committee from 1958 to 1974); Walter Heller (future chairman of President Kennedy's Council of Economic Advisers); Herb Stein (director of research for the Committee for Economic Development and later chairman of President Ford's Council of Economic Advisers); Stanley Surrey (Harvard law professor and later assistant treasury secretary for tax policy under Presidents Kennedy and Johnson); Dan Throop Smith (Harvard economist and assistant treasury secretary for tax policy under President Eisenhower); Walter J. Blum and Harry Kalven Jr. (professors at the University of Chicago Law School and coauthors of *The Uneasy Case for Progressive Taxation*, the most articulate postwar critique of progressive taxation); and the Committee for Economic Development, the National Association of Manufacturers, and the Chamber of Commerce. Growth liberalism provided these tax reformers a platform on which to form a policy network of politicians, federal officials, academics, and expert researchers.

Demand-side liberals, like conservatives and supply-siders, believed in the stimulative effects of reduced taxation. However, demand-siders did not believe that high marginal tax rates necessarily threatened economic progress by distorting economic behavior, reducing work effort, or discouraging investment. Frank Clark (D-PA), for example, refuted the "fallacy" that excessive taxes jeopardized capitalism or democracy. He scoffed at the suggestion that "the crushing burden of taxation" would destroy "the whole incentive of the free enterprise system" (1959, 2488). Demand-siders acknowledged the damaging effects that could result from excessive taxes on executives, managers, and other high-income earners. They did not feel, however, that marginal tax rates of 90 percent necessarily jeopardized work incentives. "The evidence is overwhelming," economist Roy Blough reported, "that the business executive is putting a full measure of work and energy into his regular job" (1952, 37). Demand-side economist George Break wrote that "contrary to the frequently repeated injunctions of so many financial commentators, solicitude for the state of work incentives does not under current conditions justify significant reductions in the role of progressive income taxation." In fact, Break noted, income tax rates "could be raised considerably, especially in the middle and upper-middle income ranges, without lowering unduly the aggregate supply of labor." Tax-related work disincentives, he concluded, "like the weather, are much talked about, but relatively few people do anything about them" (1957, 549). According to demand-siders, taxation was not the bane of the nation—the obsession with growth was.

Demand-side liberals explicitly criticized the supply-side "trickle-down" theory of economics. Tax cuts on wealth and capital did not lead inevitably to economic gains throughout the income distribution. What good was increased supply without sufficient demand? "It is well and good to worry about taxation effects on investment incentives when there is plenty of demand for goods and services and a lack of investment capital," argued Robert Nathan, chairman of the Americans for Democratic Action. "But we should make sure now that there is enough demand to make investment profitable in the first place." Demand created supply. "The way to increase investment," Nathan emphasized, "is to increase consumption" (1954, 879). "Continued economic growth," the AFL-CIO agreed, "will depend upon sustained and expanding levels of consumption" (Kassalow 1959, 518). Senator Russell Long (D-LA) argued for the demand-side economic vision during tax debates in 1954. "What we need at the present time is not more production but more buying power in the hands of the consumer to buy the products which are already being produced at a greater rate than they are being sold. . . . The problem," Long emphasized, "is that of keeping the consuming and the productive powers in balance. At the present time there is no question whatever but that the problem is not in producing more washing machines, more automobiles, more television and radio sets, and so forth, but in selling the products of industry" (1954, 9172).

Supply-side liberalism was a cop-out, demand-side liberals argued. It diverted the discussion from difficult and unsettling issues such as income and wealth inequalities. "The usual liberal approach today," lawyer Louis Eisenstein lamented, "is that if we can promote economic growth, if we can have a larger pie, all segments of society will necessarily have larger shares of that pie and we won't have to worry about redistribution of income anymore" (1962, 4). The rising tide thesis was a by-product of what John Kenneth Galbraith identified as the general "decline of interest in inequality as an economic issue" (1958, 82). The great economic issue in postwar America was not equity, but economic growth. Bucking the trend, demand-side liberals attacked disparities between rich and poor in an affluent society.

The theorists among this liberal cohort articulated a moral and ethical defense of distributive justice. "Ethical conceptions," not empirical analysis, argued economist Earl Rolph, "provide the fundamental defense for equalitarian devices" such as progressive taxation (1950, 393). Tax policy alternatives, Harold Groves suggested, should be evaluated in terms of "the social significance of income" (1956, 27). These theorists drew on a long tradition in public finance that emphasized the social implications of fiscal economics, or what sociologist Rudolph Gold-scheid (1917) and economist Joseph Schumpeter (1918) had called "fiscal sociology." Taxes reflected and reinforced social norms. Apprising tax justice involved evaluating the relationship between a nation's economic and social systems. It involved, above all else, appreciating a society's moral and ethical code. When talking about the "equity of taxation," fiscal theorist S. J. Chapman argued, "we are obviously talking ethics, and therefore the wants primarily dealt with must be adjudged not according to the value of their satisfaction in fact (positive value), but according to the value of their satisfaction in a moral scheme of consumption (normative value)" (1913, 34). Measuring tax justice involved apprising distribution, recognizing social-economic equality and inequality, and considering "the equity of the whole existing order" (Taussig 1921, 509).

Demand-side theorists emphasized tenets of public finance theory that taught tax justice, "along with [its] underlying image of a good society, cannot be resolved by considerations of economic efficiency alone" (Musgrave 1996a, 354). Equity considerations were essential to "good" taxation. "The equity of the tax structure," Richard Musgrave told Congress during hearings on the Kennedy-Johnson tax cut in late 1963, "is an important end in itself. The ability of a people to institute a fair and equitable tax structure is a true test of social responsibility in a working democracy." Tax reform, argued Musgrave, "is not only a matter of broadening the tax base so as to permit rate reduction to aid incentives." Indeed, economic growth was salient to tax policy debates. So was social and economic equity. "Equitable distribution of the tax burden *is* important," Musgrave emphasized. "This means an income tax law which defines income so that, in line with the demands of 'horizontal equity,' people in equal positions are treated in similar fashion. It also means that the tax burden, in line with considerations of vertical equity, should be distributed fairly among different income groups." Musgrave acknowledged that his advocacy for progressive taxation might appear as "a matter more of political philosophy than economic analysis." But that hardly lessened its power. All arguments for progressive taxation—economic, philosophical, moral—should inform the debates, "especially in the individual income tax, since the rest of the tax structure is regressive" (1963a, 2202).

Attacking tax loopholes complemented the demand-side strategy of shifting the tax burden away from low-income individuals. Demand-siders recognized that statutory rates could not—and perhaps should not—go any higher. But closing loopholes, nearly all of which bene-fited high-income individuals and corporations, would improve pro-gressivity. If demand-siders could hold the line on statutory rates while removing tax privileges, they could shrink the distance between what taxpayers should have been paying and what they really were paying. In fact, demand-siders recognized that they could give ground on rate reduction if they accomplished enough loophole closing. They traded vertical equity for horizontal equity on the theory that improving hor-izontal equity could improve vertical equity enough to justify modest tax cuts.

Closing tax loopholes also raised revenue. The money generated from reducing tax leakages could pay down the public debt, balance the national budget, increase personal exemptions, improve national defense, and raise public expenditures. Perhaps more important, closing loopholes could pay for tax cuts, which provided demand-siders bar-gaining power. "If all the controversial points in the revenue act were resolved in favor of the revenue," Harold Groves said, "the rates of per-sonal tax could be reduced 25 percent" (1955, 243). Base broadening paved the way for tax reduction. It also enhanced the ability of the fed-eral income tax to provide economic stability during periods of upswing and downswing. If Congress increased total income subject to tax, Randolph Paul explained, "we have more of a chance to decrease taxes because we have more income subject, generally, to tax and in addition we have a more sensitive income-tax structure, because the broader the base, the greater then will be the effect one way or the other of a change in the economic trend" (1955, 256).

Demand-side liberals succeeded in consolidating the wartime changes to the federal income tax and challenging efforts to carve out additional tax loopholes. Personal income tax rates never fell below 90 percent in the 1950s, and corporate income tax rates fluctuated between 52 and 77 percent. Demand-siders also demonstrated that pro-gressive taxation promoted economic growth as well as social justice. Pro-gressive equity, moreover, complemented democracy as well as capitalism. Tax loopholes, on the other hand, threatened both. They discriminated against the majority of taxpayers and distorted economic behavior. At a time when steep marginal income tax rates arguably justified tax favors to strengthen the national economy, demand-side liberals kept progressive equity at the forefront of tax policymaking debates.

In their fight for progressive tax equity, demand-side liberals put together a coalition of reformers that included Senators Paul Douglas (D-IL), Al Gore (D-TN), Wayne Morse (D-OR), and Hubert Humphrey (D-MN); academic economists Otto Eckstein (Harvard University), Harold Groves (University of Wisconsin), and Richard Musgrave (Harvard University); economists Richard Goode of the Brookings Institution and Joseph Pechman of the Committee for Economic Development and, later, of the Brookings Institution; tax lawyers Louis Eisenstein, Randolph Paul, and Joseph Sneed; organizations such as the ADA and AFL-CIO; and "high-brow" publications such as *The New Republic* and *The Nation*.

A Postwar Tax Policymaking Consensus

The three groups of postwar tax reformers occupied different positions on the spectrum between growth and equity. Members from each group came together at certain points, however, to form a tax policymaking consensus that emphasized rate reduction and horizontal equity. They viewed the policymaking debate, perhaps in an oversimplification, as a trade-off between tax cuts and tax reform. They talked in terms of balancing progressivity losses in statutory tax rates, for example, with progressivity gains through fewer tax loopholes. Regardless of the theoretical accuracy of their rhetoric, postwar policymakers correctly recognized that linking tax cuts and tax reform could prove a winning combination both economically and politically. Closing loopholes paid for rate reduction. It broadened the tax base and provided additional opportunities for cutting taxes. Lower tax rates, in turn, reduced incentives to carve out new tax preferences. The practical and theoretical foundations of the postwar tax policymaking consensus animated tax discussions for the latter half of the 20th century. Broadening the tax base and lowering marginal tax rates provided the intellectual and political foundation for the most important episodes in postwar tax policymaking: the Revenue Act of 1964, the Tax Reform Act of 1969, and the Tax Reform Act of 1986. The tax policymaking consensus reinforced postwar economic imperatives.

A clear majority of tax reformers favored tax cuts. Supply-side liberals supported tax reductions that stimulated the economy, while demand-siders sanctioned most stimulative cuts. Conservatives, unless compromised by unbalanced budgets, worked to reduce excessive taxation. Support for targeted tax incentives aimed at enhancing economic growth garnered less support in the early postwar years. However, an extensive lobbying effort on behalf of supply-side liberals, in combination with the perceived necessity of meeting the Soviet economic threat, delivered both liberal and conservative endorsements for growth-oriented tax subsidies.

Finding support for reform was harder. The two liberal factions agreed generally on the need to eliminate inequities in the tax code, but they differed on the margins. These distinctions often involved the relative importance of growth versus equity. Demand-side liberals criticized the income tax treatment of capital gains, for example, because the provision discriminated against earned income in favor of investment income. Supply-siders, on the other hand, welcomed certain tax subsidies, particularly those for investment income, which they believed could promote economic growth. Despite their policy emphases, the two liberal factions found enough common ground to trade modest tax cuts for modest tax reform in the postwar period. On those occasions when the two liberal groups supported the same legislative measure, they formed a formidable alliance. But it was a precarious alliance, particularly for demand-side liberals. Without support from their liberal brethren, demand-side liberals had nowhere to turn. If supply-siders decided to abandon equity concerns, the demand-side agenda for achieving progressive equity would stall. Or if they decided to endorse horizontal equity only insofar as it helped them accomplish tax reduction, the policy "trade-off" between losses in vertical equity and gains in horizontal equity could yield substantial progressivity losses.

Conservatives made the alliance between the two liberal cohorts more precarious. If conservatives refused to budge on the horizontal-equity side of the equation, or if they forged an alliance of their own with supply-side liberals (around their shared affinity for promoting investment, for example), demand-siders would again be left on the losing end of the battle for progressive equity. Demand-side liberals walked an uncertain path. Conservatives generally accepted the Swiss-cheese nature of the federal income tax because it resulted in a less progressive tax system. But conservatives also recognized that tax loopholes distorted free-market operations and business decisions. In addition, conservatives disparaged the idea of using the tax code to achieve social and economic goals other than revenue collection. Also, conservatives recognized that loopholes were blatantly unfair; they could not afford to ignore all discriminations in favor of wealthy taxpayers. Thus, they supported limited tax reforms.

In order to achieve progressive equity, demand-side liberals needed more than "limited reform." They needed to politicize tax policymaking, publicize tax inequities, and lead a taxpayer revolt against tax loopholes. However, neither the political culture nor political institutions would allow it. The official government institutions of tax policymaking—the House Ways and Means Committee and the Senate Finance Committee—consciously eschewed politics and demagoguery during postwar tax policy debates. In particular, the Ways and Means Committee, under the direction of Wilbur Mills (D-AR), cultivated an aura of impartiality around tax policymaking. Mills relied on his own expert knowledge of the tax code, as well as the expertise of an influential network of tax professionals and economists both inside and outside government (Zelizer 1998). The numerous tax hearings Mills convened throughout the 1950s and 1960s were forums for neutral, technocratic, and objective tax policy discussions. Ostensibly, they accomplished a comprehensive, impartial, nonpartisan review of the federal taxing process.

Unfortunately for demand-siders, these tax discussions also focused on supply-side tax policies. Tax reform characterized by technocratic, impartial, expert, or numbers-driven discussions subordinated class politics and philosophical questions of tax justice. The supply-side emphasis on economic growth and efficiency overwhelmed concerns regarding income and wealth inequality. To the extent the tax-writing committees discussed redistributive tax policies, they condemned them as threats to the economy's incentive structure. The aggregate economic benefits of taking from the rich and giving to the poor were difficult to quantify. But demonstrating the effects on capital formation that flowed from an investment tax credit, for example, could be determined readily through empirical analysis.

Postwar tax reform involved objective considerations. Determining appropriate levels of vertical equity, on the other hand, required making value judgments. It was a matter of taste. "If A's income is twice B's," economist Herb Stein posited in 1959, "should A's tax be twice B's, or one and one-half times or three times as large? Intuitive standards of equity," Stein counseled, "seem to throw no light on questions of 'How much' " (1959, 114). Reaching consensus on degrees of vertical equity in the rate schedule was indeterminate and should be avoided as a matter of policy. Subjective considerations of progressive equity belied the aura of impartial precision that Mills and his network of supply-side tax reformers cultivated. Moreover, debating progressive equity from the standpoint of tax rates threatened to disturb the tacit compromise among the members of the postwar tax policymaking consensus regarding the incremental reduction in tax rates. Demand-siders enjoyed some success debating progressive equity from the standpoint of tax loopholes. Their success, however, derived more from their ability to characterize tax loopholes as deviations from horizontal equity than from their ability to engage supply-siders and conservatives in a discussion over how tax loopholes undermined progression.

The concept of horizontal equity generated more agreement than discord. Horizontal equity amounted to "the first, basic rule of taxation" (Stein 1959, 110). Everyone could agree on the principle of taxing equals equally. It was hard to imagine someone arguing for the *unequal* taxation of equals. Yet, postwar tax reformers allowed exceptions to the rule. Businesses could deduct "ordinary and necessary" expenses, but individuals could not. Farmers who raised four-legged livestock for purposes of "draft, breeding, or dairy" paid taxes at a special rate of 25 percent on the sale of their livestock; farmers who raised and sold two-legged poultry, meanwhile, paid taxes according to the more penal graduated rate schedule. In addition, working parents with 12-year-old children received a tax deduction for child-care expenses, but identically situated working parents with 13-year-old children did not.

In the end, debates over horizontal equity, like debates over vertical equity, amounted to value judgments and were equally subjective. They prompted as much disagreement among tax reformers as debates over vertical equity because the participants rightly perceived the two principles as linked. Improvements in horizontal equity could improve vertical equity. Conversely, creating new loopholes could reduce progressivity.

Ostensibly, all three tax-reforming groups stood the same chance of accomplishing their distinct vertical-equity goals in the battle over horizontal equity. Demand-siders faced a stacked deck, however. Not only were "tax-cutting provisions . . . hard to dislodge," but they also "tend[ed] to fan out and bring other tax reductions in their wake" (Hellerstein 1963, 22). Each additional subsidy further undermined progressive equity, which, in turn, justified still more subsidies. Demand-side liberals were left fighting a losing battle. It was only a matter of time before their agenda for progressive equity was overwhelmed by the combination of tax politics and the supply-side agenda of economic growth and efficiency.

Growth: Declaring Victory

In 1953, Walter J. Blum and Harry Kalven Jr. published the most careful study of progressive taxation to date. They acknowledged the weaknesses of graduated rates: High marginal tax rates yielded little revenue; progressivity complicated the tax system, both structurally and administratively, and it created economic inefficiencies, encouraged tax evasion, promoted "political irresponsibility," stifled incentives for risktaking, and overtaxed saving (Blum and Kalven 1953). Ultimately, Blum and Kalven offered a "stubborn but uneasy" case for progressivity. Like Simons 20 years earlier, they reconciled the adverse consequences of progression with its "ethical or aesthetic" effects on income and wealth inequality.

By the end of the 1950s, the case for progressive taxation had become less stubborn and more uneasy. In fact, the debate between growth and equity ended in the early 1960s with growth emerging triumphant. Postwar supply-side anxieties about the stagnant U.S. economy finally compelled legislators to enact deep tax cuts. The rate cutting that began with the 1964 Revenue Act and continued for the next 22 years represented a triumph of economy and efficiency over equity. Richard Musgrave observed this trend firsthand. During a Treasury Department consultants' meeting in 1963, Musgrave lamented that President Kennedy's tax reform package emphasized growth while subordinating equity. "I am bothered by the Administration's failure to emphasize the importance of the equity objectives in the whole reform issue," Musgrave stated. "To argue for base broadening as needed merely to permit rate cuts (required on incentive grounds), and not urge it on equity grounds, is a pretty weak position from which to defend the reform case. One cannot but note a change in flavor, in this respect, between the tax messages of '62 and '63" (1963b). Horizontal equity, the "first, basic rule of taxation," was being used to accomplish tax cuts, not tax fairness.[10]

Supply-side liberals within the Kennedy administration convinced the president to support stimulative tax policies primarily for their effects on the economy. Kennedy lobbied for a controversial investment tax credit in 1962. In 1963, he argued for across-the-board cuts in personal and corporate income taxes, reduced capital gains taxes, and accelerated depreciation. The Kennedy proposal became the Kennedy-Johnson tax cut of 1964. It represented the triumph of "growthmanship" and Keynesian countercyclical policies. Cutting taxes while the budget was in deficit could stimulate economic growth. Some liberal supply-siders peddled the comforting assumption that the rising tide would lift all boats: poverty could be eliminated without significant redistribution of wealth. Rather than reslicing the economic pie, policymakers could enlarge it. Tax cuts could benefit everyone.

For demand-side liberals, the 1964 tax bill was cause for less celebration. They perceived the wisdom of using taxation as a countercyclical tool, but they were discouraged by the subordination of progressive equity to economic growth and efficiency. The 1964 tax cuts signified a definitive policy turn away from progressive, ability-to-pay taxation. Gone was the conflation of social justice and tax reform. Gone, too, was the conceptualization of tax justice as a moral and ethical construct. In its place emerged a single-minded emphasis on taxation's economic effects.

Economy and Efficiency: Falling Rates and Relative Burdens, 1964 to 1999

The years 1964 to 1999 witnessed significant declines in the U.S. income tax system's statutory progressivity. The 1964 Revenue Act cut individual rates by an average of 20 percent, with the top rate falling from 90 to 70 percent and the bottom rate from 20 to 14 percent. The Tax Reform Act of 1969 reduced the maximum rate on wage and salary income to 50 percent. The Economic Recovery Tax Act of 1981 decreased individual income tax rates by 23 percent over a period of three years, and reduced the rate on unearned income from 70 to 50 percent. The Tax Reform Act of 1986 finished the business of rate cutting. It lowered the top rate to 33 percent, and consolidated the rate schedule to three brackets (15, 28, and 33).[11] In 1992 and 1993, Congress raised the top statutory rate—but only slightly—to 39.6 percent.

The top corporate income tax rate also fell during this period, from 52 percent in 1963 to 38 percent by 1994. Decreases in the corporate tax rate resulted in declining corporate income tax revenues as a percentage of federal receipts. In 1964, the corporate income tax made up 20.86 percent of federal tax revenues. By 1997, it had fallen to 11.7 percent, up from a low of 6.16 percent in 1982 (Moody 1998). The taxation of another form of capital—property—also declined during this period.

Both the corporate income tax and the property tax, long-standing symbols of tax justice, assumed minor roles in a postwar tax system that emphasized lower rates and pro-growth policies. In fact, according to one study, without accounting for any shifting of the corporate income, property, or payroll taxes, the tax burden on capital income declined by nearly 50 percent from 1966 to 1985 (Pechman 1985).

While taxes on capital income fell, taxes on labor income increased. Lower- and middle-income groups experienced higher marginal tax rates because of rising payroll taxes (Bakija and Steuerle 1991). From 1964 to 1990, the combined employee/employer payroll tax rose from 7.25 to 15.3 percent. The maximum taxable earnings increased as well, and the portion of tax receipts from payroll taxes grew from 19.5 to 36.8 percent (Moody 1998).

Meanwhile, the personal exemption declined dramatically, both as a percentage of personal income and the poverty level. In 1948, the personal exemption equaled 27.2 percent of personal income. By 1960, it had fallen to 19.8 percent, and by 1986, to 6.2 percent (Bakija and Steuerle 1991). Periodic increases in the standard deduction for married couples did not offset declines in the personal exemption, and tax-exempt thresholds remained well below the poverty line for nearly the entire period—1964 to 1986. The 1986 tax law increased tax-exempt thresholds, and removed over six million individuals from the income tax rolls by raising the standard deduction and personal exemption, and by liberalizing the Earned Income Tax Credit (EITC) (Conlan, Wrightson, and Beam 1988). Additional increases to the EITC in 1990 and 1993 raised the tax-exempt threshold still further. These increases, however, occurred during a period of rising payroll taxes on low-income workers as well as dramatic changes in welfare policy; the EITC expansions merely offset increased regressivity and retrenchment in other areas of the tax-transfer system (Ellwood 2000; Ventry 2000).

Low-income taxpayers also faced deteriorating wages. Beginning in the early 1970s, real earnings reversed their post–World War II upward trend and approached stagnation. For the next two decades, earnings inequality accelerated, creating a "hollowed out" earnings distribution with large percentages of workers at the top and bottom of the distribution, and smaller percentages in the middle (Levy and Murnane 1992). Income inequalities widened throughout the 1990s, with explosive growth in earnings and capital gains at the top of the distribution and modest growth at the bottom (Cohen 2000). Indeed, the entire period from 1968 to 1998 was characterized by increased income inequality. Census Bureau data indicate that shares of before-tax family income decreased for families below the 80th percentile in the income distribution, with the poorest 20 percent of families losing the most ground. By comparison, the share of income for the top 20 percent of families increased by an average of 14 percent, with the richest 5 percent receiving a 33 percent increase (Cohen 2000).[12]

The tax system contributed to this trend by taxing higher levels of income at reduced rates (Gramlich, Kasten, and Sammartino 1993; Pechman 1985, 1990; Slemrod 1992; U.S. Census Bureau 1992). From 1980 to 1997, effective income tax rates declined for the wealthiest Americans. According to the Internal Revenue Service, the richest 1 percent of taxpayers experienced an effective income tax rate of 34.5 percent in 1980. By 1997, that rate had fallen to 27.6 percent. Effective tax rates during the same period also fell for the top decile of taxpayers, from 23.5 to 21.4 percent (Bartlett 1999). Although wealthy taxpayers paid a larger percentage of total federal income taxes in 1997 than in 1980, income and wealth inequalities also increased. From 1983 to 1998, the after-tax income share for the wealthiest 20 percent of taxpayers increased by 5 percent, and by 16 percent for the richest 5 percent. Meanwhile, the after-tax income shares for all other households decreased (Cohen 2000). Thus, both the before-tax and after-tax distributions of income and wealth became more unequal.

The policy trends of the last 40 years have created a tax system that appears much less just from the standpoint of the republican/democratic tradition, which emphasized progressive, ability-to-pay taxation. Why have Americans accepted such a system?

The Role of Economists: Explaining the Rate Changes, 1964 to 1999

Unlike previous changes to the U.S. tax system, the transformation that began in 1964 was not the result of war, politicians, or social movements. Rather, it largely reflected changes within the economics profession and its influence within the tax policymaking process.[13]

Postwar economists de-emphasized progressive equity. The question they faced was not whether a corporation should be allowed to retain profits or whether the tax system should redistribute wealth. Rather, the question concerned whether high marginal tax rates prevented businesses from maximizing growth or an entrepreneur from maximizing aggregate welfare. Although some economists vigorously resisted these trends, their arguments for tax reform based on moral and equity considerations became difficult to sustain once the economics profession shifted its focus to efficiency gains and losses. The profession de-emphasized what it considered value judgments on relative degrees of equity for more "reliable" measurements on the efficiency effects of tax subsidies and implicit taxation. Supply-side economists extended the argument, suggesting that equity considerations were irrelevant; economists and policymakers should concentrate solely on minimizing tax distortions.

As the economics profession gained status in postwar America, economists sold their expert, efficiency-minded advice to policymakers and presidents.[14] Government economists peddled a particular kind of advice. According to Charles Schultze, chairman of President Carter's Council of Economic Advisers, government economists served as spokespersons for economic principles and especially as "partisan advocate[s] for efficiency" (Schultze 1982, 62). During the 1950s, when the U.S. economy slowed relative to that of the Soviet Union, calls for increasing economic efficiency resonated with particular clarity. Economists used efficiency arguments to advocate across-the-board cuts in personal and capital income taxes throughout the 1960s. Encouraged by the stimulatory effects of the cuts, economists turned to rate reduction again in the 1970s. And when the U.S. economy could not shake the paralysis of stagflation, economists played the efficiency card once more. In the process, they reduced taxes on capital income and high-income taxpayers to postwar lows. Their efforts resulted in a flatter, less-progressive tax system that favored corporations and high-income individuals.

Economic research justified these dramatic transformations. Public finance theory had held for generations that the least distorting tax-transfer system (one with a marginal tax rate of zero) involved lump-sum transfers whereby taxpayers paid a fixed amount of taxes or received a fixed amount of subsidy. However, such a system required that tax officials know more than they possibly could about the ability of every taxpayer to pay. Theorists and policymakers were forced to use other observable proxies to measure ability to pay. Like income, however, these proxies created efficiency losses involving a range of individual decisions about work effort, saving, and risk taking. Tax theorists struggled to create an efficient tax system with second-best strategies and asymmetric information—that is, until Peter Diamond and James Mirrlees ushered in the "optimal tax" tradition (Diamond and Mirrlees 1971a, b; Mirrlees 1971). According to the two theorists, the optimal second-best tax system contained relatively flat marginal tax rates through most of the income range and declining marginal tax rates at the top. Overall, an optimal tax system achieved progression because average rates rose with income, with the marginal rate remaining higher than the average rate through most of the income range. Other theorists extended the optimal tax model and argued that the highest-earning individual (the most able person in theory) should encounter a marginal tax rate of zero (Phelps 1973; Seade 1977). Still others advocated negative rates on the highest-income earners (Stern 1982; Stiglitz 1982). Indeed, Diamond and Mirrlees's findings created a race to the bottom of the rate scale. Researchers fiddled with calculations to see how much equity could be sacrificed in the interest of efficiency. By the early 1980s, tax "efficiency" in some circles meant the same thing as tax "equity." Under these assumptions, equity had to be sacrificed for equity's sake.

Optimal tax theory hardly initiated the postwar penchant for cutting taxes. However, it swept the economics profession, in part because economists had been "thinking along the same lines," and "were concerned with the development of models of optimal second best taxation" (Sandmo 1999, 179). Even economists who did not consider themselves optimal tax adherents absorbed many of its suppositions and used them to advocate stimulative tax cuts. It is impossible to ascertain the extent to which the optimal tax tradition has influenced individual economists over the last generation. It is safe to say, however, that modern-day economists have inculcated its concern for reducing distortions. We can observe these influences and hypothesize about their effects on policy by comparing two relatively under-appreciated tax-policy opinion polls.

The first survey, conducted in 1934 and administered by the Tax Policy League, polled public finance professors in the country's leading universities (Walker 1935). The second poll, conducted in 1994 and administered by the National Tax Association (NTA), asked American and Canadian members of the NTA to respond to many of the same questions found in the 1934 survey (Slemrod 1995, 1999). Comparing the survey results indicates that modern-day economists express less interest than their predecessors do in wielding the tax system as an instrument of social justice.

A larger percentage of economists in 1934 supported progressive income taxation for individuals. One hundred percent of surveyed economists in 1934 favored a "graduated personal income tax," compared with 80 percent in 1994. A significant number of economists in 1934 believed so strongly in the power of progressive personal income taxation that 45 percent of respondents favored abolishing all taxes except the federal personal income tax. By contrast, the 1994 response rate was 12 percent.

Economists in 1934 also favored transfer taxes and opposed sales taxes at higher rates. Ninety-two percent of respondents in 1934 and 72 percent in 1994 supported federal inheritance taxes, while 90 percent in 1934 favored a separate tax on gifts, compared with 70 percent in 1994. On sales taxes, not a single respondent in 1934 favored a general retail sales tax at the local level, compared with 56 percent of respondents in 1994. Support for a general retail sales tax at the state and federal levels was equally low in 1934 (12 and 13 percent, respectively) and comparatively high in 1994 (91 and 33 percent, respectively).

The largest professional difference between economists in 1934 and 1994 involves their attitude toward the taxation of capital income. Sixty-six percent of respondents in 1934 favored taxing "unearned (i.e., capital) income" at higher rates than earned income, compared with 7 percent in 1994. Attitudes toward property and business taxes reinforced these preferences. In 1934 and 1994, respectively, 62 percent and 22 percent of respondents thought there should be "a special tax on [the] unearned increment of land values." With respect to business taxes, 98 percent of respondents in 1934 supported a net income tax on corporations, compared with 70 percent in 1994. In addition, economists in 1934 preferred higher taxes for industries believed to possess excessive power, including banks (54 percent), insurance companies (73 percent), and railroads and public utilities (55 percent). Economists in 1994 expressed much less support for these discriminatory taxes (27, 28, and 24 percent, respectively).

The change in tax policy preferences among economists over the last 50 years influenced commensurate changes in the nation's tax system. The economics profession was also instrumental in changing the attitudes of American taxpayers toward the "proper" structure of the U.S. tax system. To some extent, economists altered popular notions of tax justice by educating legislators and taxpayers on the negative economic effects of high marginal tax rates.

The successful effort to cut taxes in 1964 was largely a campaign of economists and did not enjoy a groundswell of popular support. In fact, for the five years preceding the 1964 tax cut, Americans expressed more satisfaction with the income tax system than in any other five-year period after World War II. In response to a Gallup poll question asked almost every year from 1947 to 1998 ("Do you consider the amount of federal income tax that you have to pay as too high, too low, or about right?"), 48.8 percent of respondents in the years 1959 to 1964 felt their federal income tax burden was "too high," much lower than the average response rate of 57.5 percent for the period 1947 to 1998. Meanwhile, 42.4 percent surveyed felt it was "about right," well above the 50-year average of 36.7 percent (Gallup 1972, 1998, 1999).

After the 1964 tax cut, however, the tax-cutting penchant of economists appeared contagious. Oddly, public enthusiasm for tax cuts seemed only loosely correlated to statutory tax rates. In the three polls conducted after 1964 (1966, 1967, and 1969)—that is, after rates were cut 20 percent— 57 percent of those surveyed indicated their federal income taxes were too high, a significant jump from the five-year period preceding the 1964 tax cut (Gallup 1972). Examining taxpayer attitudes over the longer run is even more revealing. For the years 1947 to 1964, when the top marginal tax rate never dropped below 90.0 percent, 54.9 percent of respondents considered their federal income tax burden too high. From 1965 to 1998, when the top marginal income tax rate plummeted from 90.0 to 39.6 percent, a *higher* percentage of those surveyed, 60.6 percent, indicated that they paid too much in federal income taxes (Gallup 1998). From 1965 onward, American taxpayers expressed less satisfaction with the federal income tax although rates fell steadily. Something besides high tax rates (or in addition to high tax rates) fueled the public's anti-tax sentiments.

While taxpayers followed economists along the path of rate reduction beginning in the 1960s, they diverged from prevailing economic wisdom in recent years. Public opinion polls in the 1990s indicated that a majority of taxpayers supported tax reforms that would significantly reduce progressivity. In December 1995, 50 percent of respondents to a national Gallup poll supported a flat tax with a large exemption for low-income workers (Gallup 1996). A January 1996 poll found similar support (51 percent) for a flat-tax system that did not explicitly include a low-income exemption (Gallup 1997). Furthermore, by March 1999, a clear majority of respondents (65 percent) favored a flat tax with an unspecified exemption (Bartlett 1999). Professional economic opinion, by comparison, did not support a flat tax: only 28 percent of respondents endorsed a flat tax in the 1994 NTA poll (Slemrod 1999).

Have Americans abandoned progressive equity? Hardly. Americans have merely lost confidence in the income tax system to uphold progressive rates. Over the last 30 years, their worst fears have come true: corporations and high-income taxpayers have avoided their tax obligations while average taxpayers have been left to pay the bill. In January 1969, Acting Treasury Secretary Joseph Barr told Congress that 154 of the richest Americans paid no taxes in 1967 and warned of a grassroots "taxpayer's revolt." Congress responded by enacting a "minimum tax" in 1969, but public concern over loopholes that favored the rich and big business persisted. During the 1970s, while a select group of taxpayers reaped huge economic benefits from tax shelters, the majority of Americans saw more of their income subject to taxes and their after-tax income decline in value because of inflation. Although statutory income tax rates dropped during this period, bracket creep, rising payroll taxes, and higher state and local income taxes increased the marginal rate paid by the majority of Americans.

By the late 1970s, Barr's warning appeared prophetic. Beginning at the state and local levels and spreading to the federal level, taxpayers "revolted." In California, voters passed Proposition 13, an amendment to the state constitution restricting the property tax and requiring a two-thirds vote in each house of the state legislature to pass any new taxes. Proposition 13 spawned similar tax revolts in other states (O'Sullivan, Sexton, and Sheffrin 1995). These tax reform movements fed off a larger anti-government phenomenon that included Republicans and Democrats, conservatives and liberals—a movement that rejected the rising costs of government, as well as the ineffectiveness of social programs, inadequate public services, and unresponsive legislatures at all levels of government. It reflected a well-documented cynicism toward government that revealed a simple but powerful political expression: the burdens of citizenship outweighed the benefits. Americans found expression for their cynicism by reconsidering one of the most obvious public burdens, taxation.[15]

Public support for a flat tax can be viewed as part of the process of reconsidering benefits and burdens and, some say, indicates public displeasure with progressive taxation (Mitchell 2000). The evidence presented in this chapter suggests otherwise, however. Public support for the flat tax reflects frustration with the existing tax system's inability to uphold statutory progressivity, and demonstrates the belief that a flat tax would produce a more just income and wealth distribution. In the eyes of average taxpayers, a flat tax with no dispensations could produce more progression than an income tax full of loopholes.[16]

Public discontent with income tax burdens throughout the period from 1947 to 1998 was not a function of marginal tax rates. The lowest percentage of public approval with the income tax in the postwar period correlated with periods of low marginal tax rates. Alternatively, the highest percentage of public approval with the income tax system correlated with periods of high marginal tax rates. Additional poll data indicate that Americans believe progressive tax rates produce a just distribution of the tax burden. A 1983 poll conducted by the Advisory Commission on Intergovernmental Relations asked, "Which *one* of the changes would be the single most important change that would make the nation's tax system more fair?" (emphasis in the original). Forty-nine percent of respondents checked the box, "Make the upper-income taxpayers pay more," three times the percentage for the second-place vote-getter, "Make business firms pay more even if it reduces the number of jobs" (ACIR 1986). Similarly, respondents to a 1993 Gallup poll indicated overwhelmingly that neither high-income nor business taxpayers paid enough taxes. Seventy-five percent of those surveyed thought both upper-income individuals and large corporations paid too little in taxes (Gallup 1994).

Americans still believe in using tax policy as an instrument of social justice. In the 1960s and 1970s, economic efficiency arguments facilitated public acceptance of income tax reduction. Marginal tax rates of 90 percent, and even 70 or 50 percent, appeared excessive and a likely source of tax evasion. Most American taxpayers, however, accepted rate reduction not because they desired subordinating equity to efficiency concerns. Rather, they believed improving efficiency could also improve progressive equity and by extension, tax justice. Closing loopholes was supposed to pay for more progressive equity, not less.

Bridging the Divide between Equity and Efficiency

Although considerations of equity still resonate with American taxpayers, tax theory and tax policymaking currently downplay equity as an orienting principle. This last section examines the consequences of subordinating equity to efficiency in modern-day tax discussions and considers the benefits of reinserting equity into the debate. It also evaluates whether theorists are justified in separating efficiency concerns from equity concerns. The section concludes by suggesting that bridging the divide between the two principles would result in tax policies more consistent with widely shared perceptions of tax justice.

When designing (or redesigning) a tax system, participants should agree on the pattern of effective tax rates before they consider the tax instrument that will uphold these rates (Musgrave 1996a). This process encourages both the public and policymakers to consider acceptable levels of burden and benefit in relation to widely understood concepts of justice. Presently in the United States, the formula is backwards; that is, most tax reformers (legislators and economists especially) consider tax forms first and sets of rates later. In fact, many tax reformers purposely obscure the resultant pattern of effective rates. Flat-tax proponents, for example, fail to mention that their proposals will tax Bob Gates's forty-thousandth dollar of income at the same rate as Bill Gates's ten millionth dollar. They concentrate, instead, on how their proposals might reduce complexity, minimize tax evasion, or reduce the size and power of the Internal Revenue Service—all commendable concerns, but not the value-based considerations that preoccupied previous generations of tax reformers. The usual results are an empty and misleading public debate, deficient tax policies, and a cynical citizenry.

Refocusing the debate on the desired pattern of effective rates would undoubtedly make some people uneasy by raising questions about societal norms and values. However, reinserting distributive justice and competing levels of progression into the policymaking mix would restore a much-needed degree of morality into the public discourse over taxes.

Evaluating the desired distributive effects of taxation would impel policymakers to consider tax and expenditure programs as part of an integrated budget policy. Viewing tax burdens (or benefits) in isolation presents only a partial picture of relative government benefits and burdens. Both taxes and expenditures influence distribution; it does not matter, practically speaking, whether the tax side or the expenditure side impacts individuals. Thus, Musgrave (1996a) suggests viewing equity in terms of net benefits and burdens, an approach that provides policymakers with a better understanding of how individual tax policies (as well as expenditure policies) interact with the rest of the tax-transfer system and therefore helps them determine an equitable pattern of effective tax rates.

Economists have resisted considering equity too seriously, arguing that they "have no special competence in determining which distribution of resources is appropriate" (Heckman 1997, 327–28). In the interest of scientific rigor and gaining "some relative advantage to non-economists" (Steuerle 1999, 1593), the profession has avoided what it considers the "naïve and dogmatic set of judgments" required "to decide on the kinds and extent of inequality" that should prevail (Stigler 1952, 285). Economists divorce their professional duties from their duties as citizens, leaving society's pedestrian equity concerns to their citizen selves rather than their professional selves. "Since we get our notions of equity from the community," George Stigler wrote, "we can hardly play a large role in the community's choice of policies with respect to income distributions" (1982, 65). In the end, many economists seem untroubled that the "separation of efficiency and equity creates a void that often leads to neglect of the distribution/redistribution question entirely" (Heckman 1997, 332).

Both in theory and practice, the divide between efficiency and equity is not as wide as many economists would have us believe. When economists measure efficiency, they assume given and various levels of income distribution. To the extent economists prioritize certain efficiency outcomes, they also prioritize the levels of distribution associated with those outcomes. The very meaning of a given efficiency outcome depends on the initial distribution of resources. Maximizing aggregate welfare "depends on tastes, on what people want, on what they value. But what they value depends on what they have to begin with" (Calabresi 1982, 90) and, it follows, on what they end up with. On a more practical level, economists consider equity outcomes every time they evaluate competing costs and benefits of public policies.

By de-emphasizing equity, economists fail to fully use their professional training. Economics "emphasizes understanding and quantifying relationships and determining how well various measures work, such as in identifying who are equals and who are not" (Steuerle 2000, 692). Competing equity schemas are as pertinent to tax policymaking as competing consumption desires, particularly when equity preferences are viewed as "revealed preferences" analogous to other consumption preferences that cannot be neglected by economists (Steuerle 2000, 692).

Attempts to partition off equity from efficiency when considering tax policies also ignore the relationship between horizontal and vertical equity. Gains and losses in horizontal equity can, respectively, increase and decrease vertical equity. Moreover, efforts to improve horizontal equity can improve both equity and efficiency, respectively, by taxing equals equally and by reducing distortions caused by taxation.

The lingering resistance among economists to consider equity alongside efficiency involves a professional ethos that purports objectivity and rejects ideology. However, economics itself comprises an ideology by putting its faith in the competitive market economy, and by favoring policies and behaviors that reinforce the values of competition and efficiency. The free markets, within which consumers theoretically evaluate efficiency gains and losses, "are not really free," legal scholar Neil Duxbury has argued. "Rather, they are markets within which the economically powerful are able to dominate the economically weak. To express a preference for such markets is arbitrarily to uphold the legitimacy of existing power relationships" (1995, 404). With the recognition that economics reflects a system of values, maintaining a distinction between efficiency and equity based on scientific rigor becomes indefensible.

Evaluating equity alongside efficiency recognizes the inherent sociopolitical inputs of taxation. "Tax policy is a product of politics," economist Randall Holcombe suggests. "A complete understanding of tax policy requires an explicit recognition of the political environment within which tax policy is made" (1999, 397). It requires an evaluation of both social and economic equity. Although many economists are reluctant to recognize it, they are well positioned to evaluate the political and sociological variables associated with competing tax policies and systems. The economics profession resides "at the boundary where efficiency and value considerations are difficult to keep apart" (Musgrave 1996b, 257). Perhaps economics is destined to play only a supporting role to politics in the formation of tax policy (Holcombe 1999). But it shouldn't. Perhaps, too, the tools of economic analysis "can provide only limited guidance" with respect to the distribution of taxes (Sheffrin 1996, 324). But they don't have to. If economists can "transcend what is usually defined as economics" (Musgrave 1985, 13), they will once again be able to apply their valuable analytical and empirical skills to creating a tax system more in line with the realities of tax policymaking and more reflective of tax justice as defined by the group that matters most in a democracy—the taxpayers.

Conclusion

Tax theorists like to say that horizontal equity provides the one basic rule of taxation on which everyone can agree. Nonetheless, vertical equity, not horizontal equity, animates the history of tax justice in the United States. Whether in the form of the property tax, the progressive income tax, or the estate and gift tax, Americans have preferred tax policies that regulate concentrations of wealth and privilege. Similarly, whether in the form of high exemptions, lower rates for earned income, or refundable tax credits for the working poor, Americans have desired a tax system that favors low-income individuals. This is not to say that lawmakers would (or should) consider raising marginal income tax rates to approximate levels of the 1940s or 1950s. It does suggest, however, that policymakers and theorists should facilitate public debates over progressive tax equity. Moreover, it indicates that policymakers and theorists should be explicit about what various tax schedules and tax systems mean—economically as well as morally—for all income classes.

Within the last 20 years, tax experts have adjusted their models to better simulate real-life tax policymaking. They assign greater weight to the social cost of income and wealth inequality, for example, and they allow for more egalitarian social welfare functions. While experts have become slightly more amenable to equity considerations, the taxpaying public has become more sensitive to efficiency concerns, particularly the costs of high marginal tax rates. Nevertheless, tax theory and tax practice remain separated. "Optimal taxation" for economists and tax theorists still subordinates equity to efficiency. "Optimal taxation" for the majority of taxpayers, on the other hand, sacrifices efficiency for the sake of equity and emphasizes progressive tax policies. Public perceptions of tax justice may have evolved with respect to specific tax policy instruments and the relative importance of efficiency concerns, but American taxpayers still prefer tax policies that reinforce egalitarian, progressive forms of equity.

NOTES

I am indebted to Dan Shaviro, Joe Thorndike, and the reviewers from the Urban Institute Press for their instructive suggestions on earlier drafts of this chapter.

    1. For Roosevelt's proposal to impose a 100 percent tax on all incomes above $25,000, see Treasury Department, Division of Tax Research, Memorandum for the Secretary, "A Supertax on Individual Incomes above $25,000," May 1942; and Roy Blough,

"Comments from Harriss, Hewett, and Slitor on Super-Tax on Individual Incomes above $25,000," May 5, 1942; both documents in the Records of the Office of Tax Analysis/ Division of Tax Research, Box 54, General Records of the Department of the Treasury, Subject Files, Record Group 56, National Archives, College Park, Md.

2. Vertical and horizontal equity are not mutually exclusive, of course. Improvements in horizontal equity can result in improvements in vertical equity, while losses in horizontal equity can create losses in vertical equity. Throughout the history of taxation in the United States, theorists, policymakers, and the public have recognized these relationships. For purposes of this chapter, however, unless otherwise indicated, "equity" is defined as the opposite of "efficiency" and indicative of societal norms involving morality, ethics, and social justice.

3. Not all modern-day economists ignore issues of equity and distribution. The welfare economics tradition, for example, makes distribution issues central to its analysis, and the optimal tax tradition measures equity issues alongside efficiency issues. Both groups of theorists, however, de-emphasize the social value of equality, theoretically as well as empirically.

I should emphasize that this chapter could not have been written absent previous research on tax equity and income distribution. Several contributions deserve especial comment: Slemrod's individual research and a series of conferences on progressivity (Slemrod 1983, 1992, 1996, 2000; Slemrod and Bakija 2000); Blank (1997), Danziger and Gottschalk (1995), Ellwood (1988), and Wolff (1995, 1998) on income distribution and wealth inequality; Pechman (1985, 1990) and Bakija and Steuerle (1991) on progressivity trends, and Steuerle's numerous written and professional efforts to increase progressivity at the bottom of the income distribution; Atkinson (1975, 1983) and Sen (1973, 1992) on liberal welfare economics and inequality; and the entire career of Musgrave (1959, 1989, 1992, 1996a). Despite these important contributions, economists generally consider equity issues as (1) qualitative matters about which their profession should say little; (2) measurable variables that, although important, should be subordinated to efficiency concerns when there exists an observable trade-off; or (3) salient only when they contribute to further efficiency gains.

4. Only 1.5 percent of households paid an income tax in 1913, and only 2 percent paid income taxes on average from 1913–1915 (Brownlee 2000; Witte 1985).

5. As Brownlee has shown, the term "soak-the-rich" taxation was a contemporary designation used in both the United States and England by critics of progressive taxation (Brownlee 2000).

6. For Roosevelt's New Deal tax programs, see Lambert (1970), Leff (1984), Witte (1985), and Brownlee (1996). Of the four, only Brownlee and Witte perceive the radical nature of Roosevelt's pre–World War II tax policy, and only Brownlee sees a commitment to soak-the-rich taxation. Lambert emphasizes Roosevelt's moral commitment to ability-to-pay taxation, but does not consider New Deal tax policies as radical. Leff, for his part, sees only hollow, symbolic victories for the American people in New Deal taxation; Roosevelt's tax reforms were all bark, no bite, according to Leff.

7. The balance of this paragraph relies heavily on Brownlee (1996).

8. For the legislative efforts to limit the taxing powers, see H.R. 8545, Ralph Gwinn (R-NY), *Congressional Record*, March 24, 1954, p. 3804; H.J. Res. 16, Frederic Coudert Jr. (R-NY), *Congressional Record*, January 5, 1955, p. 49; H.J. Res. 608, Ralph

Gwinn (R-NY), *Congressional Record,* April 23, 1956, p. 6809; H.J. Res. 171, Russell Keeney (R-IL), *Congressional Record,* January 1, 1957, p. 791; S.J. Res. 25, Everett Dirksen (R-IL), *Congressional Record,* January 1, 1957, p. 404; H.J. Res. 67, Noah Mason (R-IL), *Congressional Record,* January 3, 1957, p. 90; H.J. Res. 218, Overton Brooks (D-LA), *Congressional Record,* February 2, 1957, p. 1508; H.J. Res. 232, Clare Hoffman (R-MN), *Congressional Record,* February 2, 1957, p. 2062; H.R. 12879, Gerald Flynn (D-WI), *Congressional Record,* June 29, 1960, p. 15040.

9. The liberal supply-siders of the 1950s and 1960s should be differentiated from the conservative supply-siders of the 1970s and 1980s. The former group pursued policies that stimulated economic growth, but they also recognized the economic and social benefits of stability in the form of a progressive income tax, welfare transfers, unemployment insurance, and farm subsidies. The latter group of supply-siders pursued economic growth to the near exclusion of economic stability (except to the extent lower taxes stabilized investment planning for businesses and high incomes). They argued for reduced taxes on capital income, and they attacked programs that provided stability during economic upswings and downswings, such as the progressive income tax and welfare payments.

10. Musgrave was not alone in suggesting that the Kennedy administration had abandoned equity in advocating the tax bill. Economist Joseph Pechman, for one, noted, "In the hullabaloo over the tax reduction, the tax reform part of the package has been virtually forgotten" (1963, 20).

11. For practical purposes, TRA 86 created two tax brackets (15 and 28 percent). The 33 percent "bubble" bracket applied to only a narrow band of income.

12. The trend toward increased income inequalities between 1968 and 1998 stands in stark contrast to the period from 1947 to 1968. During this period, shares of before-tax income for families below the 80th percentile increased, while shares of before-tax income for the richest 20 percent of families decreased (Cohen 2000). Although researchers have discussed the effect of taxes on after-tax income inequality by comparing pre-tax income distributions with after-tax income distributions, they have spent less time trying to understand the effect of taxes on before-tax income distributions. It would be worth studying the relationship between taxes and before-tax income inequalities for each of the two distinct periods (1947–1968 and 1968–1998), particularly because decreases in before-tax income inequalities seem to be correlated to periods of high marginal tax rates while increases in before-tax income inequalities seem to be correlated to periods of low marginal tax rates.

13. The evidence presented in this section challenges George Stigler's conclusion that economists "exert a minor role and scarcely detectable influence on the societies in which they live" (1982, 63).

14. For government economists as political actors, see Stein (1986) and Nelson (1987).

15. According to a May 1999 poll conducted by the Council for Excellence in Government, many Americans still perceive an imbalance between government burdens and benefits. Forty-six percent of respondents felt they paid too much in taxes for what they received from government, while only 19 percent considered their taxes a fair price for the benefits they received. Cited in Bartlett (1999).

16. Slemrod and Venkatesh (1999) conclude similarly that Americans believe a flat tax would improve progressivity. Slemrod and Venkatesh also argue that most tax-

payers misunderstand the distributive effects of flat-tax proposals. My research supports these conclusions. Consider, for example, that a January 1996 Gallup survey revealed that 51 percent of respondents believed a flat tax would help middle-class Americans (Gallup 1997). The majority of flat-tax plans, however, most certainly redistribute tax burdens from wealthy taxpayers to everyone else, including the middle class.

REFERENCES

Advisory Commission on Intergovernmental Relations (ACIR). 1986. *Changing Public Attitudes on Governments and Taxes.* Washington, D.C.: ACIR.

Atkinson, Anthony Barnes. 1975. *The Economics of Inequality.* Oxford: Clarendon Press.

———. 1983. *Social Choice and Public Policy.* Cambridge: MIT Press.

Bakija, Jon, and C. Eugene Steuerle. 1991. "Individual Income Taxation Since 1948." *National Tax Journal* 44 (4, December): 451–75.

Bartlett, Bruce. 1999. "The Trouble with Tax Cuts." *Tax Notes* 85 (11, December 13): 1457–63.

Blakey, Roy G. 1914. "The New Income Tax." *American Economic Review* 4 (1, March): 25–46.

Blank, Rebecca M. 1997. *It Takes a Nation: A New Agenda for Fighting Poverty.* New York: Russell Sage Foundation.

Blough, Roy. 1952. *The Federal Taxing Process.* New York: Prentice-Hall.

Blum, John Morton. 1959. *From the Morgenthau Diaries: Years of Crisis, 1928–1938.* Boston: Houghton Mifflin.

Blum, Walter J. 1955. Remarks of. In U.S. Congress Joint Committee on the Economic Report. *Federal Tax Policy for Economic Growth and Stability.* Washington, D.C.: U.S. Government Printing Office (GPO).

Blum, Walter J., and Harry Kalven Jr. 1953. *The Uneasy Case for Progressive Taxation.* Chicago: University of Chicago Press.

Break, George F. 1957. "Income Taxes and Incentives to Work: An Empirical Study." *American Economic Review* 47 (5, September): 529–49.

Brinkley, Alan. 1995. *The End of Reform: New Deal Liberalism in Recession and War.* New York: Vintage Books.

Brownlee, W. Elliot. 1996. *Federal Taxation in America: A Short History.* Cambridge: Cambridge University Press and Woodrow Wilson Center Press.

———. 2000. "Historical Perspective on U.S. Tax Policy toward the Rich." In *Does Atlas Shrug? The Economic Consequences of Taxing the Rich,* edited by Joel B. Slemrod (29–73). New York and Cambridge: Russell Sage Foundation and Harvard University Press.

Calabresi, Guido. 1982. "The New Economic Analysis of Law: Scholarship, Sophistry, or Self-Indulgence?" *Proceedings of the British Academy* 68: 85–108.

Chapman, S. J. 1913. "The Utility of Income and Progressive Taxation." *Economic Journal* 23 (89): 25–35.

Clark, Frank. 1959. Remarks of *Congressional Record* (February 17).

Cohen, Stephen B. 2000. "Vanishing Case for the Flat Tax: Growth, Inequality, Saving, and Simplification." *Tax Notes* 86 (5, January 31): 675–90.

Colmer, William. 1953. "Taxation: The Power to Destroy America's Future." *Congressional Record* (February 12).

Committee for Economic Development (CED). 1946. *Fiscal Policy to Fight Inflation.* New York: CED.

———. 1948. *Monetary and Fiscal Policy for Greater Economic Stability.* New York: CED.

———. 1954. *Defense against Recession: Policy for Greater Economic Stability.* New York: CED.

Conlan, Timothy J., Margaret T. Wrightson, and David R. Beam. 1988. *Taxing Choices: The Politics of Tax Reform.* Washington, D.C.: Congressional Quarterly Press.

Curtis, Carl. 1950. "Tax Relief." *Congressional Record* (June 8).

Danziger, Sheldon, and Peter Gottschalk. 1995. *America Unequal.* Cambridge: Harvard University Press.

De Jouvenel, Bertrand. 1952. *The Ethics of Redistribution.* Cambridge: Cambridge University Press.

Diamond, Peter A., and James A. Mirrlees. 1971a. "Optimal Taxation and Public Production I—Production Efficiency." *American Economic Review* 61 (1, March): 8–27.

———. 1971b. "Optimal Taxation and Public Production II—Tax Rules." *American Economic Review* 61 (2, June): 261–78.

Duxbury, Neil. 1995. *Patterns of American Jurisprudence.* Oxford: Clarendon Press.

Eisenstein, Louis, Edmund Cahn, Thurman Arnold, and Robert J. McDonald. 1962. "A Discussion of 'The Ideologies of Taxation.' " *Tax Law Review* 18: 1–22.

Ellwood, David T. 1988. *Poor Support: Poverty in the American Family.* New York: Basic Books.

———. 2000. "Anti-Poverty Policy for Families in the Next Century: From Welfare to Work—and Worries." *Journal of Economic Perspectives* 14 (1, Winter): 187–98.

Galbraith, John Kenneth. 1958. *The Affluent Society.* Boston: Houghton Mifflin.

Gallup, George H. 1972. *The Gallup Poll: Public Opinion, 1935–71.* 3 vols. New York: Random House.

Gallup, George, Jr. 1994. *The Gallup Poll: Public Opinion, 1993.* Wilmington, Del.: Scholarly Resources, Inc.

———. 1996. *The Gallup Poll: Public Opinion, 1995.* Wilmington, Del.: Scholarly Resources, Inc.

———. 1997. *The Gallup Poll: Public Opinion, 1996.* Wilmington, Del.: Scholarly Resources, Inc.

———. 1998. *The Gallup Poll: Public Opinion, 1997.* Wilmington, Del.: Scholarly Resources, Inc.

———. 1999. *The Gallup Poll: Public Opinion, 1998.* Wilmington, Del.: Scholarly Resources, Inc.

Goldscheid, Rudolph. 1917. "A Sociological Approach to Problems of Public Finance." Translated from German by Elizabeth Henderson. In *Classics in the Theory of Public Finance,* edited by Richard A. Musgrave and Alan T. Peacock (202–13). New York: St. Martin's Press, 1964.

Gramlich, Edward M., Richard Kasten, and Frank Sammartino. 1993. "Growing Inequality in the 1980s: The Role of the Federal Taxes and Cash Transfers." In *Uneven Tides: Rising Inequality in America,* edited by Sheldon Danziger and Peter Gottschalk (225–50). New York: Russell Sage Foundation.

Groves, Harold M. 1944. *Production, Jobs and Taxes: Postwar Revision of the Federal Tax System to Help Achieve Higher Production and More Jobs.* New York: McGraw-Hill.

———. 1955. Statement of. In U.S. Congress. Joint Committee on the Economic Report. *Federal Tax Policy for Economic Growth and Stability.* Washington, D.C.: GPO.

———. 1956. "Toward a Social Theory of Taxation." *National Tax Journal* 9 (1, March): 27–34.

Gurley, John G. 1952. "Fiscal Policies for Full Employment: A Diagrammatic Analysis." *Journal of Political Economy* 60 (6, December): 523–33.

Gwinn, Ralph. 1950. "The Need of Limiting by Congressional Amendment the Spending and Taxing Powers of Congress." *Congressional Record* (January 16).

Hamby, Alonzo. 1973. *Beyond the New Deal: Harry S. Truman and American Liberalism.* New York: Columbia University Press.

Hawley, Ellis. 1995. *The New Deal and the Problem of Monopoly: A Study in Economic Ambivalence,* revised edition. New York: Fordham University Press.

Hayek, Friedrich A. 1956. "Progressive Taxation Reconsidered." In *On Freedom and Free Enterprise: Essays in Honor of Ludwig von Mises,* edited by Mary Sennholz. New York: D. Van Nostrand Co.

Heckman, James J. 1997. "The Intellectual Roots of the Law and Economics Movement." *Law and History Review* 15 (2, Fall): 327–32.

Hellerstein, Jerome R. 1963. *Taxes, Loopholes, and Morals.* New York: McGraw-Hill.

Holcombe, Randall G. 1999. "Tax Policy from a Public Choice Perspective." In *Tax Policy in the Real World,* edited by Joel Slemrod (397–409). Cambridge: Cambridge University Press.

Hull, Cordell. 1948. *The Memoirs of Cordell Hull, Volume 1.* New York: Macmillan.

Jones, Carolyn. 1988. "Split Income and Separate Spheres." *Law and History Review* 6 (2, Fall): 259–310.

Kassalow, Everett. 1959. Representing the AFL-CIO. "To Restore Balance and Equity in Family Taxation." In U.S. Congress. House. Committee on Ways and Means. *Tax Revision Compendium: Compendium of Papers on Broadening the Tax Base,* vol. 1 (515–24). Washington, D.C.: GPO.

Lambert, Robert K. 1970. "New Deal Revenue Acts: The Politics of Taxation." Ph.D. diss., University of Texas, Austin.

LeCompte, Karl. 1953. "We're Following the Teachings of Karl Marx." *Congressional Record* (March 30).

Leff, Mark. 1984. *The Limits of Symbolic Reform: The New Deal and Taxation.* New York: Cambridge University Press.

Levy, Frank, and Richard J. Murnane. 1992. "U.S. Earnings Levels and Earnings Inequality: A Review of Recent Trends and Proposed Explanations." *Journal of Economic Literature* 30 (September): 1333–81.

Long, Russell. 1954. Statement of. *Congressional Record* (June 29).

Lutz, Harley. 1947. *A Tax Program for a Solvent America.* New York: Committee on Postwar Tax Policy.

Magill, Roswell. 1959. "Federal Income Tax Revision." In U.S. Congress. House. Committee on Ways and Means. *Tax Revision Compendium: Compendium of Papers on Broadening the Tax Base,* vol. 1. Washington, D.C.: GPO.

Mirrlees, James A. 1971. "An Exploration in the Theory of Optimum Income Taxation." *Review of Economic Studies* 38 (April): 175–208.

Mitchell, Daniel J. 2000. "The Inevitability of the Flat Tax." *Tax Notes* 86 (5, January 31): 669–74.

Moody, Scott, ed. 1998. *Facts and Figures on Government Finance,* 32d ed. Washington, D.C.: Tax Foundation.

Musgrave, Richard A. 1959. *The Theory of Public Finance.* New York: McGraw-Hill.

———. 1963a. Statement of. In U.S. Congress. Senate. Committee on Finance. *Revenue Act of 1963.* Washington, D.C.: GPO.

———. 1963b. "Comments on Tax Policy." May 4, 1963. The Stanley S. Surrey Papers. Harvard Law School Library. Box 176. File 1.

———. 1985. "Public Finance and Distributive Justice." In *Public Choice, Public Finance, and Public Policy: Essays in Honour of Alan Peacock,* edited by David Greenaway and G. K. Shaw (1–14). Oxford: Basil Blackwell Ltd.

———. 1989. "Horizontal Equity, Once More." *National Tax Journal* 42 (2, June): 113–22.

———. 1992. "Social Contract, Taxation and the Standing of Deadweight Loss." *Journal of Public Economics* 49: 369–81.

———. 1996a. "Progressive Taxation, Equity, and Tax Design." In *Tax Progressivity and Income Inequality,* edited by Joel Slemrod (341–56). Cambridge: Cambridge University Press.

———. 1996b. "The Role of the State in Fiscal Theory." *International Tax and Public Finance* 3: 247–58.

Nathan, Robert. 1954. Statement of. Representing the Americans for Democratic Action. In U.S. Congress. Senate. *The Internal Revenue Code of 1954, Part II.* Washington, D.C.: GPO.

Nelson, Robert H. 1987. "The Economics Profession and the Making of Public Policy." *Journal of Economic Literature* 25 (March): 49–91.

Noyes, C. Reinold. 1947. "The Prospect for Economic Growth." *American Economic Review* 37 (1, March): 13–33.

O'Sullivan, Arthur, Terri A. Sexton, and Steven M. Sheffrin. 1995. *Property Taxes and Tax Revolts: The Legacy of Proposition 13.* Cambridge: Cambridge University Press.

Paul, Randolph. 1947. *Taxation for Prosperity.* New York: The Bobbs-Merrill Co.

———. 1955. Remarks of. In U.S. Congress. Joint Committee on the Economic Report. *Federal Tax Policy for Economic Growth and Stability.* Washington, D.C.: GPO.

Pechman, Joseph A. 1963. "The Case for Tax Reform." *The Reporter* (June 6): 20–23.

———. 1985. *Who Paid the Taxes, 1966–85?* Washington, D.C.: The Brookings Institution.

———. 1990. "The Future of the Income Tax." *American Economic Review* 80 (1, March): 1–20.

Phelps, Edmund S. 1973. "The Taxation of Wage Income for Economic Justice." *Quarterly Journal of Economics* 87 (August): 331–54.

Rawls, John. 1971. *A Theory of Justice.* Cambridge: Harvard University Press, Belknap Press.

———. 1974. "Concepts of Distributional Equity: Some Reasons for the Maximin Criterion." *American Economic Review* 64 (2, May): 141–46.

Reed, Chauncy. 1955. "Limiting the Power of Congress to Tax Incomes, Inheritances, and Gifts." *Congressional Record* (January 31).

Rich, Robert. 1950. "To Lower Taxes and Balance the Budget Our Job." *Congressional Record* (June 8).

Rolph, Earl R. 1950. "Equity Versus Efficiency in Federal Tax Policy." *American Economic Review* 40 (2, May): 391–404.

Roosevelt, Theodore. 1906. Remarks of. *Congressional Record* (December 4).

Sandmo, Agnar. 1999. "Asymmetric Information and Public Economics: The Mirrlees-Vickrey Nobel Prize." *Journal of Economic Perspectives* 13 (1, Winter): 165–80.

Schultze, Charles L. 1982. "The Role and Responsibilities of the Economist in Government." *American Economic Review* 72 (2, May): 62–66.

Schumpeter, Joseph A. 1918. "The Crisis of the Tax State." Translated from German by W. F. Stolper and R. A. Musgrave. In *International Economic Papers* No. 4. Edited by Alan T. Peacock, Wolfgang F. Stolper, Ralph Turvey, and Elizabeth Henderson (5–38). New York: The Macmillan Co., 1954.

Seade, Jesus K. 1977. "On the Shape of Optimal Tax Schedules." *Journal of Public Economics* 7 (April): 203–35.

Seligman, Edwin R. A. 1894. "The Income Tax." *Political Science Quarterly* 9 (4): 610–48.

Sen, Amartya. 1973. *On Economic Inequality.* Delhi: Oxford University Press.

———. 1992. *Inequality Re-Examined.* New York and Cambridge: Russell Sage Foundation and Harvard University Press.

Shafer, Paul. 1951. "Statement of Republican Principles and Objectives." *Congressional Record* (June 8).

Sheffrin, Steven M. 1996. "Perceptions of Fairness in the Crucible of Tax Policy." In *Tax Progressivity and Income Inequality,* edited by Joel Slemrod (309–40). Cambridge: Cambridge University Press.

Shere, Louis. 1948. "Taxation and Inflation Control." *American Economic Review* 38 (5, December): 843–56.

Simons, Henry C. 1938. *Personal Income Taxation: The Definition of Income as a Problem of Fiscal Policy.* Chicago: University of Chicago Press.

Slemrod, Joel. 1983. "Do We Know How Progressive the Income Tax Should Be?" *National Tax Journal* 36 (3, September): 361–69.

———. 1992. "Taxation and Inequality: A Time-Exposure Perspective." In *Tax Policy and the Economy,* vol. 6, edited by James M. Poterba. Cambridge: MIT Press.

———. 1995. "Professional Opinions about Tax Policy: 1994 and 1934." *National Tax Journal* 48 (1, March): 121–47.

———, ed. 1996. *Tax Progressivity and Income Inequality.* Cambridge: Cambridge University Press.

———. 1999. "Professional Opinions about Tax Policy: 1994 and 1934." In *Tax Policy in the Real World,* edited by Joel Slemrod (435–61). Cambridge: Cambridge University Press.

———, ed. 2000. *Does Atlas Shrug? The Economic Consequences of Taxing the Rich.* New York and Cambridge: Russell Sage Foundation and Harvard University Press.

Slemrod, Joel, and Jon Bakija. 2000. "Does Growing Inequality Reduce Tax Progressivity? Should It?" NBER Working Paper No. 7576. Cambridge, Mass.: National Bureau of Economic Research.

Slemrod, Joel, and Varsha Venkatesh. 1999. "Public Attitudes about Taxation and the 2000 Presidential Campaign." *Tax Notes* 83 (12, June 21): 1799–801.

Stanley, Robert. 1993. *Dimensions of Law in the Service of Order: Origins of the Federal Income Tax, 1861–1913.* New York: Oxford University Press.

Stein, Herbert. 1959. "What's Wrong with the Federal Tax System?" In U.S. Congress. House. *Tax Revision Compendium: Compendium of Papers on Broadening the Tax Base,* vol. 1. Washington, D.C.: GPO.

————. 1986. "The Washington Economics Industry." *American Economic Review* 76 (2, May): 1–9.

————. 1990. *The Fiscal Revolution in America: Policy in Pursuit of Reality,* 2d revised edition. Washington, D.C.: American Enterprise Institute.

Stern, Nicholas H. 1982. "Optimum Taxation with Errors in Administration." *Journal of Public Economics* 17 (2): 181–211.

Steuerle, C. Eugene. 1996. "Financing the American State at the Turn of the Century." In *Funding the Modern American State, 1941–1995,* edited by W. Elliot Brownlee (409–44). Cambridge: Cambridge University Press and Woodrow Wilson Center Press.

————. 1999. "And Equal (Tax) Justice for All?" Part Four, *Tax Notes* 85 (12, December 20): 1593–94.

————. 2000. "And Equal (Tax) Justice for All?" Part Eight, *Tax Notes* 86 (5, January 31): 691–92.

Stigler, George. 1952. *The Theory of Price,* revised ed. New York: Macmillan.

————. 1982. *The Economist as Preacher and Other Essays.* Chicago: University of Chicago Press.

Stiglitz, Joseph E. 1982. "Self-Selection and Pareto Efficient Taxation." *Journal of Public Economics* 17 (2): 213–40.

Taussig, Frank W. 1921. *Principles of Economics,* 3d ed. New York: Macmillan.

Tobin, James. 1949. "Taxation, Saving, and Inflation." *American Economic Review* 39 (6, December): 1223–32.

Trilling, Richard J. 1980. *Realignment in American Politics: Toward a Theory.* Austin: University of Texas Press.

U.S. Census Bureau. 1992. *Measuring the Effect of Benefits and Taxes on Income and Poverty: 1979–1991.* Current Population Reports, Series P-60, No. 162. Washington, D.C.: GPO.

Ventry, Dennis J., Jr. 2000. "The Collision of Tax and Welfare Politics: The Political History of the Earned Income Tax Credit." *National Tax Journal* 53 (4, Part 2, December): 983–1026.

Walker, Mabel L. 1935. "Opinion of American Professors of Public Finance on Important Tax Questions as of January 1, 1935." In *Tax Systems of the World,* edited by Tax Research Foundation. Chicago: Commerce Clearing House, Inc.

Williamson, Jeffrey G., and Peter H. Lindert. 1980. *American Inequality: A Macroeconomic History.* New York: Academic Press.

Witte, John F. 1985. *The Politics and Development of the Federal Income Tax.* Madison: University of Wisconsin Press.

Wolff, Edward N. 1995. *Top Heavy: The Increasing Inequality of Wealth in America and What Can Be Done about It.* New York: Twentieth Century Fund.

————. 1998. "Recent Trends in the Size Distribution of Household Wealth." *Journal of Economic Perspectives* 12 (3, Summer): 131–50.

Zelizer, Julian. 1998. *Taxing America: Wilbur D. Mills, Congress, and the State, 1945–1975.* Cambridge: Cambridge University Press.

3

Economic History and the Analysis of "Soaking the Rich" in 20th-Century America

W. Elliot Brownlee

I n the United States, political interest in establishing tax justice has focused heavily on adopting tax policies that "soak the rich."[1] This interest has produced a mix of policies that tax wealth: Personal and corporate income taxation rates are sharply progressive; until World War II, the income tax focused on the taxation of profits and interest rather than on the taxation of earned income; the system of estate and gift taxation is highly progressive; and the property tax is the highest in the world. Some analysts believe that the interest in taxing the wealthy has been sufficiently pronounced to establish progressivity as one of the distinguishing characteristics of American taxation.[2]

America's high taxation of the wealthy may seem paradoxical, given the social value attached to the accumulation of private capital and a historical reluctance to erect governmental barriers to the individual "pursuit of happiness." Some historians have explained away the paradox by arguing that taxing the rich in the United States has been far more symbolic than real. These commentators argue that the impetus to tax the rich largely reflects a manipulative invocation of progressive symbolism by capitalists and their political trustees. By contrast, other historians, including this author, regard the intent to tax the rich as a deliberate, influential tack. According to this view, the continuing importance of republican ideology helps explain the apparent dissonance of tax policy within American capitalism. Until the 1960s, classical republicanism, adapted to industrial conditions, led progressive tax reformers to believe that taxing the rich would, in fact, stimulate the accumulation of private capital and the advance of economic growth. Only during the 1960s did such reformers see the trade-off between equity and growth. With that realization, they concluded it was time to abandon the effort to enhance progressive equity for the sake of promoting economic growth (Brownlee 2000).

Economic historians have not contributed significantly to the understanding of taxation in the United States. They have failed to systematically test the validity of the conflicting assertions regarding trade-offs between equity and growth. In addition, they have not sought structural explanations for the intensification of "soak-the-rich" taxation in the early 20th century or for the decline of this practice during the 1960s. This chapter attempts to point to ways in which the "new" economic history might advance knowledge of the political economy of taxation in the United States.

This chapter examines the state of historical knowledge about the effects of taxing the rich on the distribution of income and wealth, economic growth, and economic stability. A comprehensive history of tax justice in the United States must include the effects of tax policy as well as the nature of the interrelationships between the development of tax policy and its effects. The chapter evaluates prospects for assessing the historical effects, both growth and distributional, of taxation within the scholarly context of the new economic history. The new economic history has mobilized economic theory and quantitative data to describe and account for long-term patterns of economic growth, stability, and the distribution of income and wealth. In so doing, the new economic history has created a theoretical and quantitative platform for analyzing the economic effects of technological and organizational change. This platform may be of value in assessing the growth and distributional effects of taxing the wealthiest Americans.

The chapter then considers how an improved understanding of the economic context of tax policy would assist in understanding how and why policymakers have sought particular methods of advancing tax justice. The work of the new economic historians is also helpful here, particularly in terms of theoretical, rather than quantitative, efforts to understand the linkages between institutional development and economic performance.

The goal of the new economic historians is to reconstruct neoclassical economic theory, which has disregarded institutional development and the dimension of time. Some new economic historians argue that with a better sense of institutional history and social learning, the discipline of economics could better explain economic development, especially the emergence and spread of incentive systems that promote technological advances and investment in human capital. A prominent example of this theoretical work is that of Nobel Prize winner Douglass C. North, who has labored to develop a theoretical understanding of issues such as the emergence of capitalistic systems of property rights in the early modern era.[3] In such theoretical efforts, the new economic historians have converged with the historians in the disciplines of history, political science, and sociology who have explored the way in which economic changes shape American political and social organization. These scholars commonly describe themselves as historians of "political economy," and in fact, they share ancestors with the new economic historians. Both groups of scholars practice modern variants of the institutionalism that began with the discipline of economics during the late 19th century.[4]

Within this literature of political economy lies most of the recent research on the history of American tax policy. The literature features a variety of assertions about the economic effects of tax measures. Historians of the political economy of taxation have made assumptions about the rationality and perceptiveness of the actors who shape tax policy, and have posited strong, continuing feedback effects between intentions and consequences.

Political Economists and the Economic Effects of Taxation

Scholars of tax history have different assumptions regarding two central categories of economic change—the distribution of income and wealth, and economic growth or productivity improvement.

Distribution of Income and Wealth

The "progressive" school of tax historians launched the modern history of taxation. Sidney Ratner, the school's first architect, assumed that progressive taxation effectively promoted a more equitable, vertical distribution of income, describing such taxation "as preeminently fit for achieving and preserving the economic objectives of a democracy" (1942; 1967, 14). Ratner praised the income tax not only because it seemed progressive, but also because, in his view, it created the basis for a well-funded welfare state and for a federal government that could defend the cause of economic democracy around the world. Thus, the adoption of progressive income taxation facilitated an expansion of social democracy at home and abroad. In other words, Ratner argued that an evaluation of the federal income tax ought to take into account the progressively redistributional effects of the revenues raised by the tax.

A wide variety of "postprogressive" tax historians have challenged the assertions of Ratner and his colleagues regarding the distributional effects of federal taxation in the 20th century. Within the new, postprogressive tax histories, four interpretive options regarding the distributions of political power and economic wealth have emerged.

- *The "capitalist-state" view.* Capitalists and their agents have captured the state and concentrated the distribution of wealth in their own hands. Historian Mark Leff, for example, argues that even the New Deal's tax program catered to capitalist power. The New Deal's income tax initiatives, including the radical tax on undistributed earnings, were no more than hollow, purely symbolic efforts to appease the forces of democracy.[5]
- *The "pluralist" view.* Competitive interest groups have ground down the state and distributed wealth to benefit middle-class groups. The progressive intent of the tax system has been modest. Carolyn Webber and Aaron Wildavsky, political scientists and authors of *History of Taxation and Expenditure in the Western World* (1986), summarized the pluralist point of view by quoting Pogo: "We—the broad middle and lower classes—have met the special interests, and 'they is us' " (531).[6]
- *The "neo-conservative" view.* Narrowly selfish "tax-eaters" have subverted democracy and distributed wealth in their favor. Economists who practice economic history, especially Ben Baack, Edward J. Ray, and Robert Higgs, are primarily responsible for crafting this neoconservative interpretation. They see the passage of the Sixteenth Amendment, for example, as the thin edge of the wedge for interest groups that want to use government to redistribute income in their direction—through the revenue effects as well as the incidence of the income tax.[7]
- *The "democratic-institutionalist" view.* Both progressive redistributionists and capitalist interests have been influential in the highly

contingent process of making tax policy. At different times, each category of interests decisively shaped what has been a rather chaotic flow of policy. Their effect on the distribution of wealth has varied greatly, depending on which group prevailed in the highly contingent battles over tax policy. This "democratic-institutionalist" take on tax history is the one associated with my work (Brownlee 1996a,b).

Economic Growth and Productivity

Contending schools of tax scholars treat the issue of the impact of federal taxation on economic growth—that is, growth in productivity—in ways that parallel their analyses of the issue of distribution.

The progressive historians maintained that the progressively redistributional effects of income taxation had a decidedly positive advance on economic productivity. Ratner argued that progressive taxation effectively attacked monopoly power and encouraged competitive forces. Therefore, Ratner claimed, it enhanced the ability of the marketplace to increase productivity.

Ronald King, making just the opposite assumption about the source of productivity, reached the same conclusion. Progressive taxation in America reinforced the interests of monopoly capitalism and thereby enhanced productivity—as measured by the capitalist marketplace. The tax preferences that capitalist "elites" embedded in the tax code promoted capital accumulation and increased productivity. King argues that all U.S. presidents after World War II invoked this logic in devising their tax programs. He finds, however, that the administration of John F. Kennedy was the most creative in mobilizing investment tax subsidies to accommodate the potentially conflicting interests of business and labor.

In contrast with the progressives and the capitalist-state theorists, the pluralists, neocapitalist, and democratic-institutionalist historians all regard progressive income taxation as having *limited* the productivity of the American economy. These groups all stress the economically dysfunctional character of federal tax policy; they all recognize the ways in which the introduction and expansion of tax expenditures within the tax code have created a welter of incentives and disincentives for economic behavior that prevents the American economy from making optimal use of its resources. In addition, the neocapitalists and democratic-institutionalists also tend to criticize the system's progressivity. They suggest that "soak-the-rich" taxation has significantly raised the cost of capital and thereby inhibited investment and the advance of productivity.

The democratic-institutionalists add a further complication to the assessment of productivity effects. They alone identify episodes of reform on behalf of horizontal equity and praise their economic effects. They point, in particular, to the process of social learning that led a bipartisan coalition, after World War II, to abandon "soak-the-rich" taxation as a central element of tax policy. By the 1960s, elements within the tax policy community built support for tax uniformity. Historian Julian Zelizer, for example, finds that even Wilbur Mills contributed to this movement by embracing significant base-broadening reforms in the Revenue Act of 1962. That base-broadening movement gathered force in the late 1970s and played a crucial role in the passage of the Tax Reform Act of 1986. Certain experts and political entrepreneurs within the tax-policy community tracked, through systematic investigation, the effects of taxation of productivity and economic growth, and reached consensus on the need for a broader-based, more uniform system of income taxation. Thus, the democratic-institutionalists find the effects of tax policy on productivity significantly more variable than do other schools of tax history, and they see greater possibilities for significant discontinuities in tax policy.[8]

The New Economic Historians and the Economic Effects of Taxation

Rigorous quantitative research might assist in discriminating among the powerful, competing claims of the political economists regarding the economic impact of tax institutions. In turn, economists could strengthen the historical foundations of the models they have designed to explain changes in distribution, productivity, and stability. But have economic historians done such research?

The short answer is that they have not. The powerful research by economic historians on the patterns of growth, stability, and distribution, and on the sources of those patterns, has not extended to taxation and public finance. The quality and scope of even the basic data on the characteristics of public finance has improved little over the last generation. For example, the call more than 30 years ago by Lance Davis and John Legler for the development of a comprehensive set of time series on the basic trends of public finance has gone largely unanswered (Davis and Legler 1966).[9]

Public finance economists, however, have provided some useful preliminary research on the impact of the federal tax system on the distribution of income and wealth (e.g., Kasten, Sammartino, and Toder 1994; Slemrod 1994). Bajika and Steuerle (1991) have clarified the initial incidence of the federal income tax since World War II. The group has not, however, addressed the thorny problems surrounding the ultimate incidence of taxation.[10]

In my own work (Brownlee 2000), I have tried to expand upon this preliminary research by measuring, back to 1913, the effective tax rates imposed by the federal income tax on the rich—the nation's wealthiest taxpayers.

"The rich" here uses the definition of households with income in the top 1 percent of all households (Slemrod 1994). But at least one historian of American taxation, Mark Leff, has questioned the wisdom of paying close attention to the wealthy in evaluating the progressivity of the tax system. He has dismissed, in particular, the redistributional efforts of the New Deal by charging that if the plan had been serious about redistribution, it would have focused less on the very rich. The resources owned by the wealthiest 1 percent of households, however, are very substantial. In 1991, the average income of these households was nearly $675,000 a year, and they received nearly 16 percent of all household income. In addition, they owned 36 percent of total household wealth and 46 percent of total household financial wealth. Even before the tax increases undertaken by the Clinton administration in 1993 and the stock-market bubble of the late 1990s, the wealthiest 1 percent of the nation's families remitted about a quarter of the federal income tax (Wolff 2000).

"Effective rates" refers to the average percentages of taxable income actually paid in income taxes. Effective rates are invariably lower than marginal rates for two reasons. First, the marginal rates refer to the tax rate on the last dollar earned; in a progressive system, dollars earned earlier are taxed at lower rates. Second, the effective rates take into account the deductions and exemptions taken by the wealthy. Indeed, the measurement of effective rates is attractive precisely because of the tendency of tax complexity, specifically deductions and exemptions, to reduce progressivity.

The estimates cited in this chapter significantly understate the real level of effective rates. This outcome occurs partly because the estimates ignore the incidence of corporate income taxation on the rich. Kasten, Sammartino, and Toder (1994) have estimated that in 1980, the corporate income tax would have increased the effective rate of all federal taxes on the top 1 percent of households from 28.7 percent (assuming that all of the corporate tax fell on labor income) to 34.9 percent (assuming that all of the corporate tax fell on capital income).

To summarize the findings: the rates of effective taxation of the richest Americans increased in a series of major surges during World War I, the later phases of the New Deal, and World War II. A reduction in rates followed during the 1920s, and a stabilization of rates characterized the 1950s and the 1960s. In other words, beginning in the 1950s, rates of taxing the rich fluctuated less than they did during the first half of the century. The following sections provide a bit more detail on these trends.

Mobilization for World War I: Taxing the Rich

Mobilization for World War I included the introduction of serious "soak-the-rich" taxation. In 1918, even without taking into account the incidence of the corporate income tax on the rich, the wealthiest 1 percent paid marginal income tax rates that ranged from 15 to 77 percent, and effective rates that averaged 15 percent, up from 3 percent in 1916. The understatement of effective rates resulting from ignoring corporate taxation is potentially very important during World War I. The understatement would have been far greater in 1918 than in 1980 because of the introduction of estate taxation and the relatively heavy taxation of corporate incomes in 1918. Taxation of corporate incomes was aggressive during World War I. The Democratic program of finance embraced the concept of taxing corporate "excess profits." The Revenue Act of 1917 increased the tax on corporate incomes to 6 percent and expanded the excess-profits tax on munitions-makers to a graduated tax on all business profits above a normal rate of return. The rates of taxation were graduated progressively by rates of return on invested capital. In 1917, the tax rates ranged from 20 percent on profits over the normal rate of return to 60 percent on profits earned over a 33 percent rate of return. The Revenue Act of 1918 doubled the basic corporate income tax to 12 percent and further increased excess-profits taxation. The act reduced the number of tax rates from six to two, but increased the lowest rate to 30 percent and the top rate to 65 percent (on profits earned by more than a 20 percent rate of return). The excess-profits tax accounted for about two-thirds of all federal tax revenues during World War I and added to the tax burden on the rich imposed by the personal income tax. Only the United States and Canada taxed excess profits in this way, and only the United States placed excess-profits taxation at the center of wartime finance.

Post–World War I: Rollback of Taxes on the Rich

During the 1920s, Republican administrations rolled back taxation of the rich. The Republicans eliminated corporate excess-profits taxation; reduced estate taxes; and reduced the progressivity, or the vertical equity, of the individual income tax. At the same time, the Republicans, although they did not admit it, abandoned their goal of horizontal equity—the goal of taxing all forms of incomes with the same rate structure. Beginning in 1921, in response to intense lobbying, Republican administrations and Congress installed a wide range of special tax exemptions and deductions, most of which were disproportionately valuable to wealthy taxpayers. The cuts in marginal rates and the increases in tax expenditures on the taxation of the rich swiftly halved the effective rates of taxing the rich. As early as 1923, the effective rate on the richest 1 percent of American families had fallen to less than 8 percent, and it remained at this general level through the rest of the decade. It would have fallen even further if the economic growth of the 1920s had not pushed the less-rich households within the top 1 percent into higher tax brackets. The decline was even more dramatic in light of the demise in excess-profits taxation and the reductions in estate taxation.

The Great Depression: Three Waves of Taxing the Rich

The Depression years saw nearly a tripling of the effective rate of taxing the richest Americans. The increase occurred in three waves.

The first wave followed the Revenue Act of 1932, President Herbert Hoover's budget-balancing measure, which imposed the largest peacetime tax increases in the nation's history. This act raised the top marginal rate from 25 percent to 63 percent, nearly restoring it to World War I levels, and dramatically increased estate taxes. In 1934, as a consequence of the 1932 act, some economic recovery in 1933–34, and a closing of a New Deal loophole in the Revenue Act of 1934, the effective income tax rate on the rich rose to about 11 percent, a rate higher than at any time during the years of Republican "normalcy."

The second wave resulted from the Revenue Act of 1935, which increased marginal tax rates on the rich, and from the effects of some measure of economic recovery. Together, these factors pushed households into higher tax brackets. By 1936, effective rates on the rich had increased by nearly 50 percent. In 1936, the effective rate paid by the rich increased to 16.4 percent, higher than any year during World War I. This effective rate was, in fact, the highest it had ever reached. It remained roughly at that level until 1940. In this period, New Deal tax reform also expanded estate taxation and, in 1937, the New Deal launched the radical tax on undistributed profits. The effective tax rates among the wealthiest Americans, to the extent that this new tax reached their capital income, would have been even greater.

The third wave of effective tax rates during the 1930s occurred as a consequence of further closings of tax loopholes and the effects of economic recovery. Enough taxpayers paid higher marginal rates to increase the effective rate to more than 20 percent in 1940.

Mobilizing for World War II: More Taxing of the Rich

Mobilizing for World War II produced a doubling of the effective rates on the rich. The Revenue Act of 1942 imposed a surtax that was graduated from 13 percent on the first $2,000 to 82 percent on taxable income over $200,000. The act raised the marginal rates of taxation on personal incomes higher than at any other time in the history of the income tax in America. The higher marginal rates, coupled with wartime inflation, produced effective rates on the rich that, from 1942 through 1945, were more than 40 percent, or roughly twice the rate in 1940. In 1944, the effective rate reached an all-time high of nearly 60 percent, or almost four times the highest level during World War I. The rates were high enough so that in 1945, even with a much broader base of taxation, the richest 1 percent of households produced 32 percent of the revenue yield of the personal income tax.

Post–World War II: Slow Reduction in the Wealthy's Taxes

During the two decades following World War II, both Democratic and Republican administrations reduced the effective rate of taxing the rich. However, they did so slowly—more slowly than Republican administrations had reduced those taxes during the 1920s. They also accepted levels of taxation of large incomes and corporate profits that were substantially higher than before World War II. These levels were viewed by the rich and the business community as unconscionable at the time World War II ended. In the immediate postwar years, Republicans accepted marginal rates of personal income taxation on the rich that were as high as during World War II. Moreover, the normal tax on corporate incomes reached a postwar peak of 52 percent, which held until 1964. (During the Korean War, an excess-profits tax pushed the marginal rate for some firms to 77 percent.) From 1964 until 1986, the normal rate was usually either 46 percent or 48 percent.

In effect, the two political parties made the reforms of the New Deal and World War II an enduring part of the nation's fiscal order. As late as 1952, effective rates of taxing the rich were nearly one-third—higher than at any time during the 1930s. Even in the early 1960s, rates were still more than 25 percent, higher than at any point during the 1930s. By 1981, as a consequence of inflation-driven creep into higher tax brackets as well as high marginal rates, the effective rate on the rich had risen to nearly 30 percent.

Early 1980s: Further Reductions

The most significant post–World War II cut in effective rates of taxing the rich came in 1981. The Economic Recovery Tax Act of that year (ERTA) indexed tax rates for inflation and slashed the marginal rates on the rich. The result was a decline in effective taxation rates to the levels that had prevailed in the early 1960s. The Tax Reform Act of 1986 broadened the base of income taxation and may have thereby restored some progressivity to the federal income tax system as a whole. The measure, however, further reduced the marginal rates of taxation on the rich and sustained ERTA's reductions in the effective rates paid by the rich.

What is the significance of these trends for the economic history of the 20th century? An awareness of this pattern narrows the range of historical possibilities that can help determine the impact of income taxation on economic development. Moreover, when we couple these results with the findings of the new economic history, we may be able to isolate further how taxing the rich affects long-term trends in the distribution of wealth and income as well as in productivity.

Historians of political economy have not paid much attention to economists' histories of income and wealth distribution. They have ignored, for example, Jeffrey G. Williamson and Peter Lindert's path-breaking book *American Inequality: A Macroeconomic History.* Written more than two decades ago, the book rarely figures in analyses by political economists. The reasons are not entirely clear. Many historians of political economy probably find the research dense and arcane. In addition, and more troubling, the findings of Williamson and Lindert may repel political economists who would prefer to regard the distribution of income and wealth as having been stable or shifting in favor of the rich throughout the 20th century. But it is important not to map back the trends of the last 20 years to the century as a whole, and it is also important to consider the effects of progressive taxation and its spending effects on the earlier trend. The challenge that Williamson and Lindert gave us more than 20 years ago still stands. In their words, "The 20th-century leveling, like the rise in inequality almost a century earlier, was real and of sufficient magnitude to require explanation" (1980, 285).

If political economists attempted to answer the challenge, they might learn much that is new about the distributional effects of taxation before and after the era of Reaganomics. In the process, they ought to consider that more than coincidence may account for the early-20th-century peak in the concentration of income at the eve of American entry into World War I and the beginning, in 1916, of the first wave of "soak-the-rich" taxation. At the same time, they ought to reckon with the possibility that the recurring waves of 20th-century enthusiasm for taxing the wealthiest Americans contributed to the leveling of incomes that extended through the 1970s (Williamson and Lindert 1980).

We lack a strong economic narrative that describes large trends in economic productivity during the 20th century. There is no equivalent of the Williamson and Lindert study on distribution within the literature on productivity, despite the fact that since World War II economists have bestowed a great deal of attention on productivity trends.

The recent work of the new-growth economists, such as that of Paul Romer, has gained much visibility. The assumptions they use about the dynamics of change, however, cripple their analysis as a framework for historical narrative. The productivity trends described by Romer and his colleagues take place in a world essentially without institutions. On the one hand, this genre of economics strengthens the case that neoclassical economic historians like Douglass North and Robert Fogel have made on behalf of a reconstruction of economic theory that would increase understanding of the "historical evolution of economies" and provide "a crude guide to policy in the ongoing task of improving the economic performance of economies" (North 1996, 343).[11] On the other hand, the new economic historians have recorded significant accomplishments primarily in the well-controlled, short-term world of partial equilibrium analysis. They have been less persuasive in the world of general equilibrium analysis, where all significant variables, including capital stocks, may change simultaneously. Only general equilibrium analysis, however, can provide a comprehensive, quantitatively framed narrative of economic growth and its sources in the 20th century.[12]

Consequently, we know relatively little about the long-term relationships between the tax burdens of the wealthiest Americans and their economic behavior. All we know for certain about the relationship between taxation and productivity changes over the 20th century is that substantial, and often increasing, taxation of the rich has not blocked the remarkable gains in productivity. Perhaps these gains, however, would have been even greater if such taxation had been lower and more encouraging. Notably, accelerations in productivity gains have often followed marked reductions in taxes on the richest Americans. Of particular interest are, on the one hand, the productivity surges during the 1920s, the late 1950s and early 1960s, and the late 1990s, and, on the other hand, the marked reductions in taxing the rich during the 1920s, the post–World War II years, and the 1980s.[13]

The near-term prospects for developing rigorous and comprehensive analysis of the long-term relationship between taxation of the rich and economic growth are dim, especially in light of the problematic nature of general equilibrium analysis. An incremental, yet strategic, accumulation of research projects of modest scope is more feasible.

Of particular value would be the selection of significant episodes of stagnant productivity or slow economic growth for research on the connections between significant increases in taxation of the rich and the economic behavior of the rich. One such episode was the New Deal's experiment with the taxation of undistributed corporate profits. This tax, perhaps more than any other dimension of the New Deal, aroused fear and hostility on the part of the leaders of large corporations. These leaders correctly viewed the tax as a threat to their profits, their control over capital, and their latitude for financial planning. The tax may well have contributed significantly to the exceptionally low level of private investment during the 1930s, and, by depressing business expectations, to the severity of the 1937–38 recession. Antimonopolist New Dealers like Harold Ickes went so far as to charge that capitalists had conspired and gone "on strike" in response to New Deal taxes. Historians have found no direct evidence of such a conspiracy, but the significant tax-driven increases in the cost of capital may have slowed investment.[14]

Three decades ago, I adopted a similar approach in a study of the relationship between tax policy and business behavior in Wisconsin and found that the Wisconsin income tax of 1911 retarded economic development in that state (Brownlee 1970, 1974). This tax—the first effective state income tax—resulted from the efforts of the Wisconsin tax pioneers to finesse the considerable administrative problems posed by a state income tax by collecting most of the revenues from corporations. Corporations paid a stringently administered 6 percent tax on their profits, and manufacturers accounted for about two-thirds of the corporate burden. The tax increased the cost of capital to Wisconsin manufacturers significantly above the levels faced by their competitors located elsewhere in the Great Lakes states. Using the capital-cost model of investment developed by economist Dale Jorgenson, the study made a key assumption about the incidence and effects of the taxes. First, it assumed that the Wisconsin corporations would not be able to pass the corporate tax either backward to owners of land, labor, and capital, or forward to consumers. In other words, the study assumed either that corporations were already maximizing profits, having pushed prices as high as possible and kept factor costs as low as possible, or that the Wisconsin corporations were constrained by interstate competition. Thus, the Wisconsin corporations would have to pay their taxes out of those profits. This approach revealed that the assumptions of progressives about the shifting and incidence of taxes on corporate profits were remarkably similar to those made 50 years later by neoclassical analysts.[15]

It is worth noting that, regardless of the real effects of the Wisconsin tax, political leaders in the other Great Lakes states and industrial states elsewhere regarded the damage of industry in Wisconsin as a cautionary tale. Massachusetts and New York did not adopt income taxes until they faced the fiscal problems imposed by World War I, and they were confident that they could build the administrative machinery required to assess and collect a tax based primarily on individual incomes rather than on corporate profits. Most industrial states did not enact income taxes until the revenue crisis created by the Great Depression.

Modest-scope studies could embrace the partial equilibrium analysis that public finance economists have employed in studying the effects of policy changes. In fact, in addressing the important issue of the impact of federal taxation on economic stability, two economists have made substantial historical contributions. More than four decades ago, E. Cary Brown introduced the concept of the "full-employment" deficit to isolate the countercyclical thrust of New Deal tax policy. More recently, Herbert Stein, writing within a democratic-institutionalist framework, used that same concept to measure fiscal policy from 1929 through 1994 (Brown 1956; Stein 1969, 1996).

Both Brown and Stein concluded that federal taxation had a disruptive effect on the American economy. Because of New Deal tax policy, the stimulus of the New Deal's early fiscal policy (between 1933 and 1937) was either far less than it would have been otherwise or a factor in the economic downturn (i.e., the recession of 1937–38). According to these economists, from the end of World War II until the Kennedy–Johnson tax cut of 1964, tax policy contributed to the slowing of economic activity and, in particular, to three significant recessions. In 1969, when *The Fiscal Revolution in America* appeared, Stein was optimistic about the prospects for the ability of a neoclassical consensus on fiscal policy, including taxation, to enhance fiscal stability. However, by 1996, when Stein published the sequel to *The Fiscal Revolution,* he had grown more pessimistic. The deficit's "Big Bang" during the Reagan administration demonstrated the fragile nature of a consensus on maintaining a modest, relatively constant full-employment surplus (Brown 1956; Stein 1969).

The new economic history should also take into account the beneficial effects of federal spending made possible by progressive income taxation, including taxation of America's wealthiest citizens. Robert Fogel's Nobel Prize lecture ought to remind us of the potential importance and, at the same time, the great difficulty of undertaking that kind of historical analysis of government spending. Fogel considered, among many other issues, why the health of the American people improved during the two decades before World War II, despite the deprivations of the Great Depression. His answer was the "huge social investments made between 1870 and 1930, whose payoffs were not counted as part of national income during the 1920s and 1930s even though they produced a large stream of benefits during these decades" (Fogel 1994, 388). In making this assessment, Fogel wrote as a policy historian, but he also suggested the importance of the public, progressive investments in the social infrastructure of health and education prior to 1930 to improved productivity.

America's richest citizens may have had a personal interest in contributing disproportionately to ensure that such investments took place.[16]

No modest study like those proposed here can reveal very much about the *magnitude* of the economic effects of changes in tax policy. Nonetheless, they can indicate the *direction* of those effects. Firmer knowledge of even the direction of policy effects would help make debates over tax progressivity something more than quarrels between contending ideologies.

The Economic Context for Policymaking

The second possibility for advancing political economy is through research in economic history. The theoretical contributions of North and the empirical research of Chandler ought to suggest to political economists that they need to delineate more clearly the development of tax institutions within the context of the economic environment. In other words, political economists need to pay greater attention to how long-run economic changes—especially the technological and organizational changes associated with economic development—shape the agendas of policymakers and shape the institutional tools available to those policymakers. More specifically, political economists should pay attention to the relationships between economic change and ways in which policymakers study taxation, craft tax legislation, administer tax codes, and, more specifically, search for tax justice.

The postprogressive histories of taxation reveal little about *how* policymakers take economic issues into account as they enact and administer tax policy. The new political economy also does not show in a systematic way how Congress puzzled its way through the economic issues surrounding revisions of the tax code; how the economic effects of tax systems shaped the way in which Congress and the President "sold government" to the American people; how the Internal Revenue Service and the courts used economic criteria in their interpretations of the tax code; or how tax experts, especially inside government, evaluated the code's economic effects.

This lack of attention to governmental processes is ironic in that each of the major postprogressive interpretations of American tax history promises to "bring the state back in" to the history of American politics. Each interpretation pays close attention methodologically to the role of the state, and each has a more clearly articulated vision of the role of the state than did the progressive histories. However, none of them provides much detail on the administrative capacity of the federal government, including the institutions that provide government with a capacity for social learning.

Postprogressive interpretations do not study how, over time, the changing economic conditions, and related factors of organizational and technological development, have defined the nature of tax institutions. Public-finance economist Richard Musgrave has stressed the importance of the relationship between structural economic change and the development of fiscal regimes. He has gone so far as to argue that structural change in highly developed economies drives dramatic changes in tax structure, in particular, by prompting countries to shift toward income taxation (Musgrave 1969).[17]

Musgrave has perhaps attached too much importance to the force of changing economic structure. But he is right that economic development—defined to include the emergence and refinement of modern technology and organizational structures as well as economic growth—has shaped the public-finance options that are available to policymakers at any given time. One way to illustrate this issue, and to suggest its significance, is to point to the future impact of information technology and the related integration of global markets on tax systems. Arguably, the pressure of international competition will lead nations to shift their taxes even further away from the more mobile portions of the tax base, such as profits and savings, and toward the less mobile portions, such as consumption, labor, and even fixed assets. Indeed, the trend may have already begun, paralleling the convergence of state taxation rates that occurred in the United States between 1911 and 1945.

Of the leading interpretations of tax history, the capitalist-state view is perhaps most neglectful of the impact of economic change on institutional possibilities. It ignores, for example, the reality that the federal government could not embody the ideal of ability to pay until economic development created the administrative underpinnings for an effective income tax. Historians who fault the federal tax system for its lack of progressivity before World War I ignore the administrative realities that made a massive income tax, even along the lines of "soaking the rich," impossible. Commentary criticizing the New Deal for failing to reach more deeply into the middle class ignores another reality of institutional development: A progressive income tax that could effectively reach

American upper-middle-class incomes, including capital gains, was exceptionally difficult to construct. The Wilson administration found that it did not have enough time to do it during World War I, despite the serious intent to create such a system. The New Dealers were only able to consider mass-based income taxation seriously after they had made the extraordinary administrative accomplishments associated with the introduction of Social Security, including the creation of a system for collection at the source. Without the Social Security system in place, the United States might have had to rely on consumption taxation, rather than a mass-based income tax, to finance World War II. Reliance on consumption taxation would have meant a more limited effort to tax the rich.

In contrast with the capitalist-state approach, the democratic-institutionalist interpretation has attempted to clarify the economic and institutional factors shaping tax policy. This approach suggests that while long-run economic change sometimes constrains tax reform, it also creates reform opportunities by influencing administrative costs and the size of potential tax bases.

For example, both Eugene Steuerle and I (Steuerle 1992; Brownlee 1996b) have emphasized how, during the 20th century, the combination of economic growth and the proliferation of modern corporations and their administrative structures were crucial to the ability of the federal government to exploit effectively the taxation of incomes, both corporate and personal, and of payrolls. Thus, we argue that economic growth and administrative capacity, as well as the search for vertical or progressive equity, were central to the "era of easy finance" that emerged during World War II. For more than three decades, the great stimulation of the fiscal capacity of the federal government by economic growth and administrative sophistication was far more powerful than the weakening of fiscal capacity by pluralism, localism, and divided government. In fact, between World War II and the 1970s, economic growth and long-term inflation enabled the federal government to garner increasing revenues. At the same time, these factors enabled it to reduce corporate as well as excise taxes, and to avoid the politically costly process of increasing income tax rates. In other words, economic growth, inflation, and administrative-capacity inflation extended the life of the World War II tax system and provided the basis for significant reductions in the taxation of the richest Americans.

Then, during the 1980s, the era of easy finance seemed to disappear. The conservative tax revolt epitomized by Proposition 13 in California and the Reagan tax cuts of 1981 were important; but once again, the economic environment was also important. The decline of inflation, along with weakened productivity during the 1970s, pushed the makers of fiscal policy toward a series of different approaches, including a reliance on deficit financing, reductions in the progressivity of the income tax, and a search for base broadening and horizontal equity.

As it turned out, some historians of public finance, including myself, were too hasty in pronouncing the demise of the era of easy finance. The swift economic expansion of the 1990s and the increasing concentration of incomes received by the nation's wealthiest citizens during the buoyant stock market of 1995–2000, coupled with the tax increases led by Presidents George H. W. Bush in 1991 and Bill Clinton in 1993, produced the basis for budget surpluses and another round of tax cuts in 2001.[18]

Thus, the theoretical apparatus of economic history can advance a central concern of political economy: exploring the reciprocal relationships between economic performance and the shaping of political institutions. In particular, economic history can provide ways to think about the links between the development of the capacities of the state and the economic environment in which social learning has given shape to modern government. Economic history ought to remind historians of political economy that institutions of modern government have developed in an economic environment that has helped define institutional possibilities and constraints.[19] In sum, by working cooperatively in both empirical and theoretical realms, economic historians and political economists could more effectively explore the historical connections between the performance of the American economy and the development of progressive taxation and the other central institutions of a modern liberal democracy.

NOTES

1. By World War I, the description of highly progressive taxation as "soak-the-rich" taxation was common in both America and England. The term had emerged in the United States in the late 1890s, accompanied by the introduction of a new meaning of "soak": "to impose upon by an extortionate charge or price" (Simpson and Weiner 1989). See also Partridge (1984) and Wentworth and Flexner (1967).

2. See, for example, Steinmo (1993), especially pages 35–40.

3. For recent examples of North's and his associates' work, see North (1990, 1996). Economists have been the major architects of this particular form of historical institutionalism, but historians have made important contributions as well. Alfred D. Chandler and his colleagues, for example, have made similar but more empirically based efforts to comprehend the social basis for economic development. Their research has placed the history of the corporation and other economic institutions in the context of

market incentives and thereby clarified the roles of those institutions in the mobilization of technology and capital. Chandler (1977) is the classic study in this area. For the most recent contributions by Chandler and his associates, see Chandler and Cortada (2000).

4. In effect, I am exploring, through the prism of tax policy, the possibilities for reuniting the two strains of historical political economy.

5. For the intellectual foundations of this approach, see Goldscheid (1962). For more recent examples of such scholarship, see Leff (1984), Stanley (1993), and King (1983, 1993).

6. See also Witte (1985).

7. See Baack and Ray (1985a, b, and c) and Higgs (1987).

8. On the role of Wilbur Mills, see Zelizer (1996, 1998). See also Steuerle (1992).

9. An important exception is the pioneering work of Richard Sylla, which focuses on state and local trends. See, for example, Sylla (1986, 832–35).

10. See also Pechman (1989).

11. For the leading example of the new growth theory, see, for example, Romer (1986) and North (1996, 359).

12. Cliometricians have tended to invoke models of long-run change that either ignored important causal relationships among the potential variables or introduced too much complexity and uncertainty. An example of the former is Robert Fogel's hypothetical counterfactual (Fogel 1964). An example of the latter is Williamson's general equilibrium model (Williamson 1974).

13. For recent efforts to shed light on this subject, see Slemrod (2000). For a summary of the state of knowledge regarding the effects of the Tax Reform Act of 1986, see Auerbach and Slemrod (1997).

14. On the causes of the 1937–38 recession, see Roose (1954), especially pages 10–12 and 209–16, where Roose discusses the effects of the undistributed profits tax. Schumpeter (1939, 1038–40) also stressed the role of that tax. On the conspiracy charges, see Leff (1984, 212–13). On the intellectual sources of the undistributed profits tax, see Bernstein (1987, 190–92).

15. For challenges to the views expressed here, see Stark (1987, 1991) and Buenker (1998, 510–11, 551–54, 689–90). For the Jorgenson model, see Jorgenson (1965).

16. For a more ambitious statement of the importance of what Fogel calls "the egalitarian revolution of the 20th century," including the adoption of progressive income taxation, see Fogel (2000), especially pages 84–175.

17. Musgrave believes, for example, that a kind of structural imperative drove the adoption of the income tax. However, if the United States had financed World War I through adoption of major consumption taxes (a practical possibility), the federal government might have also relied on these taxes for finance during later episodes of its expansion.

18. The subtitle "The Rise and Fall of the Era of Easy Finance" of my 1996 book was excessively dramatic. See Brownlee (1996a). For the argument that the increasing concentration of incomes was largely responsible for the revenue boom of the 1990s, see Krugman (2001, 62–64).

19. In developing theories about the relationship between economic performance and institutional development, new economic historians have gone beyond the conventional econometric modeling of "cliometrics." As Douglass North put the matter, "An overall contribution that institutional analysis can make to U.S. economic history is to make it a truly historical story, something that has been lost with cliometrics" (1990, 137).

REFERENCES

Auerbach, Alan J., and Joel Slemrod. 1997. "The Economic Effects of the Tax Reform Act of 1986." *Journal of Economic Literature* 35 (June): 589–632.

Baack, Ben, and Edward J. Ray. 1985a. "The Political Economy of the Origin and Development of the Federal Income Tax." In *Emergence of the Modern Political Economy: Research in Economic History* (Supplement 4), edited by Robert Higgs (121–38). Greenwich, Conn.: JAI Press, Inc.

———. 1985b. "Special Interests and the Adoption of the Income Tax in the United States." *Journal of Economic History* 45 (September): 607–25.

———. 1985c. "The Political Economy of the Origins of the Military-Industrial Complex in the United States." *Journal of Economic History* 45 (June): 369–75.

Bakija, Jon, and Eugene Steuerle. 1991. "Individual Income Taxation since 1948." *National Tax Journal* 44 (December): 474–75.

Bernstein, Michael A. 1987. *The Great Depression: Delayed Recovery and Economic Change in America, 1929–1939.* Cambridge: Cambridge University Press.

Brown, E. Cary. 1956. "Fiscal Policies in the 'Thirties': A Reappraisal." *American Economic Review* 46 (December): 857–79.

Brownlee, W. Elliot. 1970. "Income Taxation and Capital Formation in Wisconsin, 1911–1929." *Explorations in Economic History* 8 (September): 77–102.

———. 1974. *Progressivism and Economic Growth: The Wisconsin Income Tax, 1911–1929.* Port Washington, N.Y.: Kennikat Press.

———, ed. 1996a. *Funding the Modern American State, 1941–1995: The Rise and Fall of the Era of Easy Finance.* Washington, D.C., and New York: The Woodrow Wilson Center Press and Cambridge University Press.

———. 1996b. *Federal Taxation: A Short History.* Washington, D.C., and New York: The Woodrow Wilson Center Press and Cambridge University Press.

———. 2000. "Historical Perspectives on U.S. Tax Policy toward the Rich." In *Does Atlas Shrug? The Economic Consequences of Taxing the Rich,* edited by Joel B. Slemrod (29–73). New York and Cambridge: Russell Sage Foundation and Harvard University Press.

Buenker, John D. 1998. *The History of Wisconsin, Volume IV: The Progressive Era, 1893–1914.* Madison: State Historical Society of Wisconsin.

Chandler, Alfred D., Jr. 1977. *The Visible Hand: The Managerial Revolution in American Business.* Cambridge: Harvard University Press.

Chandler, Alfred D., Jr., and James Cortada, eds. 2000. *A Nation Transformed by Information: How Information Has Shaped the United States from Colonial Times to the Present.* New York: Oxford University Press.

Davis, Lance E., and John Legler. 1966. "The Government in the American Economy, 1815–1902: A Quantitative Study." *Journal of Economic History* 26 (December): 513–52.

Fogel, Robert W. 1964. *Railroads and American Economic Growth: Essays in Econometric History.* Baltimore: Johns Hopkins University Press.

———. 1994. "Economic Growth, Population Theory, and Physiology: The Bearing of Long-Term Processes on the Making of Economic Policy." *American Economic Review* 84 (June): 369–95.

————. 2000. *The Fourth Great Awakening and the Future of Egalitarianism.* Chicago and London: The University of Chicago Press.

Goldscheid, Rudolf. 1962. "A Sociological Approach to Problems of Public Finance." In *Classics in the Theory of Public Finance,* edited by Richard A. Musgrave and Alan T. Peacock (202–13). London: Macmillan. First published as "Staat, offentlicher Haushalt und Gesellschaft, Wesen und Aufgaben der Finanzwissenschaften vom Standpunkte der Soziologie," *Handbuch der Finanzwissenschaft,* edited by W. Gerloff and F. Meisel. Vol. 1. (Tubingen 1925).

Higgs, Robert. 1987. *Crisis and Leviathan: Critical Episodes in the Growth of American Government.* New York: Oxford University Press.

Jorgenson, Dale W. 1965. "Anticipations and Investment Behavior." In *The Brookings Quarterly Econometric Model of the United States,* edited by James S. Duesenberry (35–94). Chicago: Rand McNally.

Kasten, Richard, Frank Sammartino, and Eric Toder. 1994. "Trends in Federal Tax Progressivity, 1980–1993." In *Tax Progressivity and Income Inequality,* edited by Joel Slemrod (9–51). Cambridge: Cambridge University Press.

King, Ronald. 1983. "From Redistributive to Hegemonic Logic: The Transformation of American Tax Politics, 1894–1963." *Politics and Society* 12 (1): 1–52.

————. 1993. *Money, Time and Politics: Investment Tax Subsidies and American Democracy.* New Haven: Yale University Press.

Krugman, Paul. 2001. *Fuzzy Math: The Essential Guide to the Bush Tax Plan.* New York: W. W. Norton.

Leff, Mark. 1984. *The Limits of Symbolic Reform: The New Deal and Taxation.* New York: Cambridge University Press.

Musgrave, Richard A. 1969. *Fiscal Systems.* New Haven: Yale University Press.

North, Douglass C. 1990. *Institutions, Institutional Change, and Economic Performance.* Cambridge: Cambridge University Press.

————. 1996. "Epilogue: Economic Performance through Time." In *Empirical Studies in Institutional Change,* edited by Lee J. Alston, Thrinn Eggertsson, and Douglass C. North (342–55). Cambridge: Cambridge University Press.

Partridge, Eric. 1984. *A Dictionary of Slang and Unconventional English,* edited by Paul Beale (1108). London: Routledge and Kegan Paul.

Pechman, Joseph. 1989. *Tax Reform: The Rich and the Poor.* Washington, D.C.: Brookings.

Ratner, Sidney. 1942. *American Taxation: Its History As a Social Force in Democracy.* New York: W. W. Norton.

————. 1967. *Taxation and Democracy in America.* New York: W. W. Norton.

Romer, Paul M. 1986. "Increasing Returns and Long-Run Growth." *Journal of Political Economy* 94 (5): 1002–38.

Roose, Kenneth D. 1954. *The Economics of Recession and Revival: An Interpretation of 1937–38.* New Haven: Yale University Press.

Schumpeter, Joseph A. 1939. *Business Cycles.* New York: McGraw-Hill.

Simpson, J. A., and E. S. C. Weiner. 1989. *The Oxford English Dictionary* (892–93). Oxford: Clarendon.

Slemrod, Joel B. 1994. "On the High-Income Laffer Curve." In *Tax Progressivity and Income Inequality,* edited by Joel Slemrod (177–210). Cambridge: Cambridge University Press.

———, ed. 2000. *Does Atlas Shrug? The Economic Consequences of Taxing the Rich.* New York and Cambridge: Russell Sage Foundation and Harvard University Press.

Stanley, Robert. 1993. *Dimensions of Law in the Service of Order: Origins of the Federal Income Tax, 1861–1913.* New York: Oxford University Press.

Stark, John O. 1987. "The Establishment of Wisconsin's Income Tax." *Wisconsin Magazine of History* 71 (Autumn): 27–45.

———. 1991. "Harold M. Groves and Wisconsin Taxes." *Wisconsin Magazine of History* 74 (Spring): 196–214.

Stein, Herbert. 1969. *The Fiscal Revolution in America.* Chicago: University of Chicago Press.

———. 1996. "The Fiscal Revolution in America, Part II: 1964 to 1994." In *Funding the Modern American State, 1941–1995: The Rise and Fall of the Era of Easy Finance,* edited by W. Elliot Brownlee. Washington, D.C., and New York: The Woodrow Wilson Center Press and Cambridge University Press.

Steinmo, Sven. 1993. *Taxation and Democracy: Swedish, British and American Approaches to Financing the Modern State.* New Haven: Yale University.

Steuerle, C. Eugene. 1992. *The Tax Decade, 1981–1990.* Washington, D.C.: Urban Institute Press.

Sylla, Richard. 1986. "Long-Term Trends in State and Local Finance: Sources and Uses of Funds in North Carolina, 1800–1977." In *Long-Term Factors in American Economic Growth,* edited by Stanley L. Engerman and Robert E. Gallman (819–68). Chicago: University of Chicago Press.

Webber, Carolyn, and Aaron Wildavsky. 1986. *A History of Taxation and Expenditure in the Western World.* New York: Simon and Schuster.

Wentworth, Harold, and Stuart Berg Flexner. 1967. *Dictionary of American Slang* (498–99). New York: Crowell.

Williamson, Jeffrey G. 1974. *Late Nineteenth-Century American Development: A General Equilibrium History.* New York: Cambridge University Press.

Williamson, Jeffrey G., and Peter Lindert. 1980. *American Inequality: A Macroeconomic History.* New York: Academic Press.

Witte, John. 1985. *The Politics and Development of the Federal Income Tax.* Madison: University of Wisconsin Press.

Wolff, Edward N. 2000. "Who Are the Rich? A Demographic Profile of High-Income and High-Wealth Americans." In *Does Atlas Shrug? The Economic Consequences of Taxing the Rich,* edited by Joel Slemrod (74–113). New York and Cambridge: Russell Sage Foundation and Harvard University Press.

Zelizer, Julian E. 1996. "Learning the Ways and Means: Wilbur Mills and a Fiscal Community, 1954–1964." In *Funding the Modern American State, 1941–1995: The Rise and Fall of the Era of Easy Finance,* edited by W. Elliot Brownlee (289–352). Washington, D.C., and New York: The Woodrow Wilson Center Press and Cambridge University Press.

———. 1998. *Taxing America: Wilbur D. Mills, Congress, and the State, 1945–1975.* Cambridge: Cambridge University Press.

4

Hard Shells of Community

Tax Equity Debates within the National Council of Churches after World War II

Carolyn C. Jones

In the essay "The Uneasy Case for Progressive Taxation," Walter Blum and Harry Kalven Jr. set out to understand "the extent to which progressive taxation can be justified" (Blum and Kalven 1952, 417). They concluded that the goal of reducing economic inequalities presented the strongest case for progressive taxation. Along the way, Blum and Kalven urged consideration of the claims of the more wealthy to the income taken from them under a progressive tax. While their discussion of progressive taxation primarily drew from the works of economists, they also cited a survey of Christian ministers. The survey solicited the ministers' reactions to the statement, "Some observers say a steeply graduated income tax violates the moral principle that man is entitled to the fruits of his labor." Of the responding ministers, 71 percent disagreed, supporting a steeply progressive income tax; 10 percent agreed; and the remaining respondents qualified their answers or had no opinion (496).

Blum and Kalven's citation of the ministers' survey illustrates how the worlds of law, economics, and religion intersect within the discussion of tax policy. The responses also reflect an ongoing struggle within Protestantism regarding Christian ethics and taxation.[1] The results cited were from a survey undertaken by a conservative religious group, Spiritual Mobilization, and summarized in an issue of *Faith and Freedom* (Johnson 1952).[2] Founded in 1935, Spiritual Mobilization was one of many such groups arguing for the consistency of laissez-faire capitalism and Christianity (Ahlstrom 1972; Meyer 1988). *Faith and Freedom,* its monthly publication, was sent to 22,000 clergymen (Fones-Wolf 1994). The survey report refers to another consideration of religion and economics—a three-year study by the National Council of Churches (NCC) on the relationship of Christian ethics to economic life (Johnson 1952). The NCC and its predecessor, the Federal Council of Churches (FCC), were viewed by groups like Spiritual Mobilization as the voice of liberal Protestantism, or worse.

In the years after World War II, an era in which it seemed that churches were growing in number and influence, conservative and libertarian Protestants geared up to confront positions taken by the NCC and to influence the NCC's policy pronouncements. The issue of *Faith and Freedom* describing the results of the ministers' survey concluded, "When all of the testimony is added up, this fact stands out: wanting people to be better morally and materially, many clergymen reach for governmental compulsions that will require people to act more in accordance to the clergymen's ethical concepts" (Johnson 1952, 6). Indeed, some ministers prominently associated with the NCC did take that position. Theologian Reinhold Niebuhr advocated the use of law—including tax law—to provide "an approximation of a loving community" in a selfish world (Boulding 1953, 244).

The clergy's consideration of government measures and use of law suggested a society in which church sanctions were not as effective as they had once been, despite a postwar resurgence in church membership and a perception of increasing church influence (Weisbrod 1988). Church affiliation, after remaining fairly stable during the first decades of the 20th century, increased from 49 percent of the total population in 1940 to 55 percent in 1950, and it reached 62 percent by 1956 (Ahlstrom 1972). Church attendance grew, and funds spent on church construction more than doubled between 1948 and 1954. Some business leaders, including the National Association of Manufacturers (NAM), were convinced that "the clergyman's concept of right and wrong has tremendous influence" (Ahlstrom 1972, 2).[3] These leaders thought that "people generally respect what their minister or priest tells them—even when he speaks regarding matters with which he is not thoroughly familiar."[4]

This chapter explores social justice debates about tax policy that have received little attention from tax scholars. Taxation, in addition to being the product of formal governmental decisionmaking, can be seen as a cultural phenomenon. The chapter shifts the focus away from the formal centers of power in Congress and the executive branch to an institution neither responsible for tax policy nor focused upon taxation as a central concern—the FCC and its successor, the NCC. By examining conflicts over social justice within the FCC and the NCC in the 10 years following World War II, the aim is to probe into religious views on taxation, presenting an admittedly partial case study. Much more remains to be said about tax justice and faiths other than mainline Protestantism (which dominated the FCC and NCC), and the intersection of religion and taxation at other important times. This postwar Protestant example of debate, however, provides a unique view of tax policy issues. Not only was there a postwar rise in church affiliation, attendance, and construction, but there was also a burgeoning postwar conservatism.[5]

In considering the penetration of tax debates into societal institutions, this chapter begins by setting the stage on which the postwar Protestant tax debates took place. The history of the FCC and its successor, the NCC, is described briefly. In the postwar period, the clergy was seen as particularly influential, and its economic education was the subject of intense interest by religious conservatives, libertarians, and the more liberal figures within the FCC and NCC.

In general, both liberal Protestants and conservative forces seeking to influence the NCC took similar approaches to "tax equity." For both groups, the real questions concerned foundational choices about the economic system. Specific reforms and issues were sometimes mentioned, including the inadequacy of depreciation allowances, the tax treatment of business losses, and the double taxation of corporate earnings.[6] In general, however, tax debates occurred within larger discussions of economic justice centered on the key question, Was any particular type of economic system Christian? In 1948, the World Council of Churches (WCC) issued a statement answering "no." It stated, "Christian churches should reject the ideologies of both Communism and laissez-faire capitalism," an assertion viewed by lay conservatives as another example of federated Protestantism gone awry (Fones-Wolf 1994, 219–20).

The intersection of religion and economics studied here produced two prototypes. In the first, "educative" prototype, business and other groups presented arguments concerning economics to the FCC and NCC with the aim of making the clergy more knowledgeable about economics. This approach included some discussion of Christian ethics or doctrine, but its major focus was the explanation of economic ideas.

This chapter illustrates the first prototype with two examples containing Keynesian overtones: the NCC's statement on inflation and Kenneth Boulding's tax recommendations in his book on organizations, published in an NCC series on ethics and economic life.[7]

The second, "theological" prototype involved a more explicitly religious approach to economics and Christianity. Both conservatives and liberals resorted to scriptural sources. Protestant conservatives and libertarians argued that the free market was the only Christian economic system. To the extent that taxation impaired market transactions, it violated freedom and fundamental Christian principles. Leading theologian Reinhold Niebuhr, seen as a liberal by his conservative opponents, disagreed.[8] He built a case for redistributive taxation on theological arguments about justice, love, and the innate selfishness of men.

The Federal/National Council of Churches

The FCC was formed in 1908 and became "the voice of liberal Protestantism" (Fones-Wolf 1994, 218). In many ways, it was the institutional base for the social gospel movement, which has been described as "the application of the teaching of Jesus and the total message of the Christian salvation to society, the economic life, and social institutions . . . as well as to individuals" (Hopkins 1940, 3). Individual stewardship was seen as inadequate to the problems of an industrial society. "Stewardship was then applied in a sense to the state, which, as guardian of God's gifts to the people, should oversee their just distribution" (Hopkins 1940, 324). The social gospel movement was strongest among Congregational, Methodist, Disciples, and Presbyterian leaders. Because evangelical Protestant denominations viewed individual faith, morality, and personal salvation, rather than social reform issues, as the church's central concerns, many did not ally with the FCC.

Religion, economics, and taxation intersected in the work of some prominent social gospel figures in the years before the end of World War I. Richard T. Ely, founder of the American Economics Association and an author on taxation, was associated with the social gospel movement (see Hovenkamp 1990). Congregational minister Washington Gladden, who died in 1918, was an early social gospel figure who studied taxation. Single-tax proponent Henry George influenced Walter Rauschenbusch, the foremost exponent of the social gospel of his generation.[9]

After a lull in support during the 1920s, the social gospel movement reemerged during the Depression, a time when the public lacked confidence in business. The 1930s were characterized by the FCC's difficulties in formulating its position with respect to the New Deal. Franklin Roosevelt proclaimed himself "as radical as the Federal Council" in 1932, and spoke at the organization's 25th anniversary celebration in 1933 (Meyer 1988, 314). The FCC's committees and publications provided some support for the New Deal. The organization also came out against the "coercive" aspects of the National Recovery Administration (Meyer 1988, 171). One Pennsylvania pastor noted in 1939 that "the social gospel is in the amazing and tragic predicament of being identified with the New Deal, by the haters of the New Deal" (316). During World War II, the FCC expressed openness to "experimentation with various forms of ownership and control, private, cooperative and public" (King 1989, 128–29). The group exercised greater leadership on postwar international affairs, particularly in advocating the establishment of the United Nations and the Marshall Plan.

As conservative attacks upon the FCC increased after World War II, the organization sought to move to the right of its liberal Protestant base. In 1946, Charles P. Taft, a lawyer and the brother of Republican Senator Robert A. Taft, became president of the FCC. Charles Taft was a trustee of the Committee for Economic Development (CED), a business organization seen as "moderately conservative or even liberal" (King 1989, 7). CED statements supported a role for the government in promoting economic stability and growth. The FCC welcomed a closer relationship with the CED, "one of the most constructive recent efforts of progressive business leaders" (King 1989, 233). In addition to moderating its economic views, the FCC merged with some more conservative, evangelical churches in 1950 to form the National Council of Churches.

The National Council's Lay Committee represented another effort at base-broadening (and fundraising). After approaching a number of prominent businessmen with more moderate positions, the NCC planning committee offered J. Howard Pew leadership of its Lay Committee. The retired Sun Oil executive had been a critic of the FCC, and had financed a book describing "the subversive activities" of the council (Fones-Wolf 1994, 218). Pew was quite explicit in a 1951 letter to Charles R. Hook of Armco Steel Corporation about his goals for the Lay Committee. In it, he described his conversations with church officials:

> I then pointed out to them that before this lay group would take an active participation in the affairs of the National Council, they would first need to be assured

that no group of ministerial economic illiterates would be permitted to dissemi-
nate subversive literature until such literature had been subjected to review by the
lay men, and until these lay men had had an opportunity of presenting their views
to the Board before any such literature was released to the press.[10]

The right to review, he held, would be supplemented with financial
power—"we must raise all the money necessary to finance the proper
operations of the National Council . . . because if we control the purse
strings, it will give us a position which lay people have never heretofore
held in any of these important church organizations."[11]

Pew was given a great deal of freedom in constituting the Lay
Committee, and the group reflected his views. NCC liberals, including
G. Bromley Oxnam, a Methodist bishop, and Reinhold Niebuhr, professor of ethics at Union Theological Seminary in New York, found the
shape and direction of the Lay Committee alarming, and they opposed
an overarching oversight function for Pew's committee. Disagreements
over the Committee's procedural role and powers continued until it was
disbanded in June 1955 (Fones-Wolf 1994; Meyer 1988).

Economic Education for the Clergy

Both the FCC/NCC and its detractors devoted considerable effort to the
economic education of Protestant clergymen during these years. The
FCC/NCC issued a biweekly publication called *Information Service,*
which provided social and economic data to thousands of subscribers,
mostly ministers. An October 1949 issue summarized significant books
in the field of economics. One collection of essays, *Saving American Capitalism,* included contributions from A. A. Berle Jr., Chester Bowles,
Alvin H. Hansen, Leon H. Keyserling, Arthur M. Schlesinger Jr., and
Edwin E. Witte.[12] Jasper Crane, a libertarian businessman and lay participant in the FCC and NCC, complained, "Not one of these men is a
sound economist, and I look upon several of them as being among the
most dangerous enemies of the American way of life."[13] Crane countered
by recommending the views of such "distinguished economists and
scholars" as Felix Morley, Frederic Bastiat, Ludwig Von Mises, and
Bertrand de Jouvenel, and offering to donate a "little library" to the NCC
Department of the Church and Economic Life.[14]

Some business leaders were uncomfortable with what they perceived to
be the power of the clergy. Foreign examples of such influence were cited

as warnings. Economist Friedrich Hayek based his surprisingly successful book *The Road to Serfdom* on one such example (Hayek 1944).[15] Crane wrote in 1948, "I was told by Dr. Hayek it was the Church of England that led Great Britain into socialism. Must we admit that the Federal Council of Churches is leading the United States on the road to serfdom?"[16]

An organization surveying clerical views on economic issues concluded that the "great body of clergy support the basic principles of capitalism. They are against socialism."[17] Nonetheless, they concluded that "much interpretive work remains to be done [by industry] if clergymen and businessmen are to see eye-to-eye on social legislation."[18]

Concerns about clerical views were evident in the survey commissioned by Spiritual Mobilization and cited by Blum and Kalven. One area identified for improvement was clerical attitudes toward the graduated income tax. Responding to a question of whether there was anything morally wrong with the principle of the graduated income tax, 88 percent of the ministers said no; only 6 percent thought progressive taxation was morally wrong. When asked whether it was just or unjust that "people with large incomes now must pay as much as 80 percent of their income in Federal taxes," 59 percent felt it was just, while 25 percent considered it unjust.[19] Finally, the responding clergy members were asked to agree or disagree with the following statement:

> It is said that taxing the rich to help the poor through government welfare is against Christian (ethical) principles, because it removes the voluntary aspect of true charity.

Among the nearly 500 respondents, 64 percent disagreed; 23 percent agreed. While the survey results on clerical attitudes could be viewed as a larger societal reflection of postwar bipartisan consensus on taxation, these were somewhat discouraging portraits of the relationship of business and the church for conservative industrial and religious leaders.

NAM tried to improve the communication of business views to clergy through discussions and plant tours.[20] After World War II, NAM expanded its program by increasing its contacts among Protestant, Roman Catholic, and Jewish organizations and among theological seminaries. Corporations and conservative businessmen, such as J. Howard Pew, sponsored conservative religious groups, including Spiritual Mobilization and the Christian Freedom Foundation. These two religious groups conducted summer conferences and seminars for businessmen and clergy on the free-market economy and its consistency with Christianity and the dangers of collectivism. Spiritual Mobilization hosted a radio program while the Christian

Freedom Foundation published *Christian Economics,* a newspaper sent to more than 175,000 Protestant clergymen (Fones-Wolf 1994).

The NCC responded with its own attempts to provide an economic education to clergy and lay members of its denominations. In addition to *Information Service,* the NCC and the theology faculty of the University of Chicago ran a three-week program, the School of Church and Economic Life, "established to facilitate the minister's comprehension of the issues and to increase his effectiveness as a pastor in an industrial society."[21] In 1951, the NCC offered a seminar, "Christian Business and Professional Leaders Look at Their Government" for clergy and laity chosen by their denominations. The program was to give special consideration to such issues as wage-price controls, housing, fiscal and taxation policies, and international trade relations. The NCC's Cameron Hall contacted Roy Blough, a member of Truman's Council of Economic Advisers and an NCC committee participant, to arrange a visit for seminar members to the Council. "We hope that they would feel it worth their while for us to visit them and spend some time in learning about the role and place of the Council of Economic Advisers in the government and some of the major economic problems of which business and professional leaders who are active in the churches should be aware."[22]

Hall, executive director of the FCC's Department of the Church and Economic Life (FCC/DCEL), saw the situation as less about clerical influence than about attempts to influence the clergy: "Never before, it would seem, has what the clergy thinks about economic matters seemed so important to so many non-church bodies. There is an anxiety about the economic education of clergy that is flattering and somewhat overwhelming!"[23]

The Educative Model: Translation of Economics to a Religious Audience

Statement on Inflation

In August 1950, about two months after the Korean War began, the FCC/DCEL expressed concern in a proposed statement over the effects of inflation and war and the "moral implications of the economic adjustments which involve all our people in the present situation."[24] The DCEL identified taxation as the most powerful weapon against inflation[25] and deemed inflation's effects on those with low and fixed incomes very negative.[26] The proposed statement continued:

> The details of taxation . . . [are] not within the province of the Church to specify. The writing of tax laws is a highly technical matter. But in one essential respect the economic and moral requirement[s] of tax policy are the same: the burden of the tax should be distributed so as to achieve as nearly as possible equality of sacrifice. The principle of equality of sacrifice should not be applied in such ways as to cripple the necessary economic activities of the people.[27]

The DCEL continued exploring inflation and equality under the Christian ethic through 1951 and into 1952.[28] In a draft statement on inflation prepared by a subcommittee with economist Kenneth Boulding as chairman,[29] the government was cited as responsible for keeping the economy stable: "The ability of the government to do its duty depends on the encouragement which it receives from the people. By fostering the spirit of Divine love in the hearts of men, the church lightens the task of the state in its search for just and workable policies."[30]

The published document, *Christian Responsibility toward Some Ethical Problems in Inflation* (1952), urged "just and equitable" taxation and admonished taxpayers to "refrain from bringing pressure on the government for special privileges and exemptions from measures that are designed to restrict expenditures and are in the general public interest."[31]

J. Howard Pew agreed that taxation was critical, but supported limited government. He wrote:

> As I think the matter over, I see no way of avoiding a clash with the radical elements who are desirous of using the National Council for the purpose of planting the seeds of collectivism in the minds and hearts of the American people. I know of no issue which is so clear-cut as inflation—no issue which I know so much about—no issue where your points can so easily be gotten across. Therefore, to lock horns with the radicals on the question of inflation, would be choosing our own battleground.[32]

The Lay Committee blocked NCC endorsement of the inflation statement. DCEL published the document as a discussion guide, despite Lay Committee objections.

The Series on Ethics and Economic Life

The six-volume series "Ethics and Economic Life" was a major project undertaken by the DCEL and its study committee.[33] The six volumes were *Goals of Economic Life, The American Economy and the Lives of*

People, Social Responsibilities of the Businessman, The Organizational Revolution, American Income and Its Use, and *Ethics and Economic Life.* The series received a grant from the Rockefeller Foundation and was published by Harper and Brothers. The publisher promoted the series as combining "the experience and thought of a broad variety of intellectual and religious leaders. Together they present penetrating analyses of the ethics of modern economic life and how they can be made to conform to Christian principles."[34]

J. Howard Pew did not take such a positive view of the series. The first volume, *Goals of Economic Life,* would not have ordinarily attracted much attention "because it is so badly done that few people will read it," Pew argued. "But when sponsored by the National Council, the communists, socialists, and left-wing commentators," he continued, "columnists and editors will seize upon the book to make it appear that 33 million Protestant church members in this country subscribe to their philosophy."[35] Pew protested publication of the series to Bishop Henry Sherrill, president of the NCC, and threatened to resign as chairman of the Lay Committee if the book were published under NCC auspices.[36] Pew took the matter up with the Rockefeller Foundation as well. In the end, the NCC's Committee of Reference, charged with resolving the issue, approved the publication of the volume with a clear statement that the NCC had "no responsibility for the views set forth by any of the contributors to the volume."[37]

Several of the volumes touched upon taxation, but perhaps the most interesting exploration of tax issues occurred in Kenneth Boulding's 1953 contribution to the FCC/NCC *Study of Christian Ethics and Economic Life* entitled *The Organizational Revolution: A Study in the Ethics of Economic Organization* (Boulding 1953).

Boulding saw the experience of war as drawing the people of a nation together, increasing the powers and activities of national governments, particularly those of the executive branch. He argued, "in part, this reflects the logic of organization. If government is going to play an active and positive part in organizing the life of the people, obviously only the executive branch can do this" (Boulding 1953, 181). Boulding, favorably mentioning Lord Keynes, urged "not a 'planned' economy, but a 'governed' economy" (182). In his description of the social-democratic national state, Boulding posited an automatic tax plan that would adjust tax rates to incoming statistical information. A decline in total money payments "would be automatically followed by a decline in tax rates"

(184).[38] A rise in total money payments, "indicating a spontaneous infla-
tionary pressure" (184), would automatically result in a rise in tax rates.
Boulding's essay sketched how such a system could be implemented in
the United States:

> All the machinery for such a system is already in existence. We already have an
> information system which yields moderately accurate quarterly reports of
> national money income, prepared by the National Income Division of the
> Department of Commerce. We also have, in the deductible-at-source income tax,
> a powerful and flexible instrument for the rapid adjustment of tax collections. All
> that needs to be done is to hitch these two parts of the machinery together, and to
> link changes in tax rates quarterly with changes in national income. Then the
> budget deficit or surplus could be left to look after itself. A deflationary movement
> in the economy would automatically produce a budget deficit tending to offset it,
> as declining national money income forced a decrease in tax rates; an inflationary
> movement, on the other hand, would produce a budget surplus tending to offset
> it, as rising national income forced an increase in tax rates (184).

In October 1953, John C. Gebhart, of the research department of the
National Association of Manufacturers, prepared a summary and analysis of Boulding's book. Gebhart identified the book as the one of the series
"which is likely to have the most far-reaching effects," and in contrast to
Pew's views, described Boulding as "one of our leading economists" and
as "a deeply and sincerely religious man." Gebhart's review praised
Boulding as sympathetic to the notion of a market economy. "In all cases
his treatment of different points of view is very fair and tolerant and he
has repeated at length views of those who do not agree with him."[39]

Charles Taft, chairman of the NCC/DCEL, received the fairly favorable Gebhart review and sent it to members of the NCC General
Board.[40] Just after Taft's letter to the Board, Pew contacted Percy L.
Greaves Jr., a conservative economist, asking for a response to the
Gebhart review. Greaves was blunt: "My personal opinion is that these
six books are extremely dangerous and should be opposed at every
level." Greaves took issue with Boulding's tax proposal, arguing:

> He then goes on to advocate the CED plan of controlling deflations by manipu-
> lating the government's cash surplus or deficit. He would do this by changes in tax
> rates every quarter. This means giving the Executive Department the right to
> change tax rates at will on the basis of its estimate of economic conditions. This
> of course would ruin all business calculations. No one would know his taxes or his
> income from month to month.[41]

Gebhart was a part-time consultant to the NAM. A memo dated July 13,
1954, states, "Will you please be good enough to take such steps as are

necessary to terminate Mr. Gebhart's services with the Association at the earliest possible date?"[42]

Religious Arguments about Economics and Taxation within the NCC

Rev. John Bennett noted the divisions within the NCC in an NBC radio discussion:

> As I see it, the Social Gospel emphasis upon the application of Christian ethics to social life tended, particularly in the 1930s, to become rather uncritical of collectivistic answers to our questions. Now there has developed in our Protestant churches a very extreme type of individualism which wants to go back to an absolutely unreconstructed capitalism. So we have at the present time in the Protestant churches this one-sided tendency toward collectivism and a one-sided tendency toward individualism.[43]

These two starkly different views of human nature, religion, and economics structured much of the postwar tax policy discussion within the NCC.

Scriptural Sources

Each side in this contest of stark opposites within the NCC—collectivism versus individualism—found support in parables from the New Testament.[44] Individuals with views characterized as collectivist could turn to the parable of the workers in the vineyard from the Book of Matthew. Early in the morning, the owner of a vineyard hired laborers for payment of one denarius for a day's labor. Three hours later, he hired more workers, promising to pay them "whatever is right." Every three hours, he went forth, hiring more laborers and promising to pay them "whatever is right." At the end of the day, all the workers were paid the same amount—one denarius. Those who had worked all day were disgruntled, but the owner replied, "Friend, I am doing you no wrong; did you not agree with me for a denarius? Take what belongs to you, and go; I choose to give to this last as I give to you . . . So the last will be first, and the first last" (Matt. 20:1–16, Revised Standard Version [RSV]).

Collectivism could also look to a passage in Acts 2: 44–45 (RSV), which describes the economic arrangements of Jesus' followers after the crucifixion: "And all who believed were together and had all things in common; and they sold their possessions and goods and distributed them to all, as any had need." One conservative Christian newspaper contended that these verses were not applicable to Christians in 20th-century America. "It is not a divine economic plan that is here revealed to be practiced under all circumstances, but the manifestation of divine grace, under circumstances of God's own making, for the spread of the Pentecostal revival."[45]

For those supporting a free market or libertarian view, affirmation could be found in the parable of the talents in the Book of Matthew:

> For it will be as when a man going on a journey called his servants and entrusted to them his property; to one he gave five talents, to another two, to another one, to each according to his ability. Then he went away. He who had received the five talents went at once and traded with them; and he made five talents more. So also, he who had the two talents made two talents more. But he who had received the one talent went and dug in the ground and hid his master's money. Now after a long time the master of those servants came and settled accounts with them. The first two servants were praised, "Well done, good and faithful servant . . . enter into the joy of your master." The servant who had buried his talent was rebuked:
>
> "You wicked and slothful servant! . . . Then you ought to have invested my money with the bankers, and at my coming I should have received what was my own with interest. So take the talent from him, and give it to him who has the 10 talents. For to every one who has will more be given, and he will have abundance; but from him who has not, even what he has will be taken away. And cast the worthless servant into the outer darkness; there men will weep and gnash their teeth" (Matt. 25:14–30, RSV).

One active layman summarized, "Jesus mentioned profit so favorably on several occasions. . . . Socialism attacks profit. Marx forbids interest payments."[46]

The Conservative/Libertarian Standpoint: The Ethics of Taxation

Conservatives and libertarians within the NCC emphasized the individual nature of faith. As Jasper Crane wrote:

> The Social Gospel people want to reform the world by government action. . . . [T]hey mean the use of force which is government to carry out supposedly benevolent purposes. So Dr. Ream hits the nail on the head when he says, "They believe that the basic problem in our age is the poverty and inequality and injustice characterizing society." It is a secular philosophy. On the other hand, we libertarians believe in the importance and dignity and distinct individuality of every human being. We seek spiritual ends and believe primarily in evangelism as the means for promoting the growth of the Kingdom. We think we are sincerely and explicitly following the teachings of the Gospel, but we cannot expect the intolerant left to credit us with that.[47]

In March 1953, Crane asked Leonard Read, at the conservative Foundation for Economic Education, for help in composing an alternative to the NCC draft of a statement "Basic Christian Principles and Assumptions for Economic Life." Crane wrote: "It seems to me that the starting point ought to be from the Sermon on the Mount, 'Seek ye first the Kingdom of God and his righteousness, and all these things shall be added unto you.' . . . Many Christians, and especially those who embrace the 'social gospel' seem, however, to put first, 'What shall we eat?' or 'What shall we drink?' or 'Wherewithal shall we be clothed?' "[48]

In May 1953, J. Howard Pew sent Crane a draft of a substitute statement by a Dr. Haake. This draft asserted that Christian principles could "be applied sufficiently only in a free market economy."[49] Redistributive taxation was seen as antithetical to Christian teachings. Church leaders "have on occasion approved taxation by government beyond the costs of government as such in order to equalize income and possession, to redistribute the wealth by taking it from some who have earned more than they are considered to need in order to give it to others who have less than they want, some of whom may be in real need, who have neither earned what is thus given to them or been frugal in the use of what was theirs." The draft called this redistribution "stealing." Haake's draft continued:

> It is forgotten by those who would thus have wealth and income equalized, that any giving should be voluntary. God expects His children to be charitable and to share what they have to relieve the greater need of others. But, again, this is voluntary; for He has given us freedom to choose and He has not given to some the right to take from anyone, involuntarily, to give to others of their choosing."[50]

The draft argued that inequality was ordained by God. "Artificially established and maintained equality ultimately destroys those who are relieved of the necessity to improve their own status."[51]

Reds and the NCC

Tax debates within the NCC involved what Sydney Ahlstrom has described as "a new form of patriotic piety that was closely linked to the cold war" (Ahlstrom 1972, 954). J. Howard Pew, in a lengthy letter objecting to the NCC book *Goals of Economic Life*, drew religion and economics into one coordinate. "It is my conviction that Christianity and freedom are inexorably tied together, and the free market is but one of freedom's parts. Conversely, Communism and paganism are tied together. And so Christianity and Communism become the antithesis of each other."[52] As far back as 1946, Jasper Crane saw the views of the left-ish FCC in conflict with those held by "men of good-will," arguing that "this is all part of the conflict between the ideas of Marx and Christ which is raging throughout the world."[53] Marx's advocacy of progressive income taxation in the *Communist Manifesto* placed the American post-war tax system on the negative side of the ultra-conservative worldview.[54] This view was not new in the postwar period. David Wells published his article "The Communism of a Discriminating Income Tax" in 1880 (Wells 1880). In 1895, the Supreme Court declared the 1894 income tax unconstitutional in *Pollock v. Farmer's Loan and Trust Co.,* with the tax characterized as communistic in oral argument.[55]

Journalist John T. Flynn, in his 1949 book *The Road Ahead,* alleged that "many of the men most powerful in directing [the FCC's] affairs are using its machinery to promote the interests of a socialist revolution in America" (Flynn 1949, 107). Flynn focused on G. Bromley Oxnam, for-mer FCC president and a Methodist bishop, labeling him a socialist and an apologist for the Soviet system. Critics said the FCC was promoting socialized medicine in Sunday School publications and pursuing other socialist goals: "As first one and then another issue inserts itself into the public consciousness, either through some effort of the Socialist Plan-ners in Congress or in other forms of popular promotion, the Council will be found on the job" (Flynn 1949, 118).

While church membership could be viewed as an expression of one's support for anticommunism, Pew and Crane were concerned about com-munist infiltration into the FCC and, later, the NCC. Pew offered fellow Lay Committee member Lois Hunter $1,000 to check into all the dele-gates to the council's General Assembly, asking her to determine: "Who among the ministers are modernists and who are liberals. Who among them are Socialistically minded. What about the laymen. Who among them have minds of their own and who are so flattered by being appointed that they are quite willing to be rubber-stamps."[56] The pamphlet "How Red Is the Federal/National Council of Churches?" listed FCC leaders and the "questionable" groups with which they were affiliated.[57] Some NCC lead-ers did have ties to socialist groups. Reinhold Niebuhr, for example, was a founder of the Fellowship of Socialist Christians.

J. B. Matthews, in an article titled "Reds and Our Churches" in *Ameri-can Mercury* (1953), asserted that "the largest single group supporting the Communist apparatus in the United States today is composed of Protes-tant clergymen. . . . During the [past] 17-year period, the Communist

Party has enlisted the support of at least 7,000 Protestant clergymen in the same categories—party members, fellow travelers, espionage agents, party-line adherents, and unwitting dupes" (3). J. Howard Pew sent a copy of the article to Dr. Roy G. Ross, associate general secretary of the NCC, commending Matthews as "a man of integrity and one who knows more about who does belong to the Communist Party than any man in America."[58] Pew noted that Senator Joseph McCarthy had selected Matthews as chief executive of the Senate Permanent Subcommittee on Investigations. Four senators objected to the employment of Matthews. In response to a telegram from three leaders of the National Conference of Christians and Jews, President Eisenhower replied: "Generalized and irresponsible attacks that sweepingly condemn the whole of any group of citizens are alien to America. Such attacks betray contempt for the principles of freedom and democracy." On July 9, 1953, Senator McCarthy accepted J. B. Matthews's resignation.[59] On July 21 of the same year, the liberal Methodist Bishop G. Bromley Oxnam went before the House Committee on Un-American Activities, condemning its unconstitutional methods and demanding that it clear its files of unsubstantiated charges. The committee admitted that it had no evidence that Oxnam was a communist sympathizer.

Allegations of communist infiltration of federated Protestantism were defused by these events, but they did not die away entirely. Liberal Protestants resisted efforts to align Christianity with support for free markets, but clearly the anticommunist influences caused major NCC figures to disavow left-wing associations and to moderate their advocacy on economic issues, including taxation.

Taxation and Christian Ethics—The Niebuhrian View

Reinhold Niebuhr, in his 1953 essay "The Christian Faith and the Economic Life of Liberal Society," which appeared in the first volume of the NCC series on ethics and economic life, expressed his view of the relationship between Christianity and economics. Economists, he said, could not find a source for ethical standards in pure economic analysis. Yet, they used ethical norms in making their judgments. Niebuhr viewed these norms as relating to "justice," a concept that was not only identified with the Christian faith. Niebuhr asked, "Does the Christian faith add anything significant to the concept of justice?" concluding that Christianity subordinated justice "to an even higher standard, that of love. . . . The most ideal social possibility for man may well be so perfect an accord of life with life that each member of a community is ready to sacrifice his interests for the sake of others" (Niebuhr 1953, 439). In previous works, Niebuhr had described this form of Christian love:

> Unprudential love, in which there is no calculation of mutual advantages, obviously stands in a dialectical relation to mutual love and to every scheme of distributive justice as well. In mutual love and in distributive justice, the self regards itself as an equal, but not as a specially privileged member of a group in which the rational self seeks to apportion the values of life justly or to achieve perfect reciprocity of advantages. [The will to do justice and mutual love] are mixed with a careful calculation of interest and advantages in which the self always claims an equal share. The final form of love is bereft of such calculation and meets the needs of the other without calculating comparative rights (Niebuhr 1986, 150).

Political and economic life, however, "must assume the selfishness of men" (Niebuhr 1953, 439). Niebuhr rejected the sort of religious view of economic life championed by Protestant conservatives of the time. He saw this movement as elevating middle-class prejudices, a "tendency toward extravagant individualism," laissez-faire principles, and a "lack of a sense of community or justice" to "religious absolutes" (441). He described this program as "so heavily financed by interested political and economic groups that its ideological corruption is even more evident than was the religious support of traditional 'natural law' concepts at the rise of modern commercial society" (441).

Niebuhr stated the relation of love to law in this way: "The law seeks for a tolerable harmony of life with life, sin presupposed. It is, therefore, an approximation of the law of love on the one hand and an instrument on the other hand" (Niebuhr 1986, 157–58).

In his response to Kenneth Boulding's 1953 contribution to the NCC series *The Organizational Revolution,* Niebuhr applied these ideas to taxation. As a starting point, Niebuhr argued that "the quasi-coercive contrivances of statecraft, on the one hand, offer the possibilities of community and justice beyond the natural limits of the primitive kinship society; and, on the other hand, they contain the perils of injustice and tyranny" (Boulding 1953, 241).[60] Niebuhr's comments should be placed within the context of his neoorthodoxy, a theological view that rejected perfectibility and emphasized man's sin and selfishness. With such a view of human nature, law and even tax law had a role to play:

> Taxation schedules are another case in point. Any system of taxation is coercive as it impinges upon the individual taxpayer. But the same taxpayer who feels the

coercion when he pays the tax may vote for it as the most equitable way of distributing the common burdens of a community. In a democratic society there are many policies in which consent and coercion are compounded in varying proportions. The consent to the coercive measure may be freely given, not only because the citizen regards the coercive measure as the best method of achieving common standards of sacrifice, but also as a method of supporting his own long-range sense of duty toward the community as against a short-range disinclination to do so (Boulding 1953, 239–40).

But, Niebuhr argued, "from the Christian standpoint at least, we cannot regard as evil the structures, systems, laws, and conventions by which partly selfish and partly unselfish men are held together in large-scale cooperation. The order and justice which they achieve must be regarded as an approximation of a loving community. It is merely an approximation under conditions of sin. So long as men are selfish, these hard shells of community must be preserved" (Boulding 1953, 244).[61]

Conclusion

As the United States entered into a period of postwar abundance, the years after World War II have been described as a time of bipartisan consensus about the federal tax regime. One element of that consensus was support for a "progressive but mass-based personal income tax for general revenues" (Brownlee 1996, 102). While politicians operated in a world of consensus and compromise, productive of a *pax tributorem*, federated Protestantism provided a battleground for opposing visions of justice, including tax justice, and of Christianity during this same period. Conflicting ideas about social justice were arrayed as collectivism *versus* individualism and were mapped onto the geopolitical struggle of the Cold War.

This case study suggests that tax scholars, in attempting to analyze tax equity and justice, can gain a richer sense of thinking about taxation by exploring "nonpolitical" cultural contexts. Blum and Kalven's use of the ministers' survey provides a step in this direction. The example of federated Protestantism provides, first, an illustration of the translation of economic debates into a religious context. Because of the perceived influence of the clergy, both conservative/libertarian and liberal Protestant activists sought to understand and influence the thinking of ministers in their parishes and in more nationally prominent settings. Explications of Keynesianism and other economic doctrines were presented to clergy in newspapers, schools, pamphlets, and more ambitious efforts such as the NCC's series on economics and ethics. As the government took a more active role in the economy, partly because of the continuation of the World War II tax regime, discussions of economics became more contentious and central to federated Protestantism. While effects on the poor and on taxpayers in general were considered, the focus of this first type of discussion of the intersection of religion and taxation was, largely, educative.

A second sort of discussion was more overtly religious and centered on fundamental questions of the role of government and the nature of man. Here, both sides cited scriptural authorities. Libertarian and conservative Protestants involved in these debates advocated an individualized approach to faith and salvation, relegating to government a minimal role. These advocates saw redistributive taxation as misguided and un-Christian. The Cold War setting led to stark dualities between freedom and Christianity on one side, and government oppression and communism on the other. Redistributive taxation smacked of communism and the antireligious stance associated with it. Reinhold Niebuhr was perhaps not representative of the views of NCC liberals, but he was certainly a figure of influence within Protestant circles. For Niebuhr, taxation was a means of coercing sinful and selfish people into doing what they knew was right in their better moments. One could not always be counted upon to be charitable in the moment to moment, and "hard shells of community," like taxation, provided an intermediate place short of *agape*. Niebuhr criticized the "Christian Economics" movement's opposition to unemployment insurance as unnecessary "because Christians of sensitive conscience will organize private charity for the needy." Niebuhr said: "The effort to confine *agape* to the love of personal relations, and to place all structures and artifices of justice outside that realm, makes Christian love irrelevant to the problems of man's common life" (Niebuhr 1986, 155).

The economic expansion seemed to have ameliorated many problems. Some economists, like Kenneth Boulding, viewed such expansion as the most important tool in addressing poverty and need. Reinhold Niebuhr disagreed. He saw human existence as inherently limited. "The serenity of man and the sanity of his life with others finally depend upon a wisdom which knows how to come to terms with these limits. This wisdom of humility and charity must be derived from a faith which measures the ends of life in a larger context than that which the immediate desires of man supply" (Niebuhr 1953, 457).

It is hard to know the more general impact of these debates, but their participants thought that within the context of a resurgent Protestantism, these ideas mattered economically, politically, and spiritually. Decisions about tax policy implicated justice and even divine love. The hint of the religious survey in Blum and Kalven's landmark essay provides an opening to alternative forums for debates about tax policy and alternative ways of approaching the notion of tax justice.

NOTES

1. There is, of course, a wealth of materials on these issues as they relate to other religious traditions over the centuries. Research into economic and tax policy debates would contribute to our understanding of taxation and culture. This chapter, however, covers a more limited period and a limited range of religious traditions.

2. Johnson reports that the opinion survey was of close to 2,000 ministers of all faiths and that a reputable opinion survey organization conducted the survey for Spiritual Mobilization. Other archival evidence identifies the polling organization as Opinion Research Corporation (ORC). The ORC's report indicates that both Protestant and Catholic clergymen were surveyed. ORC, "Gaining the Clergyman's Understanding," Public Opinion Index for Industry (August 1951), J. Howard Pew Personal Papers, Clergy & Business & Industry, Box 162, NCC Church Conference of Social Work 1953 to NCC World Council of Christian Education. Two years earlier, the same organization surveyed Protestant, Catholic, and Jewish religious leaders on their views concerning business, profits, and economic justice. One question was, "Are Christianity and capitalism in conflict?" In response to the statement "Our business system achieves a high degree of economic justice in the distribution of wealth," 39 percent of Protestant clergy agreed, while 30 percent of Catholic priests and 15 percent of Jewish rabbis agreed. ORC, "Business and the Clergy," Public Opinion Index for Industry (June 1949), J. Howard Pew Personal Papers, Clergy & Business & Industry, Box 162, NCC Church Conference of Social Work 1953 to NCC World Council of Christian Education, Hagley Mills Library.

3. "Churchmen Assent as Industry Voices Its Position at Conference," NAM News (March 1, 1947), p. 11, col. 2, Jasper E. Crane Papers, Box 31, Federal Council of Churches, 1947–51, Hagley Mills Library.

4. "Gaining Clergymen's Understanding of Business and Industry" (October 18, 1951), p. 1, Jasper E. Crane Papers, Box 60, National Council of the Churches of Christ in the USA, January-February 1954, Hagley Mills Library.

5. American conservatism can be seen as including various strands from individualistic, antistatist classical liberalism (which after the appropriation of the term "liberal" by Rooseveltian reformers came to be called libertarianism) to a more normative conservatism with special concerns for "moral traditions, universal values, and inherited social hierarchies" to "a cultural and religious fundamentalism" (Brinkley 1998, 282–91). Scholars have identified other strands as well. Jerome Himmelstein identified three elements of

conservatism—economic libertarianism, social traditionalism, and militant anticommunism (Himmelstein 1990). The story of postwar conservatism is the attempt to develop intellectual and political force despite the conflicting ideas animating conservatives' efforts (see Brinkley 1994; Nash 1998). For the purposes of this chapter, the term "conservative" refers to these various strands as a group and is used in more specific terms when referring to particular currents of conservative thought (e.g., libertarianism).

6. Noel Sargent, "Ethics, Economics and Church," at 51–52, NAM, Accession 1411, Box 163, Series I 100-QQ Religion, Church & Industry, 1955–41 (November 1954), Hagley Mills Library. Take another case: "Is it ethical to tax income when it is earned by a corporation and again when the corporation pays out the same money in dividends to the stockholder?" Sargent also pointed to his concerns about this brand of double taxation in an address delivered at a luncheon at the National Study Conference on the Church and Economic Life convened by the Federal Council of Churches in Detroit, February 16–19, 1950. *See* Department of the Church and Economic Life, Federal Council of the Churches of Christ in America, *National Leaders Speak on Economic Issues,* p. 29 (March 1950), NAM, Accession 1411, Series I 100-QQ Religion, Religion-General Folder, Hagley Mills Library.

During the 1950s, the NAM continued to express its disagreements with the prevailing depreciation and corporate tax regimes in publications concerned with the relationship between church and industry. *See* "Program for Progress," *Church & Industry Dateline* (February 1957), p. 2, NAM, Accession 1411, Series I 100-QQ Religion, Dateline 1957–59; "In the Public Interest," *Church & Industry Dateline* (November 1958), p. 2, NAM, Accession 1411, Series I 100-QQ Religion, Dateline 1957–59; "The Philosophy of Blur," *Church & Industry Dateline* (September 1959), pp. 2, 4, NAM, Accession 1411, Series I 100-QQ Religion, Dateline 1957–59.

7. Kenneth E. Boulding (1910–93) was a professor of economics at the University of Michigan during the period covered in this chapter. In 1968, he served as president of the American Economics Association and spent much of his career as an economics professor at the University of Colorado. In his obituary in the *New York Times,* Boulding was described as being "from a family of deeply religious Methodists." He "became a Quaker as a young man and remained a passionate if unconventional Christian throughout his life. An ardent pacifist, he opposed World War II and lost his wartime post as an economist at the League of Nations." "Kenneth E. Boulding, an Economist, Philosopher and Poet, Dies at 83," *New York Times* (March 20, 1993), p. 10, col. 1.

8. For a biography of Niebuhr, see Fox (1985).

9. Walter Rauschenbusch argued for the adoption of the single tax in order to "resocialize the land" (Ahlstrom 1972; Beckley 1992; Rauschenbusch 1913). "Rauschenbusch argued for a progressive inheritance tax and direct taxation . . . of corporations and individuals as the best means to socialize income and wealth" (Beckley 1992, 99).

10. Letter to Charles R. Hook (July 9, 1951), J. Howard Pew Personal Papers, Box 152, NCC, General Board, 1955–56 to NCC Solicitation 1951, at 2.

11. Id., 3.

12. *Saving American Capitalism* had its origins in the detection of "some backsliding from the Roosevelt economic program." Important officials and advisers in the Roosevelt administration and some academics "in general agreement with them" were asked to "express their views on what should be done" (Harris 1948, 3–4). The figures

mentioned were allied with the Roosevelt administration or with the Truman administration. A. A. Berle Jr., one of Roosevelt's Brain Trusters, was a Columbia law professor
in 1948 and former assistant secretary of state. Chester Bowles was director of the Office
of Price Administration. Alvin H. Hansen, America's most prominent Keynesian, was a
Harvard economics professor. Leon Keyserling helped draft major New Deal legislation
and was chairman of the Council of Economic Advisers under President Truman. Arthur
M. Schlesinger Jr. was a Harvard history professor, and Edwin Witte, a Wisconsin economics professor, served as executive director of the President's Committee on Social
Security during the Roosevelt administration.

13. Letter to Dr. Stanley B. High (October 20, 1949), Jasper E. Crane Papers,
Box 31, Federal Council of Churches, 1947–51.

14. Letter to Rev. A. Dudley Ward (December 24, 1952), Jasper E. Crane Papers,
Box 59, National Council of the Churches of Christ in the USA, January–April 1953.

15. Hayek's *The Road to Serfdom* was a surprising success upon its American publication in September 1944. The book was condensed in the *Reader's Digest* and distributed by business groups. Hayek argued that planning led to dictatorship, although he did
allow some scope for government planning to maintain competition (Rosenof 1974).

The Federal Council of Churches' *Information Service* published a mostly critical
review of *The Road to Serfdom* in a piece that described William Beveridge's *Full
Employment in a Free Society* as "the most comprehensive, detailed and reasonable program [for a socially controlled economy]" (Federal Council of Churches 1946b).

16. Letter to Dr. James W. Fifield Jr. (December 24, 1948), Jasper E. Crane Papers,
Box 88, Spiritual Mobilization, 1943–52, Hagley Mills Library.

17. ORC, "Gaining the Clergyman's Understanding" (Executive Summary)
(August 1951), p. 5, J. Howard Pew Personal Papers, Box 162, NCC Church Conference
of Social Work 1953 to NCC World Council of Christian Education, Clergy & Business
& Industry, Hagley Mills Library.

18. Id., 44.

19. Id., A-35.

20. Memorandum to John Harmon from Wm. R. Darragh (May 25, 1953), NAM,
Accession 1411, Box 163, Series I 100-QQ Religion, Religion.

> Let's keep at it until we get every minister in every task force city through some
> plant that they might understand clearer the functions of industry as relate to
> such items as production, taxes, labor relations, distribution, service of industry
> to community, how the ministers can help, etc.

NAM's efforts with respect to the clergy dated back to the 1940s and included local and
regional conferences.

21. The University of Chicago, School of Church and Economic Life (Summer
1952), Roy Blough Papers.

22. Letter from Cameron P. Hall to Roy Blough (March 29, 1951), Roy Blough
Papers, Harry S. Truman Library.

23. Major Lines of Needed Growth in the Program and Outreach of the Department, pp. 1–2, Roy Blough Papers.

24. Proposed Statement on the Moral Implications of the Economic Adjustments
in the Present Situation, (n.d.) p. 1, Roy Blough Papers.

25. Id., 2.

26. Id., 3.

27. Id.

28. Letter from Cameron P. Hall (January 11, 1951), Roy Blough Papers.

29. Department of the Church and Economic Life, Meeting of the General Committee (April 20–21, 1951), p. 2, Roy Blough Papers.

30. Statement on Inflation (second draft), p. 4, Roy Blough Papers.

31. Christian Responsibility toward Some Ethical Problems in Inflation (1952), p. 6, Roy Blough Papers.

32. Letter to Mrs. Lois B. Hunter (November 14, 1951), J. Howard Pew Personal Papers, Box 166, Mrs. Hunter, 1951 & 1950.

33. Donald Meyer has described the importance of the series:

Shortly after the Second World War, the Federal Council . . . set out again to study relationships between religion and economic life. The fruits of this project—six penetrating volumes—far surpassed any other inquiry in the history of the churches. Their guiding feature was that they were, for the most part, studies. They were not, like the Council's 1920 tract, *The Church and Industrial Reconstruction,* blueprints for action, or, like Interchurch's report on the steel strike, intervention in the world of power. . . . The council's six volumes betrayed few of the old perfectionist elements; old habits of thinking in terms of alternative "systems," of "new" social orders, of "Christianized" and "un-Christianized" areas of society had faded (Meyer 1988, 404).

34. "Harper and Brothers are proud to announce . . . ," Jasper E. Crane Papers, Box 61, National Council of the Churches of Christ in the USA, Miscellaneous Folder.

35. Letter to Luther A. Weigle (October 15, 1952), J. Howard Pew Personal Papers, Box 146, National Council of Churches, Statements & Publications, 1952–54, p. 1.

36. Memorandum from Mr. Hamilton to Mr. Pepper (September 26, 1952), J. Howard Pew Personal Papers, Box 146, National Council of Churches, Statements & Publications, 1952–54, p. 1.

37. Draft of Report of Committee of Reference, J. Howard Pew Personal Papers, Box 146, National Council of Churches, Statements & Publications, 1952–54, p. 1.

38. This idea was not unique to Boulding. For example, economist Alvin Hansen urged:

Just as Congress has, within limits established by law, empowered the executive to make adjustments in tariff rates, and just as Congress in the Federal Reserve Act has allocated to the monetary authority, within limits established by legislation, the power to raise and lower reserve ratios, so also it becomes highly important, and, indeed, essential to permit executive adjustment of the basic income-tax rate within limits imposed by Congress. Only in this manner is it possible to get quick timing and an adequate flexibility in our tax structure (Hansen 1948, 224).

39. John C. Gebhart, *Ethics and Economic Life: A Summary and Analysis of the Organizational Revolution: A Study in the Ethics of Economic Organization by Kenneth E. Boulding* (October 1953), p. 1, J. Howard Pew Personal Papers, Books, "The Organizational Revolution by Kenneth E. Boulding" (Rockefeller Foundation), Box 146, National Council of Churches, Statements and Publications, 1952–54.

40. Letter from Charles P. Taft to General Board Members (March 16, 1954), J. Howard Pew Papers, Box 146, National Council of Churches, Statements and Publications, 1952–54, Book, "The Organizational Revolution by Kenneth E. Boulding" (Rockefeller Foundation).

41. Letter from Percy L. Greaves Jr. (March 30, 1954), J. Howard Pew Personal Papers, Box 146, National Council of Churches, Statements and Publications, 1952–54, Book, "The Organizational Revolution by Kenneth E. Boulding" (Rockefeller Foundation).

42. Memorandum to Messrs. Bosted and Hansen from Kenneth R. Miller (July 13, 1954), J. Howard Pew Personal Papers, Book, "The Organizational Revolution by Kenneth E. Boulding" (Rockefeller Foundation), Box 146, National Council of Churches, Statements and Publications, 1952–54.

43. Kermit Eby, "The Protestant Ethic," *The Goals of Economic Life: An NBC Radio Discussion,* The University of Chicago Round Table, p. 3 (March 1, 1953), J. Howard Pew Personal Papers, Box 146, National Council of Churches, Statements & Publications, 1952–54, Goals of Economic Life (Rockefeller Foundation), Hagley Mills Library.

44. In his contribution to *Goals of Economic Life,* one of a series of books produced by a study committee of the Federal Council of Churches in 1953, John Maurice Clark, professor of political economy at Columbia University, highlighted these conflicting parables in his description of "An Early Marginal Theory, 1871–1900":

> In the matter of incomes, the marginal-productivity theory—companion of marginal utility—rounded out a system in which, under competition, factors of production were allocated where they would be most productive, and their owners, including laborers received the worth of their marginal contribution to the joint product. And this was not without an ethical element, though few would claim that it settles all ethical problems. It is the ethics of the parable of the talents, not that of the workers in the vineyard (Clark 1953, 36).

45. "God and Free Enterprise," *The Herald* 66 (February 9, 1955), p. 1, NAM, Accession 1411, Box 163, Series I 100-QQ Religion, Religion-General Folder, Hagley Mills Library.

46. Letter to Dr. Samuel McCrea Cavert (September 8, 1941), Jasper E. Crane Papers, Box 31, Federal Council of Churches, 1939–46, Hagley Mills Library.

47. Letter from Jasper E. Crane to Mrs. Lois B. Hunter (March 19, 1954), Jasper E. Crane Papers, Box 60, National Council of the Churches of Christ in the USA, March–April 1954, Hagley Mills Library. The Federal Council of Churches' *Information Service* provided an example confirming Crane's charge of "use of government to carry out supposedly benevolent purposes":

> It is the responsibility of the Christian community to seek continually to create social conditions under which it will be less difficult to express in daily living the spirit of redemptive love that is enshrined in the New Testament. This means that the principles of the Christian gospel are to be applied to the structure of social relations, to the organization of society, no less than to the personal relations of human beings (FCC 1946a, 2).

48. Letter from Jasper E. Crane to Mr. Leonard E. Read (March 13, 1953), Jasper E. Crane Papers, Box 59, National Council of the Churches of Christ in the USA, January–April 1953.

49. Letter and Attachment from J. Howard Pew to Mr. Jasper E. Crane (May 28, 1953) at p. 5 in attachment, Jasper E. Crane Papers, Box 59, National Council of the Churches of Christ in the USA, May–September 1953.

50. Id., 7.

51. Id., 11.

52. Letter to Dr. Luther A. Weigle (October 15, 1952), J. Howard Pew Personal Papers, Box 146, National Council of Churches, Statements and Publications, 1952–54, Books, Goals of Economic Life (Rockefeller Foundation).

53. Letter to W. O. H. Garman (December 2, 1946), Jasper E. Crane Papers, Box 31, Federal Council of Churches, 1939–46.

54. Church and Industry Dateline (February 1958), NAM, Box 164, Series I 100-QQ Religion, Dateline 1957–59, Kellems, Knutson.

55. Mr. Choate's Argument for Appellants, *Pollock v. Farmer's Loan and Trust Co.,* 157 U.S. 429, 532 (1895):

The act of Congress which we are impugning before you is communistic in its purposes and tendencies and is defended here upon principles as communistic, socialistic—what shall I call them—populistic as ever have been addressed to any political assembly in the world.

56. Letter to Mrs. Lois Black Hunter (July 8, 1950), J. Howard Pew Personal Papers, Box 162, Planning Committee for the NCC 1950.

57. "How Red Is the Federal/National Council of Churches?" Jasper E. Crane Papers, Box 59, National Council of the Churches of Christ in the USA, January–April 1953, Hagley Mills Library.

58. Letter to Roy G. Ross (June 24, 1953), J. Howard Pew Personal Papers, Box 147, NCC #1—Ross, Dr. Roy.

59. Memorandum on the Protestant Clergy and the McCarthy-Matthews Episode, J. Howard Pew Personal Papers, Box 147, "Clergy-McCarthy-Matthews Episode, July 1953," Text of Documents in Matthews Case, *New York Times,* July 10, 1953.

60. These ideas evoke later work on the concept of precommitment, most notably associated with Jon Elster (1979). Elster uses precommitment as binding oneself to a long-range goal. I am indebted to Brian Glenn's (2001) paper, "Collective Precommitment against Temptation: The Case of the Amish" for this connection.

61. Niebuhr's use of "hard shells" evoked not only creatures with hard shells, but also, in American English, someone "rigid and uncompromising in religious orthodoxy (i.e., hard-shell Baptist)," according to the *Oxford English Dictionary.*

REFERENCES

Ahlstrom, Sydney E. 1972. *A Religious History of the American People.* New Haven, Conn.: Yale University Press.

Beckley, Harlan. 1992. *Passion for Justice: Retrieving the Legacies of Walter Rauschenbusch, John A. Ryan, and Reinhold Niebuhr.* Louisville, Ky.: John Knox Press.

Blum, Walter, and Harry Kalven Jr. 1952. "The Uneasy Case for Progressive Taxation." *University of Chicago Law Review* 19 (3): 417–520.

Boulding, Kenneth E. 1953. *The Organizational Revolution: A Study in the Ethics of Economic Organization.* New York: Harper and Brothers.

Brinkley, Alan. 1994. "The Problem of American Conservatism." *American Historical Review* 99 (2): 409–29.

———. 1998. *Liberalism and Its Discontents.* Cambridge: Harvard University Press.

Brownlee, W. Elliot. 1996. *Federal Taxation in America: A Short History.* Cambridge: Cambridge University Press.

Clark, John Maurice. 1953. "Aims of Economic Life as Seen by Economists." In *Goals of Economic Life,* edited by A. Dudley Ward (23–51). New York: Harper.

Elster, Jon. 1979. *Ulysses and the Sirens.* Cambridge: Cambridge University Press.

Federal Council of Churches. 1946a. "Christianity and the Economic Order." *Information Service* 25 (February 23): 2.

———. 1946b. "Christianity and the Economic Order." *Information Service.* Department of Research and Education. Study No. 5 (December 21) 25: 4–5.

Flynn, John T. 1949. *The Road Ahead: America's Creeping Revolution.* New York: Devin-Adair.

Fones-Wolf, Elizabeth. 1994. *Selling Free Enterprise: The Business Assault on Labor and Liberalism, 1945–60.* Urbana: University of Illinois Press.

Fox, Richard Wightman. 1985. *Reinhold Niebuhr: A Biography.* Ithaca: Cornell University Press.

Glenn, Brian J. 2001. "Collective Precommitment from Temptation: The Amish and Social Security." *Rationality and Society* 13(2): 185–204.

Hansen, Alvin H. 1948. "Needed: A Cycle Policy." In *Saving American Capitalism,* edited by Seymour E. Harris (218–25). New York: Knopf.

Harris, Seymour E. 1948. "The Issues." In *Saving American Capitalism,* edited by Seymour E. Harris (3–12). New York: Knopf.

Hayek, Friedrich A. 1944. *The Road to Serfdom.* London: G. Routledge and Sons.

Himmelstein, Jerome. 1990. *To the Right: The Transformation of American Conservatism.* Berkeley: University of California Press.

Hopkins, Charles Howard. 1940. *The Rise of the Social Gospel in American Protestantism, 1865–1915.* New Haven, Conn.: Yale University Press.

Hovenkamp, Herbert. 1990. "The First Great Law & Economics Movement." *Stanford Law Review* 993: 1021–25.

Johnson, William. 1952. "The Preacher Speaks on Social Problems." *Faith and Freedom* 3 (February): 3–6.

King, William McGuire. 1989. "The Reform Establishment and the Ambiguities of Influence." In *Between the Times: The Travail of the Protestant Establishment in America, 1900–1960,* edited by William R. Hutchinson (122–40). Cambridge: Cambridge University Press.

Matthews, J. B. 1953. "Reds and Our Churches." *American Mercury* (July 3): 3–13.

Meyer, Donald. 1988. *The Protestant Search for Political Realism, 1919–1941,* 2d ed. Middletown, Conn.: Wesleyan University Press.

Nash, George H. 1998. *The Conservative Intellectual Movement in America since 1945.* Wilmington, Del.: Intercollegiate Studies Institute.

Niebuhr, Reinhold. 1953. "The Christian Faith and the Economic Life of Liberal Society." In *Goals of Economic Life,* edited by A. Dudley Ward (433–59). New York: Harper and Brothers.

———. 1986. "Love and Law in Protestantism and Catholicism." In *The Essential Reinhold Niebuhr: Selected Essays and Addresses,* edited by Robert McAfee Brown (142–59). New Haven: Yale University Press. First published in the *Journal of Religious Thought* (spring–summer 1952).

Rauschenbusch, Walter. 1913. *Christianizing the Social Order.* New York: Macmillan Co.

Rosenof, Theodore. 1974. "Freedom, Planning, and Totalitarianism: The Reception of F. A. Hayek's *Road to Serfdom." Canadian Review of American Studies* 5 (2): 149–65.

Weisbrod, Carol. 1988. "Family, Church and State: An Essay on Constitutionalism and Religious Authority." *Journal of Family Law* 26: 741–70.

Wells, David A. 1880. "The Communism of a Discriminating Income-Tax." *North American Review* 130 (280): 236–47.

5

Endowment and Inequality

Daniel Shaviro

Tax policy literature, particularly that written by lawyers, often cites either income or consumption as an "ideal" tax base—the very thing we want to tax. Warren (1980), for example, embraces the admitted tautology that "the personal income tax follows from, and is justified by, a societal judgment as to the appropriate distribution of income" (1093). If we want to redistribute "income," then of course it *is* the right thing to tax—although *why* it is the thing we want to redistribute remains unclear.[1] On the other side of the debate, Andrews (1974) favors a consumption tax because "it ultimately imposes a more uniform burden on consumption, whenever it may occur, than does an [income] tax" (1167). This distinction "keeps the tax from bearing more heavily on one person than another on account of differences in need or taste for particular goods and services, now or in the future" (1168).

As we will see, there may be considerable appeal to Andrews's argument that mere taste differences should not lead to unequal tax burdens. However, this argument can be taken a step further, as demonstrated in the following examples (Bradford 1986):

1. Two individuals differ only in their taste for consumption goods; otherwise, their circumstances are the same. One prefers to spend more on clothing, less on food; the other likes high-quality food but does not care so much about clothing.

2. Two individuals have the same wage rates and in all other respects
   are in similar circumstances. However, one prefers to work long
   hours in order to purchase more goods; the other prefers less work
   and therefore accepts having fewer goods.

That the two individuals in the first example deserve to bear the same
taxes probably seems obvious. We are not likely to regard the differences
in taste as relevant to the sharing of tax burdens. Example two is essentially the same, except that the choice is not between food and clothing,
but between leisure and goods.

Bradford's reasoning about the first example, and its extendability to
the second, rules out any possibility that consumption, income, or
wealth could be the very thing we really want to tax. Consumption taxes
burden decisions to work and thus the taste for work (or market consumption), while income and wealth taxes burden work and saving.
Estate and gift taxes burden decisions to work, save, and engage in gratuitous transfers. All of these taxes, therefore, penalize tastes that have no
obvious distributional relevance, and burden behavior that is not bad in
and of itself and does not, at least not as obviously as pollution, impose
external burdens on others.[2]

The defense of any of these tax bases therefore lies in its capacity to
provide a crude proxy for some set of attributes that are relevant to distributive justice but cannot be observed directly. But what are these
underlying attributes? While analysts are unlikely to agree on them completely, most would say that they have something to do with inequality.
After all, if society did not agree that people who are better off should
bear a greater tax burden, it presumably would not object to raising revenue through a uniform head tax (at least where benefit taxation was
infeasible). Inequality, therefore, has a prominent place in a variety of
views of distributive justice, although under any view it rests at least one
"turtle" from the bottom. (I refer to the old story of the woman who
claimed that the earth rests on the back of a turtle and, when asked what
the turtle rests on, responded that it was "turtles all the way down.")[3]
That is, the move from describing who is better off under some metric
to claiming that tax burdens should vary by reason of the differences
identified by this metric requires motivation.

Many tax policy experts have recognized the conceptual need for a
lower-lying distributional "turtle" than merely some definition of a

tax base, such as the Haig-Simons income definition.[4] The true, but unobservable, underlying measure that income is thought to represent, for reasons lying at least one more turtle down, can be termed "ability" or "ability to pay." However, the spirit in which analysts typically discuss this hypothetical measure (or, more often, deliberately do not discuss it) was well illustrated by Simons's (1938) argument that efforts to poke too far behind the supposed objectivity of an income definition "lead . . . directly back into the utter darkness of 'ability' or 'faculty' or, as it were, into a rambling, uncharted course pointed only by fickle sentiments" (31).

Such "hard-nosed" views notwithstanding, this chapter argues that consideration of the presumed underlying measure of inequality—for which wealth, income, and consumption are merely rough proxies—is crucial to developing a coherent and defensible view of distributive justice. The following section attempts to flesh out an underlying measure, which we might call "endowment," "ability," or "wage rate." The third section considers this measure's possible significance under two leading distributional approaches: utilitarianism, or weighted welfarism, and the liberalism, or liberal egalitarianism, much discussed in recent legal literature about taxation.[5] It argues that conventional rejections of endowment taxation as an orienting idea—usually on the grounds that such taxation would require enslaving a beachcomber who could have been a Wall Street lawyer—are confused in key respects. The last section briefly concludes.

"Endowment" As an Underlying Measure of Inequality

Inequality Measures Based on Welfare or Opportunity

The idea that some people are better off than others is both familiar and uncontroversial. As already noted, wealth, income, and consumption are flawed measures of such differences, unless we assume that people who fail to grab every last penny within their reach no matter what the nonmonetary cost (e.g., time or effort) are making a mistake. This section sketches out the rough contours of an underlying measure that at least comes closer to bedrock (a more hopeful metaphor than that of the unending turtles).

At this point, this section will establish *why* we might say one person is better off than another, without yet considering the relevance of this statement for tax-transfer policy. Obviously, ways of judging inequality may differ, and once we examine several views of distributive justice, we might find that one measure rather than another ought to have been used, depending on the view. As it happens, however, a look ahead reveals that this problem is less serious than it initially appears.

One obvious measure of inequality between people focuses on a presumed psychic state that might be called one's welfare, subjective well-being, or utility. This concept is the most familiar economic measure, both descriptively (i.e., people optimize their utility given their preferences) and normatively (i.e, social welfare functions depend on the welfare of individuals). One could perhaps question how meaningful this concept is, since evolution appears not to have equipped us with comprehensive, single-metric "hedometers," or "utility counters," that are readable, even by ourselves. And one could certainly challenge the usual thinking that the more preferences you satisfy, the greater your subjective well-being.[6] Nonetheless, the concept evidently has enough intuitive appeal to be widely accepted as descriptively meaningful.

Liberal egalitarians, for example, disparage welfare-based views on normative grounds, not on the grounds that such views rely on something that is not descriptively meaningful. Their normative views do, however, lead them to favor an alternative measure of inequality. Ackerman and Alstott (1999), for example, advocate equality of "opportunities, not outcomes" (24). Other liberal or liberal egalitarian writers have suggested similar ideas, which may go by such varied names as "fair equality of opportunity" (Rawls 1971), "equality of resources" (Dworkin 1981), "equality of opportunity for welfare" (Arneson 1989), or "equality of fortune" (Rakowski 1991).

The descriptive difference between the inequality measure that such views suggest and the welfare-based measure can be illustrated by comparing a miserable millionaire to a happy beggar, where the difference in their material fortunes results purely from the millionaire inheriting wealth and having greater innate business ability. By stipulation, the happy beggar's subjective welfare is greater, but his opportunities, at least in a material sense, are not as great because of the circumstances of his birth. One need not subscribe to the liberal normative view in order to accept the descriptive meaningfulness of an inequality measure based on people's opportunities or broadly defined resources.

While welfare- and opportunity-based inequality measures can be coherent descriptively, their differences potentially pose difficulty at the normative stage in distribution debates between welfarists and liberal egalitarians. For example, even if both groups are willing to use a distributional proxy such as "wealth" or "income," the interpretation they give the proxy may differ. Nonetheless, in describing measures of inequality (leaving aside for now what to do about them), these differences can, to a considerable extent, be ignored. The substantial reconcilability of the welfare- and opportunity-based measures of inequality relates to two factors: the economists' credo that increased choice is generally advantageous (Diamond 1999) and the view that, so far as we can tell, two people who make different selections from among the same choices tend to be equally well off. If we assume that greater choice is advantageous—but that we cannot assess how well people have chosen and have no other information about utility—then the alternative measures should produce the same rankings.[7]

As an illustration, consider consumer sovereignty, defined as an evidentiary inference about people's choices. It may seem reasonable to assume that people generally have the best information about their own preferences and thus incentive to act according to these preferences. Thus, it might be sensible to assume that people make the best choices for themselves given what they know. There are, of course, exceptions such as compulsive gamblers or people who undersave because they lack self-discipline. But in general, it would be arrogant and fatuous to assume that everyone should make a given choice in a particular way.

Having said that, suppose we observe people with the same earnings opportunities (and no known differences in other opportunities) make different choices in a case where there is no reason to question consumer sovereignty. One person works more than another because of differences in affinity for work versus leisure or in market versus nonmarket consumption. Or, one person saves more than another because of different consumption preferences. Either way, without more information, there may be no basis for concluding that one is better-off than the other. Identical opportunities may imply the achievement of identical welfare, if only out of ignorance about the welfare actually achieved in each case.

A simple hypothetical example may help illustrate the similarity of the two measures of inequality. Imagine a world with only two goods, leisure and food. People can freely allocate their time between enjoying leisure and working to earn food. For each of the two goods, they always prefer a larger quantity to a smaller one, but they experience declining marginal utility (unit $n + 1$ always yields less satisfaction than unit n).

Individuals in such a world differ from each other in just two respects. First, some have higher wage rates than others; that is, they can earn more food per unit of effort or time. Second, under identical circumstances, their tastes for an extra unit of leisure versus one of food may vary. These tastes can be portrayed graphically by "indifference curves" showing what combinations of the two goods a given individual regards as equally valuable. Suppose, for example, that an individual is indifferent about receiving either (a) 10 units of food plus 12 hours of leisure or (b) 15 units of food plus 11 hours of leisure. These two combinations, along with all others regarded by the individual as of identical value, can be depicted as lying on the same indifference curve. The same amount of one of these goods plus less (or more) of the other lies on a higher (or lower) indifference curve.

In this world, each individual has a "budget line" depicting the largest food-leisure bundles that he or she can procure. For example, if individuals have 24 hours a day to allocate as they choose and can earn 1 unit of food per hour, then they can choose 24 hours of leisure and no food, 24 units of food and no leisure, or various intermediate combinations (such as 16 hours of leisure and 8 units of food, or 14 hours of leisure and 10 hours of food). Given wage rate variations, people face different budget lines. For any quantity of leisure less than 24 hours, a person with a higher wage rate can get more food than one with a lower wage rate.

Figure 5.1 depicts a situation where an individual chooses the option, from among the bundles available at his or her budget line, that lies on the highest indifference curve. This individual, who can earn 1 unit of food per hour, picks B, the point of tangency between budget line AA^1 and U_1 (the highest indifference curve that touches AA^1). (All attainable points on U_0 are less desirable, and none on U_2 is attainable.) Someone who faces the same budget line but has different tastes, portrayed by a distinct set of indifference curves, will pick a different point along AA^1.

Suppose two individuals face the same budget line but have distinct indifference curves, leading one to work more, amassing more food but less leisure. We cannot say which individual is better off. Each prefers

Figure 5.1 *Commodity Choice at a Given Budget Line*

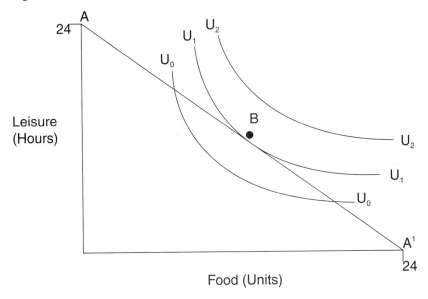

Food (Units)

where he or she is over the position of the other individual and, indeed, chose it for that reason.

Suppose, however, that the individuals have the same indifference curves but different budget lines because one of them has a higher wage rate. In this case, each prefers the point achieved by the individual whose wage rate and budget line are higher. Moreover, if each individual has the same utility function (not just the same preferred rate of trade between the goods) and nothing else about their utility levels differs, then the individual with the higher budget line is better off. Admittedly, these assumptions go far beyond anything we can really discern. They can be defended, however, as a reasonable best guess, given our ignorance.[8]

In short, under the stated assumptions, the higher an individual's wage rate and resulting budget line are, the greater the utility he or she experiences. Wage rates and budget lines therefore provide a rough measure of inequality if the standard is well-being. Moreover, an opportunity standard should lead to the same set of equality rankings under these circumstances as one based on well-being. If the wage rate is exogenous (beyond the individual's control), then anyone with a low

wage rate has "less valuable opportunities available to him . . . simply in
virtue of some chance occurrence the risk of which he did not choose to
incur" (Rakowski 1991, 1).

It should be clear, therefore, that under both inequality measures,
high-wage-rate individuals may exhibit less wealth, income, or market
consumption than low-wage-rate individuals, simply because their
different tastes lead to different commodity choices (e.g., leisure versus
goods earned through work). When this happens, high-wage-rate individuals misleadingly appear worse off rather than better-off. Figure 5.2
provides an example.

In this example, Andrea has a higher wage rate than Brian, thus giving her a budget line of AA^1 to his AB^1. However, she works so much less
that she ends up at point X, compared with his point Y. (Perhaps, solely
because of differences in taste, she is a law professor and he is a practitioner?) She therefore earns less, yet presumably is better-off since she
could have matched his earnings and had more leisure, or matched his
leisure and had more earnings. (For now, this analysis ignores the
"lumpiness" of some work decisions, which may prevent people from

Figure 5.2 *Example of High-Wage-Rate (Better-Off) Individual
with Lower Earnings than a Low-Wage-Rate Individual*

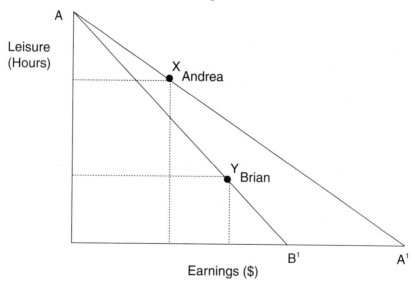

fine-tuning their work levels as precisely as they would like.) A tax on earnings, however, would likely burden Brian more than Andrea, although the outcome depends on how each person responds to the tax. Under either inequality measure, therefore, a tax on earnings seems likely to increase inequality between Andrea and Brian because of its greater adverse impact on the individual who was already worse off to begin with.

From Simple Hypotheticals to the Real World

Despite being extremely reductive, these examples capture something important about the real world. People have different opportunities to acquire material resources, and they take advantage of these opportunities to different degrees. Further, the outcomes that people experience reflect both choice and nonchoice. This distinction might matter either because choice is morally important (as under a liberal egalitarian view), or because choice reveals preference (as under a welfarist view).

The notion of an exogenous wage rate is meant to capture the unchosen element. It differs from, say, a lawyer's hourly billing rate because (1) it does not just reflect time on the clock but expresses a relationship between earnings and effort, and (2) a lawyer who charges $400 an hour did not start out at that level but is in part earning a return on past efforts to acquire skills and connections. "Endowment" and "ability" are synonyms for "wage rate" that may help to avoid confusion with a skilled professional's hourly billing rate.

Endowment or ability should not, however, be interpreted smugly as a measure of personal worth. These terms merely describe some aspect of the available interactions between individuals and the world in which they find themselves. Intellect may be part of ability, along with sound judgment, self-discipline, and the other aspects of what has been dubbed "emotional intelligence" (Goleman 1997). The same, however, may go for good looks, parental influence, possessing a white skin if customers are racists, having profitable bad taste as an artist or performer, and the capacity for fraud or violence.[9]

While the wage-rate hypotheticals capture something important about the world, they overlook many things, for example:

- They ignore the element of time, which is crucial to assessing income and wealth taxation. People's income and wealth depend not only on their earnings from work, but also on *when* they consume and their investment choices with respect to saving. However, the decision to defer consumption and thus gain greater income and wealth down the road can be conceptualized in much the same way as the decision to choose work over leisure.

- They treat wage rates, once drawn, as leading to determinate outcomes that are risk-free, begging the question of to what extent, say, Bill Gates was skillful rather than lucky. Assessing risk after one has drawn a wage rate complicates the analysis (although, as discussed in Shaviro [2000], the "social insurance" issues arising are quite similar to endowment risk), but the issue of risk is beyond the scope of this chapter.
- They use a model of rational consumer choice in an unrealistically frictionless world (for example, a world without "lumpy" labor supply decisions).
- They ignore (or dump into the undifferentiated leisure category) all the nonmaterial things that may affect individuals' lives, such as the quality of their personal relationships, interests, and health, or such personal characteristics as "a puckish sense of humor, a lovable disposition, or a melting smile" (Rakowski 2000, 267 n. 10).

These limitations suggest the need for care in generalizing from the wage-rate analysis, but do not suggest the basic premise be modified in any particular way. Wage rate (or endowment or ability) is still likely to be the best available measure of inequality under either a welfarist or liberal-egalitarian standard. Thus, if we cannot make any constructive use of taste differences, the beachcomber who could have been a Wall Street lawyer is ideally grouped (for purposes of measuring inequality) with the individual who actually *is* a Wall Street lawyer, not with the one for whom beachcombing is the only option.[10] Use of tax bases, such as wealth, income, and consumption—insofar as they are designed to adjust tax burdens in response to inequality—can be justified only as rough proxies for endowment or ability that are more observable.

Not yet considered, however, is why the observation that one individual is better-off than another suggests differentiating their tax burdens. We normally think of this notion in terms of tax bases rather than endowment. However, to illuminate the distributional issues that arise in real-world tax systems, it is worth asking why endowment (if observable) might matter under a welfarist or liberal-egalitarian view.

Differing Endowment Levels and Distributive Justice

An Endowment Tax and "Slavery"

Certain writers have tended to dismiss endowment out of hand as a distributional measure. Rakowski (2000), for example, notes the practical difficulty of measuring endowment, and also mentions an aversion to "compel[ling] somebody to pay taxes on the value of his talents . . . if he chooses not to use them productively" (267, n. 10). Levying an endowment tax, he says, "would effectively enslave the able, by forcing them to put their highly taxed talents to their most lucrative employ, however unpalatable . . . on pain of sitting in a debtors' prison" (267, n. 10).

More sweeping expressions of this concern abound in the literature, such as Kelman's (1979) comment that "[an endowment tax] would violate the simple libertarian principle that the state should not require people, directly or indirectly, to engage in particular activities. . . . The widespread principle that people ought to be taxed only when they voluntarily convert property rights into marketable form may seem simply a matter of neutrality, a reluctance to force people to make nontax decisions for tax reasons. But this principle, in more refined form, may really be a political recognition of a basic human resistance to commoditization" (842).

These arguments can be challenged on several grounds. For example, what motivates this particular use of the "simple libertarian principle"? In distributive justice, libertarianism often is used to make the case against progressive redistribution[11]—a position not agreeable to Kelman (1979). Why use it in one place and not the other?

One could also challenge Kelman's definition of neutrality. To people who have a work-leisure choice, he characterizes the decision to tax one choice but not the other as "neutral." Is a speeding ticket similarly neutral between speeding and not speeding?

Finally, consider the issue of "commoditization." Kelman (1979) expands on this point by saying that the beachcomber's "refusal to treat potentially marketable resources as commodities represents a desirable anticapitalist strain in a market-obsessed culture" (880). He is mistaken if he thinks that the beachcomber is not, like people in general, making a deliberate commodity choice. The beachcomber chooses that particular lifestyle over Wall Street "lawyering" because it best utilizes his or her talents. Entering the explicit labor market and working for a wage simply means that one has reduced self-production (including leisure) to engage in exchange transactions with other people, presumably because of what an international trade economist would call comparative advantage. Deciding whether to enter the explicit labor market is hardly different, in principle, than deciding whether to trade baseball cards with a fellow collector. Why should we think that people who eschew trades are somehow nobler, happier, or, for that matter, less-calculating optimizers than those who decide that a trade has something to offer them?

There is, of course, a vast literature about commodification, alienation, and the like that may underlie the apparently empirical claim about the perils of more extensive and explicit exchanges. However, the more than 20 years since Kelman's article have helped to clarify that viewing one's labor as a valuable, and valued, commodity may actually be empowering. In practical terms, today's main "beachcombers," or people who stand poised between entering the explicit labor market and sticking to home production, are households' secondary earners (e.g., the wife of a working husband in a traditional family). Should we want to keep the "little woman" home, too, as a valiant anticapitalist holdout in our sadly market-obsessed culture? Other less-sweeping attacks on the endowment tax approach emphasize a consideration that could be called "ease of payment." Because exchange transactions in the labor market typically involve cash, it is easier to commandeer a portion of the Wall Street lawyer's return to work than any portion of the beachcomber's return to leisure. Therefore, we expect that paying tax will in practice be more onerous for the beachcomber.[12] Now, this expectation may be both true and relevant, but in implementing a tax system it is largely an administrative problem (albeit a very important one). It has no bearing on the question of how to think about inequality or who is presumptively better-off.

Suppose that Wall Street lawyers were paid in yogurt that spoiled within five minutes if not eaten. In addition, suppose that a percentage of the beachcomber's imputed return from beachcombing could be transferred to other people, just like a portion of a cash wage, without requiring him or her to leave the beach or detracting from enjoyment of the remaining return. These mere "technological" changes in compensation transferability would reverse the character of the administrative problem. Consequently, we would conclude that Wall Street lawyers could not pay the tax unless they were dragged in chains to federal office buildings after hours to mop the floors, and we would associate slavery with taxing lawyers rather than beachcombers.

Ease-of-payment concerns and measurement problems clearly affect the desirability of implementing endowment taxation. However, these factors, given their irrelevance to measuring pretax inequality, should not affect endowment's standing as an inequality measure that is more fundamental than income, consumption, and wealth, potentially helping to orient real-world policy choices in cases where the administrative problems are not insuperable. As an analogy, consider the measurement and liquidity arguments for not taxing unrealized income from the appreciation of property. These administrative arguments do not refute the view that "economic income" lies closer to bedrock than does "realized income." Such a view might motivate lawmakers to deny deductions for investment interest and capital losses suspected as being arbitraged against unrealized gain in the taxpayer's portfolio.

Completely collapsing the plausibility of "income" or "consumption" as a coherent fundamental measure of inequality requires only one more step. Unrealized gains might be considered an example of imputed income, that is, gains not directly evidenced by an observable market transaction.[13] (Another example of such economic income is the imputed rent enjoyed by a homeowner who forgoes the money she could have earned by charging someone else to live in her home.) Implicitly paying oneself the market value of one's labor by choosing housework or leisure over a cash wage could be considered imputed income by the same logic. Nonetheless, these gains are not typically assumed to be within the boundaries of "income" or "consumption," as these terms are hypothetically defined for tax purposes.

Why do accepted notions of economic income (and consumption) reflect the use of imputation in some, but not all, cases in which no observable market transaction has occurred? Presumably, the decision reflects such considerations as ease of payment, measurability, the degree of ready comparability and/or substitutability (at least in the mind of the observer) between actual and implicit transactions, and a sense of what extensions are politically plausible or, at least, minimally explainable to nonspecialists. Clearly, however, no one really thinks an observable market transaction is needed for conceptual includability, despite all the rhetoric to the contrary. In addition, given considerations such as ease of payment, the terms "income" and "consumption," even if ultimately good descriptions of what we might actually choose to tax are not sufficiently coherent, well defined, or focused on relative well-being to serve as ideal inequality markers.

To help show the advantages of using an endowment concept to assess relative well-being, consider stay-at-home spouses, potential secondary earners for their households. That stay-at-home spouses are valuable producers[14] makes adding a tax burden if they enter the explicit labor market a questionable distributional policy and one that is likely to promote inefficient tax avoidance behavior (staying home). An endowment measure helps show that if two individuals with high-earning spouses and the same job opportunities make different choices, then the earnings difference between them may be a poor measure of their relative positions.[15]

Another implication of the secondary-earner problem is worth noting here. Imposing a tax burden on a household that has two or more potential earners may induce explicit labor market participation by members of the household who otherwise would have preferred to stay home. Suppose, for example, that a tax increase on the husband's earnings in a traditional family "forces" the wife to get a job and hire childcare providers for the time she will be spending at an office. No one seems to think that this scenario suggests a "libertarian constraint" on taxing households with two or more potential earners, and some commentators might even welcome the possible effect of discouraging traditional family structures.

So far, we have seen that endowment may provide an important orienting principle for the distributional component of tax-transfer policy, although surely we do not want to force talented beachcombers to put away their surfboards, don jackets and ties, and start reviewing loan documents or arranging interest rate swaps. However, further evaluating endowment requires specifying why the inequalities such evaluation helps to identify are pertinent to tax-transfer policy to begin with. Here the answer may vary, depending on the perspective in question (welfarist or liberal egalitarian being the two considered here).

Taxing Endowment from a Welfarist Perspective

The optimal income tax literature inspired by the work of James Mirrlees (1971) generally treats endowment as the thing we would like to tax. The available tax instrument is typically an earnings tax, reflecting the assumption that only earnings (which reflect both wage rate and effort) are observable. An earnings tax redistributes earnings from people with high wage rates to those with low wage rates, but it also discourages individuals' work effort. From a welfarist perspective, under which the desirability of a state of affairs depends purely on people's well-being in it (Sen 1992), the tax rate should optimize the value of the progressive redistribution that can be accomplished relative to the deadweight loss resulting from deterring people's work effort through the tax.

These models, however, abstract from the liquidity or ease-of-payment problem underlying the hypothetical scenario of the beachcomber who could have chosen to be a Wall Street lawyer. This omission reflects the extreme reductionism required to make the models analytically tractable. In particular, the models generally leave out differences in taste that might cause two individuals with the same wage rate to make different commodity choices. Thus, everyone with the same wage rate ends up with the same earnings,[16] works enough to be able to pay the tax, and suffers the same utility loss from having to pay the tax.

Under a utilitarian calculus in which social welfare depends purely on the sum of people's utilities, the motive for progressive redistribution comes mainly from the assumption of declining marginal utility.[17] An extra dollar is worth more to a low-wage-rate individual than to one with a high wage rate because the former has fewer dollars to spend. (For simplicity, a higher wage rate is assumed to imply greater earnings; however, if money were an inferior good,[18] this assumption would not hold up as endowment increased, although the analysis of declining marginal utility likely would endure.) However, the choice of a "weighted" welfarist alternative to utilitarianism, or a metric that weights the welfare of worse-off individuals more heavily than that of better-off individuals in the social-welfare calculus, would add an additional motive for pursuing progressive redistribution.

Under either a utilitarian or a weighted welfarist approach, the acknowledgment of taste differences—and the possibility that two individuals with the same endowment will end up as Wall Street lawyer and beachcomber, respectively—complicates the analysis in several ways. Presumably, the beachcomber has greater work aversion than the Wall Street lawyer and/or places less value on the market consumption opportunities that come with earnings. Work aversion may suggest that the beachcomber would suffer extra disutility from the income effect of having to work at least enough to pay the tax. In addition, this effect might get a lot worse if the realistic assumption of "lumpy" labor market decisions are added to the mix; for example, earning $400 per hour on Wall Street without years of training followed by a full-time commitment is difficult. Conversely, the beachcomber's lesser interest in market consumption might suggest that he or she would suffer less, rather than more, disutility than the lawyer by paying the tax. Every dollar of tax paid would deprive the beachcomber of market consumption opportunities that apparently are less interesting or valuable to him or her.

In practice, it is safe to say that few, if any, welfarists believe that overall social welfare will increase if talented beachcombers are taken in chains to labor in the corporate vineyards of recapitalizations and public stock offerings. Note, however, that weighted welfarists may place less importance than utilitarians on the disutility to high-endowment beachcombers of working a little to pay the tax, until the point where the disutility is great enough to make these beachcombers worse off than others.

Labor market lumpiness may significantly deepen welfarists' reluctance to follow through on the endowment standard. Suppose, for example, that law professors who have deliberately passed up higher-paying law jobs would be greatly inconvenienced by owing the same tax as their practitioner peers. That is, they would have to give up some of the more limited consumption opportunities that they valued a lot or else give up on serious academic effort. This problem may reflect a lumpy labor market, where it is hard to generate high billings with just a few hours of scattered effort here and there. Lumpiness suggests the possibility that, for two individuals with the same endowment, an extra dollar may be more valuable to the one who has chosen lower earnings because that individual cannot fine-tune his or her personal choices in a way that equalizes the marginal utility of the last earned dollar versus the last unit of leisure.

Now consider a more politically prominent version of the beachcomber problem—the tax treatment of secondary earners. For the wives of high-earning husbands, taxing their market work but not their home production clearly tends both to discourage labor market participation and disfavor two-earner households relative to one-earner households with similar opportunities. Lowering the tax burden on a secondary earner's market work (e.g., by permitting income splitting among couples, an option that might lower the marginal tax rate on extra earnings if the rate structure is progressive)[19] could lessen these undesirable effects. An opposite response would be to tax the home production of nonworking spouses, perhaps via an imputed measure (Staudt 1996).

Even as adjusted to raise the same overall revenue, the two approaches presumably would result in different tax-burden allocations between households. Obviously, this chapter is not the place to outline a detailed welfarist analysis of how to choose between the two approaches. Nonetheless, it is worth noting that we actually do consider problems of this sort in contemporary debates about tax policy, even when the issue of income imputed to stay-at-home spouses is not on the table. Debates about the appropriate relative treatment of different household types, such as single individuals versus married couples, often turn on how to compare need or well-being in the two settings. That a couple has two sets of hands, rather than one, is routinely taken into account, as is the fact that a couple household has two mouths, rather than one, to feed.[20] "Simple libertarian principles" (Kelman 1979, 842) apparently do not get in the way.

One of the well-recognized consequences of imposing any tax burden on a one-earner couple is the possibility of an income effect motivating the previously stay-at-home spouse to go to work. Sometimes, especially among those nostalgic for the traditional family, this effect is cause for complaint. The Christian Coalition's (1995) proposed "Contract with the American Family" blamed tax increases since the 1970s for married women's need to work. Others who are hostile to this nostalgic stance, and its possibly sexist underpinnings, cite the proponents' complaint against married women working as itself cause for complaint (McCaffery 1997). However, both sides seem to agree on one thing: the possible consequence of the income effect does not trump all other considerations (as the beachcomber example might suggest). Rather, this potential outcome belongs in the same overall stew as all the other consequences of a given household taxation scheme and should be considered in that context. Some commentators may even endorse the income effect on the labor supply among married women, arguing that the increased labor market participation has positive external effects benefiting both sexes.

From a welfarist perspective, therefore, the normative significance of endowment is complicated. There is no clear justification for imposing a straightforward endowment tax, even if we could measure endowment. This lack, however, reflects the complexity of the normative significance of inequality from a welfarist perspective. Despite the implication that, as a result of declining marginal utility (and weighted welfarism to its subscribers), we should generally favor transfers from high-endowment to low-endowment individuals, endowment ceases to provide clear-cut distribution guidance once we allow for taste differences and lumpy labor markets.

The fact that endowment does not have more decisive implications for distribution policy raises the possibility that, in practice, sticking with a proxy measure such as income, consumption, or wealth would be preferable even if endowment were directly observable. Yet the proxy measures would still be functioning as stand-ins. The justification for their use would still ultimately lie in their relationship to endowment plus other relevant factors (e.g., work aversion, materialism, and the effect of lumpy work decisions on the marginal utility of a dollar). And as a matter of analytical clarity, endowment as a tool for measuring inequality—though not for deciding what to do about inequality—remains closer to bedrock than the proxy standards.

Taxing Endowment from a Liberal Egalitarian Perspective

Turning to liberal egalitarianism, an initial methodological problem arises. This approach is generally more open-ended than welfarism, or at least open-ended in a different way. Welfarism purports to specify exactly what matters—utility—and draws a mathematical relationship between individuals' utilities and social welfare. (To be sure, the specification is not only empirically, but also analytically problematic, since "utility" is unobservable and might not exist literally.) Liberal egalitarian frameworks tend to be less definite in specifying what matters and in describing how one should choose between conflicting aims with the same rank.[21] In addition, while welfarists may differ about such matters as interpersonal weighting and the meaning of utility,[22] each liberal egalitarian (accepting the existence of such a group) may have a distinct theory altogether, making generalization about egalitarian views dangerous.

Nonetheless, some leading liberal egalitarians and a set of roughly shared principles come to mind. John Rawls, Ronald Dworkin, and Bruce Ackerman have been so labeled (McCaffery 1994a). Thomas Nagel, Amartya Sen, Thomas Scanlon, and Eric Rakowski can also be mentioned here. These thinkers generally agree that an individual's rights are independent of consequences and that distributive justice is not concerned with the welfare content of outcomes but with people's "non-welfare-based entitlements to resources, opportunities, or capabilities in consequence of their choices and of their natural and social fortune" (Rakowski 1991, 27). This claim rests on what Murphy (1996) calls the "choices thesis," under which "the distinction between wealth or income people have acquired through their own 'effort or voluntary

choices' and wealth or income obtained 'purely by chance' is of foundational importance to distributive justice" (474).

The choices thesis closely parallels the distinction (relevant to welfarists) between endowment on the one hand, and effort or commodity
choice on the other, as the determinants of earnings.[23] Once again, an
argument can be made for redistributing income from high-endowment
to low-endowment individuals, but that rationale does not extend to
earnings differences that result from differences in effort or commodity
choice. To be sure, the two schools' arguments stand on very different
grounds; thus, one could specify circumstances under which their implications would sharply diverge. For example, showing that a particular
high-endowment individual attaches the same marginal utility to a dollar as a low-endowment individual eliminates the utilitarian's—but not
the liberal egalitarian's—main reason for supporting progressive redistribution. Moreover, the utilitarian would be concerned about the
empirical consequences of discouraging effort through the earnings tax
(leading to deadweight loss) rather than about eliminating an inherently
fair reward for effort. Still, when information is limited—so that we
assume marginal utility declines (but cannot measure it) and predict
that reducing the reward to effort will discourage work (but are uncertain by how much)—the differences may lack clear implications.

A similar parallel may emerge with respect to differences in taste. A
welfarist who generally accepts consumer sovereignty will tend to think
that differences in commodity choice provide little, if any, information
about relative endowments or the utility consequences of raising or lowering a given individual's budget line. Differences in taste, therefore, are
not immediately relevant to distributional arguments, although additional information can make them pertinent (see the earlier description
of differences in materialism and work aversion). As for liberal egalitarians, they tend to place "a high value on letting people pursue their own
visions of the good" (Alstott 1996, 379), albeit within the limits of what
seems an acceptable "rational plan" (Rawls 1971, 395) as determined
through some "objective" specification of proper goods rather than
"exclusively in terms of preference satisfaction" (Rakowski 1996, 434).
This reasoning might suggest *not* redistributing on the basis of taste differences—resulting in much the same end as the welfarist view, as long
as information is limited in the right way.

Also worth mentioning is the philosophical literature on "expensive
tastes," or tastes that require a greater expenditure of scarce resources to

be satisfied. Various liberal egalitarians have criticized welfarism for its implication that "the allotment of someone who cultivated expensive tastes—for flashy cars, posh restaurants, designer clothes—be increased" at the expense of those with cheaper tastes (Rakowski 1991, 41).[24] This outcome is unfair if, under the choices thesis, expensive tastes that are deliberately cultivated should not be rewarded.

Once again, however, the choices thesis and welfarist views overlap if information is sufficiently limited. For example—illustrating anew the overlap between considering choice morally important and caring about it for incentive reasons—welfarists naturally would be concerned about the consequences of rewarding expensive tastes. Externalization of the cost of developing expensive tastes causes the individual and the optimal social incentives regarding such development to diverge. In addition, that one individual has more expensive tastes than another reveals too little about each person's utility function for us to know who would get more benefit from a given quantum of cash or change of budget line.[25]

What does all this mean for designing the tax-transfer system? Most important, the broad outlines of a liberal egalitarian's view of income, consumption, or wealth taxation should resemble those of a welfarist. Under either view, the tax bases involve a trade-off between accomplishing good redistribution based on endowment and bad redistribution based on effort or commodity choice. The choice of tax base, tax rates, and other design features must turn on complicated trade-offs between competing considerations, and undoubtedly depend, in part, on elusive empirical information. Rawls (1971) called these "questions of political judgment and not part of a theory of justice" (279),[26] presumably meaning that they could not be resolved by abstract reflection alone (rather than that his theory could not help to guide their resolution). Perhaps no plausible approach to distributive justice that treats inequality as normatively significant can hope to resolve at a broad level of abstraction the relative desirability of alternative tax instruments that burden decisions to work and/or decisions to save.

If endowment were measurable, liberal egalitarians might be more committed than welfarists to basing tax burdens on it. After all, some version of endowment appears to be what they want to redistribute under the choices thesis, and they may be inclined to disregard the utility information that might modify its use under welfarism. Thus, endowment to liberal egalitarians, unlike to welfarists, is not merely a convenient tool for getting at something else. To be sure, liberal egalitarians may generally be distressed by the case of the hypothetical beachcomber who is dragged off in golden chains to work on Wall Street. However, liberal egalitarian discussions of the problem often repeat Kelman's unexplained discontinuity between outright compulsion (such as forcing someone to work to pay the tax) and mere incentive or inducement (such as penalizing the decision to work). Although compulsion is merely a strong version of inducement (suggesting that they differ only in degree, not in kind), the inclination to put them in separate categories is apparently strong.[27]

Conclusion

Neither income, consumption, nor wealth is an "ideal" tax base, or one that plausibly reflects what we should ultimately want to tax. Rather, they are imperfect stand-ins for some underlying metric of inequality. Therefore, any choice between tax bases, as well as any effort to determine the content of the chosen tax base, should be conducted in terms of our underlying aims, not according to the outline of a definition, such as the Haig-Simons income definition.

This chapter argues for the importance of an underlying metric of inequality that might go by such names as "endowment," "wage rate," "ability," or "opportunities." Under a liberal egalitarian view of inequality, such a metric is the very thing of interest. Under a welfare-based view of inequality, limited information about people's utility functions may give endowment substantial evidentiary value concerning people's relative welfare (based on the theory that tastes differ unknowably, but that more choice tends to be better than less choice).

Even if endowment were directly observable, its normative significance would depend on why inequality matters under a given view of distributive justice. Under a variety of welfarist views, the assumption of declining marginal utility plays an important role in motivating concerns about inequality. However, if one high-endowment individual (e.g, a Wall Street lawyer) chooses to work and earn more than another (e.g, a beachcomber) with the same endowment, the additional information we have about their utility functions may modify the analysis. On the one hand, the beachcomber may have greater work aversion, suggesting that the income effect of paying tax on the endowment may be more onerous for this individual (especially if labor market decisions are lumpy). On the other hand, the beachcomber may have less taste for market consumption, so that using cash to pay tax rather than purchase market goods may be less burdensome to him or her.

Accordingly, the relationship between endowment and desired redistribution would not be entirely straightforward under a variety of welfarist views, even if endowment were directly observable. This conclusion suggests that, from a welfarist perspective, the specification of a tax base should not just aim to create a good proxy for endowment. In contrast, creating the best possible proxy of endowment might carry greater weight under a liberal egalitarian view—subject to concerns about the income effect of having to pay the tax on a high endowment.

Discussions of endowment may seem far from the real-world choices we face in our tax system, and even farther from those we would face under a more edifying political process. However, a better understanding of one's underlying aims might encourage clearer thinking about the choices we face. For example, this analysis helps show that debates over whether to shift from income to consumption taxation should hinge less on the abstract desirability of the alternative bases than on their practical consequences for efficiency and distribution (with endowment playing a key role in how we think about the distribution).[28] Similarly, in thinking about the taxation of secondary earners, the endowment idea helps reveal the reasons why a tax on earnings might have unpalatable results. The idea deserves greater prominence and acceptance, even though we will never see, and probably do not want to see, a literal, direct endowment tax.

NOTES

1. According to Warren (1980), "society's interest in the distribution of income . . . depends on the view that the importance of fortuity and the interrelationships of contemporary society deprive producers of a controlling moral claim to what would be distributed to them in the absence of a tax system" (1093). This assertion begs the question of why the fruits of production (which he calls "income") are what we should focus on as having been distributed fortuitously.

2. For a sophisticated argument that work, saving, and market consumption actually do cause external harm that is akin to pollution, see Frank (1985, 230–32). He argues that, because of people's concern about relative status, greater consumption by one individual results in harmful "positional externalities," whereby others must now work and consume more in order to achieve the same level of satisfaction.

3. On the origin of this story, see Cramton (1986, 2 n. 4).

4. See Simons (1938), defining personal income as "the algebraic sum of (1) the market value of rights exercised in consumption and (2) the change in the value of the store of property rights between the beginning and the end of the period in question" (50).

5. Recent discussions of liberalism or liberal egalitarianism by legal scholars writing on tax policy include Rakowski (1996, 2000); Murphy (1996); McCaffery (1994a, b); Alstott (1996); and Ackerman and Alstott (1999).

6. See, for example, Frank (1999, 71–74), who presents sociological evidence that increasing average income levels in recent decades have not brought significant and lasting increases in subjective well-being.

7. The assumption that we cannot assess the comparative well-being of two people who make different selections from among the same choices may seem unduly stringent if we think of people we know personally. Information gleaned from talking with or otherwise observing individuals may encourage us to think that one is better-off than the other (as a result of either choosing better or because of a better fit between available choices and personal preferences). From the standpoint of a tax administrator in society, however, the assumption is quite reasonable. As will be discussed further in the text, is there any general reason to think, say, that people who choose to work more are generally better-off than those who have the same choices but, presumably because of differing preferences, choose to work less?

8. The standard defense of the assumption that different people should be assumed to experience utility with equal intensity comes from Abba Lerner (1944, 29–32). Lerner argued that, if we are entirely ignorant of whose utility is more intense but believe that people generally experience declining marginal utility, any assumption of differential intensity (with a 50 percent chance of being wrong) reduces expected utility.

9. To simplify matters, the discussion ignores inheritance of property, which may increase one's consumption opportunities without regard to one's own work effort and is a poor fit with the term "ability."

10. Under a welfarist view, this statement would need modification insofar as we could evaluate the welfare consequences of having tastes (such as for engaging in a particular type of artistic production) that have differing payoffs in the state of the world in which an individual finds herself. A liberal egalitarian view might also suggest caring about taste differences for which individuals were not themselves responsible.

11. See, for example, Nozick (1974, 167–73), where he argues that progressive redistribution violates appropriate respect for property rights.

12. This argument, for example, appears to be Dworkin's (1981, 312) objection to "the slavery of the talented." He argues that if an individual who would prefer not to exercise his wage-earning ability must do so in order to pay the tax, that individual would envy others' resources relative to his own, leading to the same sort of unfairness as the envy of the less able for the productively employed more able. A similar objection to the "slavery of the talented" appears in Van Parijs (1995, 64).

13. At one time, however, many thought of realization as a necessary component of economic income. See *Eisner v. Macomber,* 252 U.S. 189 (1920); Seligman (1919); and the withering attack on Seligman's exclusion of unrealized gain from economic income in Simons (1938, 84–89).

14. A stay-at-home spouse need not be engaged in housework, child care, and the like to be a valuable producer. Leisure in the colloquial sense (such as reading books or watching television) is no less a way of producing utility than performing chores that someone in the household values.

15. For simplicity, this section ignores the imposition of tax on the household rather than individual level, along with the difference between employment prospects at a given point in time and underlying endowment.

16. Risk after drawing a wage rate is commonly left out of the models as well. For a model in which people face income risk until after they have made work decisions, see Varian (1980).

17. In addition, the welfare effects of observing that others are better-off or worse off than oneself may be relevant. For example, in a straight utilitarian account, envy of the better-off and the inclination to pull rank on those worse off if the pain this inflicted were typically greater than the pleasure it brought might provide added arguments for progressive redistribution.

18. An "inferior good" is commonly defined as one for which an increase in income decreases demand "other things being the same" (Rosen 1995, 551). A standard example might be hamburger—people will start replacing it with steak in their consumption baskets as they become more affluent. By extension, one could call income an inferior good relative to endowment if an increase in endowment reduces demand for it.

19. Other possibilities include ignoring marital or household status for tax purposes (thus requiring separate filing with each spouse including his or her own earnings), allowing a secondary-earner deduction, widening the tax brackets for married as compared with single taxpayers, and allowing deduction of costs (such as child care expenses) incurred when both spouses work.

20. See, for example, Pechman (1987, 107).

21. Priority rules can in some cases make a liberal egalitarian view more definitive in its verdicts than welfarism. For example, suppose that a given liberal egalitarian categorically rules out torturing an innocent individual to benefit millions of others, thus obviating the need for a determination of the overall welfare effects. See Nagel (1991, 148).

22. Consider hedonistic versus preference-satisfaction versions of utilitarianism or John Stuart Mill's controversial suggested distinction between "higher" and "lower" pleasures. See, for example, Sen and Williams (1982, 11) and Smart (1963, 12–13).

23. To simplify matters, the discussion again ignores risk or variance in the determination of earnings apart from that in the endowment lottery.

24. The quoted passage specifically criticizes "egalitarian welfarism," or the view that everyone's welfare should be equalized, as distinct from the aim of maximizing total welfare by some weighted or unweighted metric. To a utilitarian or weighted welfarist, expensive tastes could likewise have the redistributive import criticized by this passage, although that outcome depends on how the tastes affect relevant marginal utilities.

25. Suppose that of two individuals, neither is in general a more intense consumer or utility "monster," but that one develops more expensive tastes than the other—say, a taste for expensive wine rather than cheap beer. If consumption opportunities are lumpy—e.g., you can get a bottle of beer for $5 but no bottle of good wine for less than $20 (and no good wine by the glass)—we might imagine that going from $0 to $5 would benefit the beer drinker more, while going from $15 to $20 would benefit the wine drinker more. However, we need more information to say who benefits more by going from $0 to $20, and for an otherwise unspecified $5 shift we may be unable to tell where we stand.

26. Less well-supported or coherently defended was Rawls's (1971) earlier throw-away statement that "a proportional [consumption] tax may be part of the best tax scheme" (278).

27. Calling inducement merely a lesser case of compulsion should not be taken to mean that neutrality (such as leaving workers with precisely their market return) has special moral standing. As Murphy (1996) has noted, such a view would require "implicit moralization of the (suitably idealized) market" (492). Just as compulsion shades into mere inducement, so greater inducement (relative to what the market happens to offer) shades into lesser inducement and then into the opposite inducement.

28. Thus, Warren's (1975, 941–42) argument—that even a highly progressive consumption tax cannot address wealth disparities as directly as an income or wealth tax—has significance only insofar as wealth provides a better measure of endowment than lifetime income notwithstanding the savings decisions that cause one individual to hold greater wealth than another with the same earnings.

REFERENCES

Ackerman, Bruce, and Anne Alstott. 1999. *The Stakeholder Society.* New Haven, Conn.: Yale University Press.

Alstott, Anne L. 1996. "The Uneasy Liberal Case against Income and Wealth Transfer Taxation." *Tax Law Review* 51: 363–402.

Andrews, William. 1974. "A Consumption-Type or Cash Flow Personal Income Tax." *Harvard Law Review* 87: 1113–88.

Arneson, Richard J. 1989. "Equality and Equality of Opportunity for Welfare." *Philosophical Studies* 56: 77–93.

Bradford, David F. 1986. *Untangling the Income Tax.* Cambridge: Harvard University Press.

Christian Coalition. 1995. "Contract with the American Family." Nashville: Moorings.

Cramton, Roger. 1986. "Demystifying Legal Scholarship." *Georgetown Law Journal* 75: 1–17.

Diamond, Peter. 1999. "Administrative Costs and Equilibrium Changes with Individual Accounts." National Bureau of Economic Research Working Paper 7050. Cambridge: National Bureau of Economic Research.

Dworkin, Ronald. 1981. "What Is Equality? Part 2: Equality of Resources." *Philosophy and Public Affairs* 10: 283–345.

Frank, Robert H. 1985. *Choosing the Right Pond: Human Behavior and the Quest for Status.* New York: Oxford University Press.

———. 1999. *Luxury Fever: Why Money Fails to Satisfy in an Era of Excess.* New York: The Free Press.

Goleman, Daniel. 1997. *Emotional Intelligence.* New York: Bantam Books.

Kelman, Mark. 1979. "Personal Deductions Revisited: Why They Fit Poorly in an 'Ideal' Income Tax and Why They Fit Worse in a Far from Ideal World." *Stanford Law Review* 31: 831–83.

Lerner, Abba P. 1944. *The Economics of Control.* New York: Macmillan.

McCaffery, Edward J. 1994a. "The Uneasy Case for Wealth Transfer Taxation." *Yale Law Journal* 104: 283–365.

————. 1994b. "The Political Liberal Case against the Estate Tax." *Philosophy and Public Affairs* 23: 281–312.

————. 1997. *Taxing Women.* Chicago: University of Chicago Press.

Mirrlees, James. 1971. "An Exploration in the Theory of Optimum Income Taxation." *Review of Economic Studies* 38: 175–208.

Murphy, Liam B. 1996. "Liberty, Equality, Well-Being: Rakowski on Wealth Transfer Taxation." *Tax Law Review* 51: 473–94.

Nagel, Thomas. 1991. *Equality and Partiality.* New York: Oxford University Press.

Nozick, Robert. 1974. *Anarchy, State, and Utopia.* New York: Basic Books.

Pechman, Joseph. 1987. *Federal Tax Policy.* Washington, D.C.: Brookings Institution Press.

Rakowski, Eric. 1991. *Equal Justice.* Oxford: Clarendon Press.

————. 1996. "Transferring Wealth Liberally." *Tax Law Review* 51: 419–72.

————. 2000. "Can Wealth Taxes Be Justified?" *Tax Law Review* 53: 263–375.

Rawls, John. 1971. *A Theory of Justice.* Cambridge: Harvard University Press, Belknap Press.

Rosen, Harvey. 1995. *Public Finance.* Chicago: Richard D. Irwin, Inc.

Seligman, Edwin R. A. 1919. "Are Stock Dividends Income?" *American Economic Review* 9: 517–36.

Sen, Amartya. 1992. *Inequality Reexamined.* New York: Russell Sage Foundation.

Sen, Amartya, and Bernard Williams. 1982. "Introduction." In *Utilitarianism and Beyond,* edited by Amartya Sen and Bernard Williams. New York: Cambridge University Press.

Shaviro, Daniel N. 2000. *Making Sense of Social Security Reform.* Chicago: University of Chicago Press.

Simons, Henry C. 1938. *Personal Income Taxation.* Chicago: University of Chicago Press.

Smart, J. J. C. 1963. "An Outline of a System of Utilitarian Ethics." In *Utilitarianism: For and Against,* edited by J. J. C. Smart and Bernard Williams. New York: Cambridge University Press.

Staudt, Nancy. 1996. "Taxing Housework." *Georgetown Law Journal* 84: 1571–647.

Van Parijs, Philippe. 1995. *Real Freedom for All: What (If Anything) Can Justify Capitalism?* Oxford: Clarendon Press.

Varian, Hal R. 1980. "Redistributive Taxation as Social Insurance." *Journal of Public Economics* 14: 49–68.

Warren, Alvin C. 1975. "Fairness and a Consumption-Type or Cash Flow Personal Income Tax." *Harvard Law Review* 88: 931–58.

————. 1980. "Would a Consumption Tax Be Fairer Than an Income Tax?" *Yale Law Journal* 89: 1081–124.

6

Why Proportionate Taxation?

Barbara H. Fried

Over the past half century, the view that the only fair tax is a flat-rate tax has attracted support from a surprising range of political philosophers and pundits, including Friedrich Hayek, Ludwig von Mises, Milton Friedman, John Rawls, Richard Epstein, Walter Blum, and Harry Kalven Jr.[1] Notwithstanding trenchant critiques, that view has not only persisted but also gained enormous popularity in political and academic circles over the past decade.[2] There is at least some chance that in the next few years, flat-tax proponents could carry the day in Congress.

It is, of course, impossible to evaluate the claim that the flat tax is (as Hall and Rabushka [1995], two recent enthusiasts, put it) "the fairest tax of all" except in reference to a theory of fairness. It goes without saying that these odd political bedfellows cannot all have the same theory in mind. What follows is an attempt to sketch out plausible intuitions of fairness on which these claims might rest, and ask whether any of them can fully support it. I conclude not.

This chapter does not argue that a flat-rate tax scheme cannot be defended as a sensible policy solution on other grounds, for example, administrative convenience, political compromise between warring considerations, or our best guess as to how to achieve a distributive end resting on firmer philosophical grounds. Perhaps it can be so defended. Rather, this chapter aims to dislodge the apparently intractable notion that a flat tax deserves to be adopted because it is "fair" in itself, or because it is an obvious instantiation of some other fairness principle. The chapter also does not argue in favor of progressivity, regressivity, or any other rate structure on fairness grounds. The deeper moral is that no sensible theory of distributive justice would fix on rate structures themselves as fair or unfair. Rate structures are just a means to operationalize other prior moral commitments about the proper role of government. The case for any particular rate structure must stand or fall on how well it realizes those prior commitments. An examination of plausible, prior moral commitments, however, suggests that, of all the politically salient alternatives, proportionality may be the hardest to derive from any coherent theory of fairness.

The first section of the chapter considers the case for proportionate taxation in the context of two broad views of governmental power in fiscal matters. The first is an essentially libertarian view of the state. This view takes the proper role of government to be limited to solving the collective action problems that prevent private actors from spontaneously reaching optimal outcomes through voluntary agreements. While tolerating whatever minimal redistribution might occur as a consequence of solving collective action problems, the libertarian view generally rules out income redistribution as a motive for state action. In tax theory, the clear corollary to libertarianism is the so-called "benefits" theory of taxation. I start with a discussion of libertarianism, because libertarian premises are where most proponents of flat-rate taxes on fairness grounds seem to begin.

The second is a social welfarist view of the state. This approach accepts that income redistribution for the express purpose of improving the welfare of the less well-off in society is a legitimate state function, although its various proponents disagree about the optimal extent and form of redistribution. While there are no clear corollaries to the social welfarist view of the state in tax theory—likely because evaluating the social welfare effects of taxation in isolation from other fiscal policies yields incoherent results—traditional arguments for taxing on the basis of "ability to pay" or to produce "minimum sacrifice" undoubtedly reflect this view in inchoate form. Of course, other views of the legitimate role of the state in fiscal affairs exist, but most that arise in tax debates, when pushed hard enough, fall under one of these two views.

Both views—libertarian and social welfarist—evaluate taxation in the context of a comprehensive system of government (re)distribution. The last section of the chapter examines a number of defenses of a flat-rate tax viewed in isolation from the uses to which tax revenues are put. These defenses include the widespread view that a flat-rate tax vindicates some important notion of equality, the view that it leaves individuals' choices among various activities undistorted, and the view that it limits the (unfair) expropriation of the wealthiest classes by the majority. Finally, the chapter considers two other positive explanations for the popular convergence on proportionate taxation. The first is that its apparent properties of mathematical simplicity and certainty have made it a Schelling-like focal point solution to the problem of appropriate tax rates. The second is that its popularity, particularly among libertarians, is a product of political framing—of the fact that, at least in recent history, a regressive rate structure for a broad-based income tax has not been a politically viable alternative. Were that fact to change, the many who support proportionate taxation on libertarian grounds would likely find regressivity, on reconsideration, the more plausible expression of libertarian ideals.

Libertarian Justifications for Proportionate Taxation

In contemporary debates, the most vociferous advocates of a flat-rate tax—Milton Friedman, Friedrich Hayek, Richard Epstein, and David Gauthier—have been spurred at least in part by libertarian impulses.[3] The same is true of earlier defenders.[4] The classic libertarian view derives the just limits of state power from a Hobbesian and Lockean social contractarian view of the state, in which the state exists solely to provide services that, for a variety of reasons of market failure, cannot be provided optimally by private, voluntary agreement. As Richard A. Musgrave (1959) and others have noted, that view implies a quid pro quo relationship between the taxpayer and the state, with taxes functioning as the shadow price for the goods or services provided by the state. Hayek (1960) made the classic argument for deriving proportionate rates from a benefits theory of taxation: "A person who commands more of the resources of society will also gain proportionately more from what the government has contributed" to the provision of those resources, and taxation ought to be levied in proportion to the benefits so provided (316).[5]

The first big problem in assessing the case for proportionate taxation under the social contractarian view is that almost none of those who support proportionality on (vaguely) libertarian grounds, from Adam Smith forward, has, in fact, supported true proportionate taxation. A true flat-rate tax would tax all income (or consumption), starting with the first dollar, at the same rate. Instead, these proponents have supported a so-called degressive version of a progressive tax, in which the first x dollars of income (or consumption), sufficient to cover basic needs, is taxed at a zero rate, and all income (or consumption) above that amount is taxed at the same positive rate.[6]

The obvious political advantages of a degressive tax over a proportionate tax are hardly lost on its supporters.[7] The idea of a true proportionate tax that contains no exemption for basic income garners little public support. The concession to exempt basic income from taxation entirely, however, poses great difficulty to those who oppose any greater degree of progressivity through a graduated-rate structure because they view such progressivity as motivated by purely redistributive concerns. If all people earning income above the exemption level have an obligation to pick up the tab for government services provided to the poor simply because they are poor, why stop there? Why not tax the rich for government services at an even higher rate than the middle class, simply because the rich have more money than everyone else and can better afford to defray the cost? Or, for that matter, why not raise the exemption level to, say, $30,000 for a family of four; raise the proposed flat-rate tax from, say, 19 percent to 25 percent; and use the excess proceeds to finance a guaranteed minimum income to all?[8] At that point, "proportionate" taxation would start looking awfully attractive to the sorts of welfare-state liberals who reject the libertarian premises of benefits taxation out of hand.

Surely Taussig (1911) was right in declaring almost a century ago that "the demand for the exemption of the lowest tier of incomes results from the same state of mind as the advocacy of progressive taxation [through graduated rates]" (499). In the absence of any adequate libertarian justification for exempting basic income—and only basic income—from taxation, the few hearty libertarians who have rejected such an exemption as inconsistent with conventional libertarianism seem to have the better of their libertarian fellow travelers, and are to be commended, from the point of view of principle, at least, for sticking to their libertarian guns.[9]

The balance of this chapter sets aside the difficulty of justifying an exemption for basic income under libertarian premises, and turns to the central question: If taxes, as benefits theorists argue, ought to function as the shadow price for goods or services that the state provides, how do we set that price? The logical place to begin is with a determination of what a well-functioning private market would have charged for those goods or services. As Musgrave (1959) stated many years ago, "Since the relation is one of exchange, the rules of the public household are taken to be more or less the same as those of the market" (62). What then are the rules of the (private) market—or, more precisely, which of the rules of the private market ought to be applied to the public household? And once applied, what do those rules imply about appropriate tax rates?

The uncontroversial starting point for analyzing the fairness of the market is the requirement of strict paretianism—the requirement, that is, that every trade leave no side worse off and at least one side better-off. This requirement is assumed to be met automatically by any voluntary market transaction. Strict paretianism, however, is a minimally exacting standard, and gives little guidance for resolving the central problems in assigning the tax costs of providing public benefits.

First, the pareto principle provides no guidance on the level of aggregation at which the "better-offness" from being in society is to be judged. If the level of aggregation is great enough—for example, at the extreme, if we test the pareto superiority of the benefits/taxation deal offered each American against the decision whether to exit this society or not—then there is almost no redistributive mischief that cannot be justified. At the other extreme, if we insist that *each* government program satisfy strict paretianism, then almost no program can be justified, because under any feasible tax scheme some individuals are going to pay more for a particular public good, such as a road through the middle of Kansas, than the benefit they derive from it.

In practice, libertarian benefits theorists seem to employ a mixed criterion along the following lines. First, strict paretianism is used to judge the aggregate deal each of us has gotten from being in society rather than out of it.[10] This standard will almost always be met if we are comparing any plausible configuration of tax burdens in America circa 2000 to our likely individual positions in some hypothetical Crusoeian state of nature; indeed, it is met automatically as long as there is a meaningful opportunity for exit from society. Second, a potential pareto (that is, Kaldor-Hicks) test is used to judge expenditures at the maximally disaggregated level. Thus, each particular road through Kansas must be justified by showing that the social gains from building it outweigh the social costs entailed. However, it is not necessary to show that each citizen derives benefits from that particular road at least equal to his or her share of the social costs of building it.[11] Finally, strict paretianism is used to test the tax/benefits deal over some representative class of incremental public goods being considered. That is, in a just state over a representative period, each individual in the state will derive benefits from government services that are at least equal to the cost he or she bears for them. This formulation is just a guess, however, because most proponents of a benefits theory of taxation are either unclear or inconsistent on the point.

Second, the pareto principle requires only that tax prices be set so that no one is made worse off by the compulsory purchase of public goods. It says nothing, however, about the proper distribution of a surplus— that is, about the distribution of the gains from trade.

In private competitive markets, both of these problems—the level of aggregation on which to test pareto improvements and the just division of gains from trade—are automatically resolved through equilibrium prices. When dealing with public goods, however, they are not resolved through prices, because we are dealing with a hypothetical rather than an actual market. Moreover, it is a hypothetical market in which the government operates as a monopoly supplier of bundled goods and services tied to the existence of a state. As a consequence, enormous theoretical latitude exists in constructing the hypothetical exchange between government as supplier and citizens as consumers, and in particular, in resolving the two questions above: the level of aggregation at which to bundle goods or services in judging the pareto fairness of our tax scheme and the appropriate division of surplus value. Depending upon the resolution of both these questions, there exists an enormous range of acceptable distributions of tax burdens to finance public goods.

At one extreme, we can imagine the state as a monopolist with perfect information about people's reservation prices for public goods; hence, the state would have the ability to perfectly price-discriminate in setting tax prices for those goods. Consistent with the pareto principle, the state could tax each person in society at a rate that expropriates 100 percent of the surplus value of public goods. Under a broad definition of public goods, lawmakers setting tax rates could count all traditional public goods and services as well as all the benefits of being in our organized society (rather than on a Crusoeian island or in war-torn Rwanda)— benefits that are factually, if not logically, tied to membership in a particular state. This broad power to expropriate surplus value would authorize something close to a confiscatory tax on almost everyone.

At the other extreme, we can suppose that the taxable benefits are limited to identifiable costly goods or services provided by government and that the government must act as a supplier in a private purely competitive market: that is, the government must charge a uniform per unit price for all goods consumed. The most likely outcome of benefits theory under these suppositions is a highly regressive tax.

The balance of the chapter focuses on the second question: How should prices for public goods (however defined) be set within the constraints of strict paretianism and hence how should the surplus value generated by public goods be divided? As the analysis that follows shows, neither the libertarian literature approaching the benefits question from the perspective of distributive justice nor the public economics literature approaching it from the perspective of allocative efficiency fully answers that question.

The Lessons of the Private Market

There is a fatal ambiguity running through the benefits theory literature about how benefits ought to be measured. This ambiguity is evident in Hayek's (1973) statement that "a person who commands more of the resources of society will also *gain* proportionately *more* from what the government has contributed" [emphasis added] to the provision of those resources (316). Does Hayek mean by "gains . . . more" that the rich consume a proportionately greater *quantity* of public goods, or that the rich derive proportionately greater *utility* from public goods?

If the private competitive market is the benchmark, then the former interpretation is the more logical one. In a purely competitive market, all consumers face the same per unit price, set by the equilibrium price for the good. Suppliers cannot price-discriminate based on consumers' different reservation prices for the goods, because any effort to set a higher price for any consumer will be undercut by another supplier. As a consequence, the relative prices that consumers pay for a given good depend solely on the relative quantities of the good they consume. Whatever consumer or producer surplus is generated by trades at that price is retained by whomever it happens to accrue to. Assuming a conventional downward-sloping demand curve and an upward-sloping supply curve, equilibrium prices, reflecting the marginal utility (or cost) of the last unit consumed, will leave each consumer (or producer) with a surplus from all but the last unit consumed (or sold). The precise amount of the surplus depends on the fortuitous shape of the individual and aggregate demand and supply curves.

According to this perspective, benefits theory leads to proportionate taxation if, and only if, the quantity of public goods that people consume is proportionate to their income. As even proponents of a proportionate tax concede, that premise is highly implausible (a "not clearly inappropriate assumption" is the best that Friedman [1962, 175] can do). The premise is doubtful when applied to many publicly provided goods, such as fire protection, garbage collection, and schools. It is clearly wrong for goods that are truly public in the technical economic sense, with one of the defining characteristics being that everyone must consume (or have available for consumption) the same quantity of such a good. As such true public goods are the core benefits—indeed, possibly the only benefits—most libertarians believe the government (rather than the private market) ought to be in the business of providing, the difficulty of defending proportionate taxation as a just shadow price for such goods is particularly troublesome. In the end, if benefits are measured by the quantity of goods consumed, such a measure is much more likely to lead to a highly regressive tax.

If, on the other hand, what Hayek and others mean by "gains more" is that people ought to be taxed in proportion to the utility that they derive from public goods, the implications for appropriate tax rates are probably hopelessly indeterminate, because of both the impossibility of measuring the relative utility levels each income class derives from public goods and the conceptual problems involved in deciding what one ought to measure. If, for example, Bill Gates's immense well-being is a joint product of classic public goods and a host of other factors, such as social opportunities, talents, and hard work, then how much of his well-being gets credited to public goods and how much to other sources?

The choice between these two interpretations of Hayek's meaning of "gains more" boils down to the question of what is so great about market-based distribution, beyond its guarantee of strict paretianism. Is there any normative reason to preserve (or mimic) the haphazard distribution of gains from trade that happens to result from uniform, equilibrium pricing in competitive markets when we move from the private market to the shadow market for public goods? Here, we encounter a wide range of views from the libertarian camp that do not lead to any obvious conclusion.

Most libertarians treat as sacrosanct the division of surplus that happens to result from market prices, with exceptions often made for privately appropriated, scarce natural resources and other monopoly suppliers. Few libertarians agree, however, on the reasons *why* market prices are sacrosanct. Some, such as Robert Nozick and Hayek, appear to regard market prices as sacrosanct *not* because such prices effect a just division of the surplus, but because they are a necessary byproduct of freedoms independently worth protecting. (In Nozick's case, the relevant freedom is the freedom of the buyer to give away his or her money to whomever he or she wishes.[12] In Hayek's case, it is the freedom of the seller of goods or services to "use his knowledge for his own purposes" [1973, 69].) Others have defended market-based distribution as just in itself, because it rewards all individuals in accordance with their marginal product—that is, with the value they have bestowed on others.[13] Whatever merit these views may have as a justification for not disrupting the actual, haphazard assignment of surplus in a well-functioning competitive market, they do not translate well to public goods.

On the other hand, other libertarians and fellow travelers in the rational choice/social contractarian school have explicitly treated some or all of the gains from trade, or rents, as morally up for grabs. Among contemporaries, David Gauthier is a leading proponent of that view.[14] Hobbes was as well, maintaining in effect that all individual gains from moving from a Hobbesian state of nature to civilization are expropriable by an all-powerful sovereign. If we are to read Hayek's statement in the second way—that it is permissible to tax people in accordance with the utility they derive from public goods rather than the quantity they consume—then he, and all others who subscribe to that view, ought to be counted in the Hobbesian camp as well.

When dealing with private, competitive markets, most defenders of the free market would argue that it is unnecessary to resolve these internecine disagreements about the *justice* of market-based distribution. However morally arbitrary the market's division of gains from trade may be, the efficiency costs of the government's trying to alter it through price regulation or other means are simply too great to justify the effort. As one commentator has stated: "How the gains from trade are distributed [by the market] is determined arbitrarily, but since this distributional issue is resolved as a by-product of a process benefiting all parties, it need not become a bone of contention" (Mueller 1989, 37–38). When dealing with public goods, however, that response is not available. The government must set shadow prices in the first instance. As a monopoly supplier with the power to coerce payment through taxation, it *could* price-discriminate if it wished to, without being undercut by competitors. Finally, unlike in the competitive market, price discrimination may well be dictated by *efficiency* considerations, at least in the case of pure public goods. The next section looks at this last point.

Pricing True Public Goods

True public goods are those for which a private market cannot function efficiently because of the problem of nonexcludibility. They are either goods (such as clean air or defense) for which it is technologically infeasible to exclude people from use, or goods (such as roads or TV airwaves) for which it is inefficient to do so, because the incremental cost of *not* excluding is very low or zero and/or the cost of monitoring use in order to exclude is very high. From a libertarian point of view, true public goods are the only goods that *ought* to be publicly supplied; that is, the sole justification for coercive government is to correct market failure that would preclude optimal coordination in the absence of coercion. How such goods would or should be priced in the absence of a functioning market is therefore a critical, and notoriously difficult, question for any benefits theorist.

An extensive literature in public economics over the past 80 years has been devoted to devising a theoretical solution to the problem of optimal output and optimal pricing of true public goods. Since the literature is almost exclusively concerned with efficiency questions—that is, how to determine the optimal output of public goods from an efficiency point of view, it is all, in one sense, beside the point here. In a couple of other senses, however, it is not. First, the implicit or explicit indifference of the public economics literature in this area to the distributional consequences of optimal pricing schemes undercuts any claim for some broadly compelling view about the just distribution of surplus. Second, many of the optimal pricing solutions proposed on efficiency grounds have determinate distributive outcomes that are hard to square with anything resembling a proportionate tax scheme. That means, at the very least, that benefits theorists who are drawn to proportionality on fairness grounds may have to be willing to pay a theoretical price on efficiency grounds.

LINDAHL/BOWEN/SAMUELSON SOLUTIONS. The central problem in determining optimal output of public goods derives from the problem of nonexcludibility. Because we cannot exclude anyone from using pure public goods, we cannot rely on a decentralized price system to reveal true demand for the goods.[15] Eighty years ago, Erik Lindahl proposed a theoretical solution to this problem, subsequently reworked in a general equilibrium framework by Paul Samuelson. Lindahl's solution remains the starting point for any analysis of public goods.[16]

The mechanics of Lindahl-type solutions are somewhat complicated, but the basic intuition behind them can be stated simply. To achieve an efficient allocation of all resources, we want every consumer to equate his or her marginal rate of substitution between all commodities, whether privately or publicly supplied. In a competitive market, where everyone faces the same price for goods, that equilibrium is reached by each consumer varying the *quantity* of each good he or she purchases until the marginal utility of each good equals its set price. In pure public goods, where everyone must consume or have available for consumption the same quantity of the good, that equilibrium is reached by varying the *price* each consumer pays for the good, until the price equals the marginal utility derived by the individual from that set quantity of the public good.

The hypothetical mechanics for reaching a Lindahl equilibrium quantity and price are as follows. Each citizen, in effect, submits bids, revealing the marginal price he or she would be willing to pay for a given public good at each plausible quantity of that good.[17] A combined social-demand curve for that good is created by adding up the marginal unit price bids from all citizens at each quantity level.[18] The optimal level of supply is the equilibrium point where the combined demand curve, equal to the combined marginal prices for a given quantity of goods, intersects with the supply schedule for that good, equal to marginal cost of production.

Once the equilibrium quantity is determined, each citizen is assigned a tax share to pay for the cost of the goods; that share is equal to (1) the marginal price the individual bid at what turned out to be the equilibrium quantity times (2) that equilibrium quantity. The result is a set of personalized prices such that, at those specified prices, everyone demands the same level of each public good.[19]

What are the distributive effects of Lindahl tax shares? They mimic the effects of the competitive market in one respect: they divide the inframarginal surplus from public goods in a haphazard fashion. Each citizen's Lindahl tax price for a public good reflects the utility of the *marginal* unit of that good at equilibrium output times the total agreed-upon output. Assuming a downward-sloping demand curve, each citizen will therefore realize inframarginal surplus, that is gains from trade, on all but the last unit consumed. As in competitive markets, however, the amount of that surplus is arbitrarily fixed by the shape of the individual's demand curve for that good relative to the equilibrium price. In another respect, however, Lindahl tax prices differ from conventional prices in a competitive market: Lindahl tax prices are proportionate to the *marginal utility* each individual derives from a given quantity of a public good, but not to the quantity of that good consumed. In contrast, in the competitive market, total prices spent on goods would be proportionate to quantity consumed, since, facing a constant price, consumers vary their quantity until the last unit purchased generates marginal utility equal to that price.

Just as it is unclear what Hayek's "total utility" metric for tax shares may imply about tax rates, it is also unclear what Lindahl's "marginal utility" metric for tax shares implies about tax rates. For some goods, marginal utility seems unlikely to be positively correlated with income, suggesting a highly regressive tax rate. For others, it might be positively correlated with income, but it seems doubtful that such a measure would lead to proportionality.

DEMAND-REVEALING PRICE STRUCTURES. As numerous commentators have noted, Lindahl-type solutions, which tie tax shares to stated preferences, all have a central flaw. Since the government cannot exclude individuals from using public goods, whatever their stated preferences, such solutions—which in effect require each individual bidder to put her money where her mouth is—create an incentive for individuals to understate their preferences in the bidding process, thereby leading to the suboptimal production of public goods.[20]

Over the past 35 years, a number of public economists have proposed ingenious modifications to Lindahl's basic scheme to solve this central problem.[21] The modifications take different forms, but most share one key feature: the tax share that people will ultimately pay for each public good is decoupled from their stated preferences for those goods in order to induce true revelation of preferences. In most models, that result is accomplished by a two-level pricing system: (1) a first-level tax is imposed to cover the full costs of producing a public good at a given level, with the tax shares assigned independent of each person's true demand schedule for that good; and (2) a supplementary tax is imposed, the sole purpose of which is to force the true revelation of preferences. This latter tax is not used to pay for the public good in question.[22] In most schemes, the level of this supplementary tax is loosely correlated with preferences, since it tends to impose some cost on each individual to move the outcome in his or her preferred direction.[23] To that extent, the supplementary tax may reflect a loose quid pro quo for benefits received. The correlation, however, is loose at best. In the case of the leading schemes, once large numbers of voters are introduced, the tax disappears entirely.

What does this analysis imply about the appropriate tax rates to finance public goods? The critical feature of all of these proposals is that each individual's tax share must be unrelated to that individual's revealed demand for the good, and hence the level of utility he or she derives from consumption. This requirement rules out, at least in strict form, the one criterion for assigning tax shares, quid pro quo on an individual basis, that a benefit theory insists upon. Many of these schemes contemplate that the first-level tax will be apportioned among individuals on a per capita basis, a solution that would obviously be highly regressive. For some schemes, the per capita charge is a necessary feature; for others, it is not. In the latter cases, it is theoretically possible that, once optimal output (and hence full costs) are determined, one could distribute that tax burden by income class, or by other measurable, taxable voter characteristics, in a fashion that approximates Lindahl taxes for that group.[24] That decision, however, is independent of the efficiency concerns that are driving the models, and it would be dictated by wholly external distributive concerns, which require independent justification.

Just Division of the Social Surplus: Epstein's "Tale of Two Pies"

The foregoing discussion suggests that deriving anything approximating a proportionate tax scheme from benefits theory is clearly difficult. Why, then, do libertarians and fellow travelers love proportionate taxation? A partial answer lies in another line of libertarian argument, going back at least to Adam Smith. This line has argued that proportionate taxation is the obviously fair solution for dividing up the surplus value generated by civilization. It is unclear what, if any, relationship this approach to the problem of just taxation has to more traditional benefits theory; I think the best surmise is that it has none. Benefits theory tries to apportion the *costs* of government services on the basis of the benefits they bestow. "Just-division-of-the-surplus" arguments seek to apportion the *surplus* value generated by society in accordance with some baseline set of assets brought to the table in hypothetical negotiations over creation of the state. As the following analysis shows, the resulting division of tax burdens under the latter approach bears no necessary relation to that under the former. Indeed, "just division of the surplus" schemes can result in a zero, or even a negative, tax burden for some members of society, who thereby get to enjoy all the benefits of government for free.

Two notable recent studies have developed the argument that proportionate taxation can be derived from a "just division of the surplus"—Richard Epstein's *Takings* (1985)[25] and David Gauthier's *Morals by Agreement* (1986). Many of the intuitions that drive these two works seem to be widely shared in libertarian defenses of proportionate taxation, as evidenced in the Hayek statement quoted earlier. While Epstein's and Gauthier's arguments differ, the structure of the two approaches is strikingly similar. Both authors start with the conventional libertarian assumption that there exists a set of Lockean entitlements to our labor and capital that are beyond the reach of the state. In sharp contrast, though, to the more conventional libertarianism of, say, Nozick, both authors assume that those entitlements are not coincident with, and will in general be less than, the market value of each of those assets in organized society.

In Epstein's case, the entitlements protected from the state are set equal to the value that each person's assets would have had in the state of nature. In Gauthier's case, they are defined (more ambiguously) as the market prices paid for factors of production, stripped of any "rents." Both authors treat the amount by which the aggregate social product in organized society exceeds those entitlements as a "social surplus"— meaning the value generated by the existence of society to which no one (including the factor of production to whom it was paid) has in the first instance a Lockean entitlement.

Thus, to use Nozick's disparaging characterization, Epstein and Gauthier both assume that a significant component of social value generated by human effort comes into the world "unowned" as a Lockean matter, on the "manna-from-heaven" model (Nozick 1974, 219).[26] The first key step results in both schemes licensing (unintentionally, it seems in

Epstein's case, and intentionally in Gauthier's) a degree of redistribution of (pretax) factor prices from rich to poor that would be unthinkable under a more traditional (e.g., Nozickean) libertarian scheme, in which the government's fiscal power is limited to raising the revenue necessary to finance the minimal state.[27]

The first key step sets up the second: the central problem of distributive justice, in both authors' view, is figuring out who gets the social surplus. Both authors conclude that there is a unique solution to the problem. For Epstein, it is a pro rata division of the surplus, in proportion to the value of each person's assets in the state of nature (SON). For Gauthier, the solution is to divide the surplus in accordance with a formula he denominates "minimax relative concession." For both, the solution appears to be justified in part by appeal to impartial justice, in part as the hypothetical (game theoretic) outcome of an idealized bargain entered into in the SON (Gauthier 1986).[28]

Finally, both authors conclude that dividing the social surplus in accordance with their respective formulas leads to proportionate taxation. Whatever one makes of both arguments up until this point, it is impossible to make sense of their shared conclusion. Granting the authors' moral premises, their approaches are highly unlikely to lead to anything approximating proportionate taxation.

Both arguments are explored in greater detail in Fried (forthcoming [b]). In the interests of economy, the analysis here is limited to Epstein's work, the more conventional of the two. The essentials of Epstein's argument are presented in the "Tale of Two Pies" that opens *Takings* (1985). Epstein tells us to imagine society as two concentric circles. The outer circle represents the aggregate value of our assets in organized society. The inner circle represents the (smaller) value of our assets in the Hobbesian SON—or more precisely, the value of the assets we would have acquired in the SON under just Lockean principles of acquisition. The difference between the two—the outer ring—represents the increment in social value generated by the creation of the (Hobbesian) state, in which the coordination problems inherent in the Hobbesian war of all against all are solved. The central problem of distributive justice, states Epstein, is "Who gets the surplus?" (162).

For Epstein, all roads—whether constitutional, Lockean rights theory, or utilitarian—lead to the same answer: the surplus "should be divided among all citizens, pro rata in accordance with their private holdings," by which he means in accordance with the value of individuals' assets justly acquired in the SON (1985, 3, 5). That solution, central to *Takings*, appears to be fundamental to Epstein's view of a just society.[29]

For present purposes, let's set aside the constitutional and utilitarian aspects of Epstein's argument and focus solely on the argument from a Lockean perspective—the perspective shared by most of his fellow libertarians. From that perspective, two questions immediately arise. First, why should a Lockean consider the incremental value in private holdings generated by the existence of a formal state to be part of a "social surplus" that the state is entitled to distribute among the members (pro rata or in accordance with any other formula)? Why doesn't the surplus come into existence (in Nozick's terms) already owned by whoever commands it on the market through (pretax) prices? Second, why should the state distribute the surplus—assuming we can justify the state's right to do so—among the members of society in proportion to SON holdings?

The answer to both questions, according to Epstein and others with libertarian leanings, appears to derive from an unexamined analogy to private partnerships.[30] The general line of argument goes as follows. Think of the state as an *n*-person joint venture, to which we each contribute our SON assets in return for our aliquot share of the returns to investment, or surplus, that our cooperation generates. If the venture were a private partnership between two persons, with one putting up $60,000 of capital and one putting up $40,000, the parties clearly would and should agree to split the profits from their venture 60/40, in accordance with their contributions. There is no reason for that conclusion to change when we move from a two-person private partnership to an *n*-person public one. The analogy is a troubling one, in ways that call into question both Epstein's definition of surplus and his method for dividing it.

WHY IS THE SURPLUS VALUE GENERATED BY SOCIAL COOPERATION SUBJECT TO DIVISION BY THE STATE?

In the typical private joint venture envisioned in the 60/40 partnership example provided above, the boundaries between the partnership's activities and the separate activities of each partner are clearly demarcated. As a result, the portion of the partners' wealth attributable to the returns to the partnership's activities, and hence subject to division between the partners in accordance with some jointly agreed-to decision rule, is clearly demarcated.

In contrast, it is far from obvious what portion of the value generated by society, if any, should be regarded (from the Lockean perspective) as a common social surplus, subject to division by some collective decision rule. What exactly are the boundaries of the financial partnership we embark upon in the Lockean social contract? Does the contract extend only to the operations of the formal state, or does it extend to social organization in any form? Epstein and others appear to assume the latter in treating the entire (aggregate) increase in wealth we all hypothetically realize in moving from the SON to America circa 2000 as subject to division by collective decisionmaking.

That narrow view of individual entitlements, and concomitantly broad view of the social surplus, implies that the enormous gains society bestows on individuals whose natural talents have little value on their Crusoeian island—or, in the dysfunctional Hobbesian state—are all up for grabs. One *could* take this view of our implicit (Lockean) social contract; under this view, all the gains that, say, Wayne Gretzsky realizes by moving from being a man alone on a desert island—thinking of inventing a game called hockey if he could ever find ice, 11 other players, and an audience to pay to watch—to being Wayne Gretzsky in late 20th century America earning $20 million a year are thrown into a common pool for division in accordance with some norm of just distribution. This position is certainly morally plausible, with a number of respectable adherents. But it seems like an odd concession to collectivist ethics for libertarians to make.

As suggested in the following section, one would expect libertarians to insist on a more exact accounting of what precisely Gretzsky owes to whom, and why, in recompense for the benefits of social cooperation. A Nozickean would clearly take the view that Gretzsky owes society nothing, beyond, at most, his aliquot share (computed under a benefits theory) of the revenues required to run the minimal state. Limiting what is up for grabs to that portion of private gains directly attributable to the provision of specific and costly public goods is another possibility—a view that implicitly limits the scope of the social contract to the operations of the formal state. Nozick (in rejoinder to Rawls) and others have suggested yet another solution: if any common social surplus is up for grabs, it is the portion of income exceeding what the best endowed could have gotten not by *staying* in the SON but by seceding from the existing state and forming a new state populated only by the best endowed.[31]

WHY SHOULD THE SURPLUS VALUE CREATED BY THE EXISTENCE OF ORGANIZED SOCIETY BE DISTRIBUTED IN PROPORTION TO THE VALUE OF STATE OF NATURE RIGHTS?

Assuming that America circa 2000 represents one great joint venture—with each participant entitled to some share of the aggregate returns to civilization—why should those returns be divided among the participants in proportion to the value of their SON assets? Epstein defends this result in part by appealing to a (largely tautological) view of fairness: Proration is desirable because it "advances the welfare of [cooperators] in equal proportions that speak of formal equality and equality of impact" (Epstein 1993, 98). The deeper justification, however, seems to come from the view—implicit in the partnership analogy—that pro rata division is the obvious solution to the bargaining problem facing social contractarians, for the same reasons that it is the obvious solution for our private contractarians in the 60/40 partnership described earlier. SON assets represent the opportunity cost of entering into a social contract—just as the $60,000 and $40,000 respectively represent the opportunity costs of entering into the private partnership above. Those opportunity costs should be viewed as inputs in one large production process called civilization. Aggregate return to that production process is the civilization's output; hence the reward per unit of investment ought to be the same for all.

Accepting the returns-to-investment analogy, the difficulty for Epstein's argument is that dividing costs in accordance with the value of assets contributed is an obvious solution only if the inputs under question have an opportunity cost (expected return outside the partnership) equal to their value inside the partnership. That condition is presumably met in the 60/40 partnership example if we assume the partners' only contributions are (fungible) cash that is receiving a marginal (competitive) return. In this case, the constraints of the market—the opportunity cost of capital—dictate a pro rata division of the partnership's income, regardless of what justice requires. Many would, in fact, consider that result consonant with what justice requires.

But in the Lockean social contract, each person's assets are (by hypothesis) worth more if exploited within the joint venture of civilization than if exploited outside of that joint venture in the SON. That is, the Lockean social contract resembles an n-person multilateral monopoly rather than a competitive equilibrium. Imagine, for example, that in a two-person partnership, partner A contributes a really good idea, which requires $100,000 in ready cash to exploit, and partner B is the only person willing to come up with the required cash on the spot. In this example, gains from cooperation exceed the returns available to either partner from his or her next-best opportunity. Thus, the partners are locked in a bilateral monopoly. How should returns from the joint venture be divided under such a scenario?

This example presents the allocation-of-common-costs (common-surplus) problem that has been subject to extensive analysis in the game theory literature. The question posed by the problem is, How should the common costs of a value-enhancing cooperative venture be allocated among the cooperating parties? This statement might be interpreted as suggesting that the range of solutions is bounded by the actual out-of-pocket costs of the venture. In this context, that would imply that the range of solutions was bounded (at the extreme) by an allocation that assigned 100 percent of the tax costs of running the minimal state to a single party and no share to anyone else. In fact, however, in instances where the costs of a venture are low relative to the value it generates, and where that value is transferable in cash or other forms between the partners, nothing precludes one group of cooperators from extracting concessions from another that exceed the total out-of-pocket costs of the venture (but still fall short of the value generated for the latter group). To put it another way, the problem of allocating taxes or any other common costs is simply a subset of the problem of allocating common surplus (net of costs).[32]

In game theory analyses, the possible solutions ("core") of the common-costs (common-surplus) problem are taken to include all allocations that give each player in the cooperative game a payoff at least as great as the greater of (1) what the player could have secured through a noncooperative strategy, or (2) what the player could have achieved as a member of the most profitable coalition of players able to secede from the group to pursue their own cooperative strategy.[33] Clearly, the first condition requires that each person receive a return from civilization (net of taxes) at least equal to the value of his or her assets in the SON. That is, it requires that the choice to be in this society rather than out of it be individually rational. This condition, of course, correlates to the minimum constraint of strict pareto superiority that Epstein imposes on the aggregate taxes-for-civilization deal provided to each member of society by requiring that the state not touch the inner circle (representing each member's SON assets).

The second condition adds the additional requirement of group rationality. It just restates in a slightly different fashion Nozick's secession thought experiment, described earlier. Nozick is concerned with defining the extent of private gains that are up for grabs at all; the second condition is concerned with defining how such gains should be divided. But the two conditions are just different paths to the same conclusion: The best-endowed group in society (and, by extension, each lesser-endowed group in turn) will claim for itself, at a minimum, that portion of the gains from social cooperation it could have achieved by seceding from America circa 2000 and forming a new state whose membership is limited to the best endowed. From a Lockean perspective, Epstein's failure to insist on a group rationality constraint in defining either the extent of gains up for grabs or how they ought to be divided is perhaps the most surprising move in his argument.

What, if anything, do the above conditions imply about the appropriate division of surplus from society? First, the strict requirement of individual or group rationality holds as a descriptive matter (that is, it succeeds in predicting the actual outcomes in allocating common costs) only where exit from the group is possible and costless. To the extent that it is costly for the best endowed members of society (and by extension any other subgroup) to secede from America circa 2000 and form a more perfect union, the gains they could have realized in that more perfect union are, as a purely positive matter, expropriable by the less well-endowed majority. This reality describes the situation facing the very rich in this society.[34] Whether such exit costs ought to be taken into account in ideal bargaining theory is an enormously complicated question explored in Fried (forthcoming [a]).

Assume that exit is costless (or, if not, that we are morally required to treat it as such). In a large enough economy where no individual is large relative to the economy, and where there exist no increasing returns to scale for society or externalities, "the core shrinks to the competitive equilibrium" (Arrow 1971, 188). That is to say, the first and second conditions lead to whatever division of surplus happens to result from market prices, and there is, as Arrow states, no problem of social justice left at all (1971, chap. 8). If Wayne Gretzsky does not like the taxes-for-civilization deal he is getting from America circa 2000, he can pick up his hockey stick and secede with a subgroup of the most talented from whom he can extract a much better deal—a fact that will ultimately force America circa 2000 to offer him that better deal in open competition for Gretzsky's talents. In such a world, taxation is presumably relegated to a pure benefits tax, with rates set to mimic (as far as possible) the prices that the market itself would set for publicly provided goods or services.

If an organized society does exhibit increasing returns to scale, then secession imposes costs on all groups, including the best endowed, making the range of solutions in the core less clear.[35] A unique solution, however, is unlikely to be found. And a solution that assigns surplus (net of taxes) in proportion to the value of SON assets is not even necessarily in the core of the game.[36]

WOULD PRO RATA DIVISION OF THE SURPLUS VALUE OF THE SOCIAL CONTRACT, IN PROPORTION TO THE VALUE OF INDIVIDUAL RIGHTS IN A STATE OF NATURE, LEAD TO PROPORTIONATE TAXATION?

Assume that for whatever reason—some intuition of what justice as impartiality would require, or some intuition about the likely outcome of an idealized bargain—we conclude that in a just society, the surplus value generated by social cooperation would be allocated among individuals in proportion to the value of their justly acquired assets in the SON. What tax scheme would effect that result?

It is impossible to answer that question unless we arrive at a value for justly acquired SON assets—a task that requires "a very clear sense of what counts as individual rights" (Epstein 1985, 5) as well as some idea of what those rights would have been worth to each person in the SON. Given the unspecified nature of Epstein's SON, it is difficult to think about this question. Epstein does not seem to have in mind a Crusoeian SON, in which we are driven back on our private, individual assets, without markets or other less formal barter mechanisms to increase their value through exchange. He seems, rather, to have in mind a Hobbesian SON, in which some rudimentary forms of community and cooperation exist, punctuated by theft, physical violence, and various other outcroppings of the war of all against all. If this hypothetical world is very far removed from ours—that is, if the creation of the Lockean state has actually generated significant surplus value—attempting to imagine our respective positions in that world seems hopelessly speculative. Would Wayne Gretzsky be playing hockey in the Hobbesian state? Would he be earning, if not $20 million a year, still far more than anyone else? If so, could he carry his paycheck safely home at night without having it boosted from him by one of the many bands of marauders given free rein in the Hobbesian SON? And how about all of us—well-paid lawyers, academics, government officials, etc.? Would we be the well-paid consiglieres of the de facto mafia running the Hobbesian SON? Or would we be doing piecemeal physical labor for some minor warlord out in the provinces? The extraordinarily speculative and unchanneled nature of the inquiry Epstein's pro rata division rule invites here makes it doubtful that that rule could ever be operationalized so as to produce even a rough answer to the question, "Who gets the surplus?"

Assuming we could somehow surmount this problem and come up with a rough value for all SON assets, there remains the final question: What, if anything, would Epstein's pro rata division rule imply about the appropriate tax rates? Epstein, along with numerous other scholars drawn to the partnership analogy, assumes that a proportionate tax (presumably levied on income) is the answer. In fact, a proportionate tax will produce a pro rata distribution of the surplus only if two conditions are met: Everyone must derive utility from the creation of the minimal state in proportion to the value of his or her rights in a SON; *and* the utility derived by each person must be reflected in income (or whatever other tax base used). *Neither* of these conditions is likely to be met, let alone both of them.

A simple example illustrates the problem. Consider a two-person SON society consisting of person A, a hunter, and person B, a gatherer. Assume the hunter has rights, in the form of human capital, with a market value of $10 and that the gatherer has rights, in the form of human capital, with a market value of $20. The two enter an agreement to create a Nozickean/Lockean minimal state, pursuant to which they forswear Hobbesian aggression against each other, and agree to defend themselves jointly against outside aggression. To that end, they hire a mercenary police force and army, and also agree to create a variety of other public goods, including a lighthouse, a TV broadcasting system, and roads. All the goods and services together cost $100 to supply.

Because of the advances brought about by civilization, person A is now able to give up hunting and become a taxi driver for visiting tourists. She spends her spare time watching TV. The total subjective value to her of her rights in civilization equals $230—$140 in income generated by driving a cab plus the $90 value attached to the pleasures of watching TV. Person B, in the meantime, becomes a TV technician. He works all his waking hours, generating a total market income of $260, which equals the total subjective value of his rights in civilization.

Thus, in our simplified example, the total costs of civilization are equal to $100, and the total benefits of civilization are $460 ($490 total utility in civilization minus $30 total utility in the SON), yielding a net surplus value from civilization of $360. How should the $100 cost of producing that $460 benefit be divided through the tax system? Epstein's "Tale of Two Pies" requires it to be divided so that A ends up with one-third of the total $360 surplus value, or $120, and B ends up with the remaining $240. But, as table 6.1 indicates, to obtain that result A must bear the entire $100 cost of public goods, while B pays nothing. In contrast, a proportionate tax on earned income (which in this example totals $400) would take 25 percent of the earned income from each of the two, producing a $35 tax bill for A (0.25 times $140) and a $65 tax bill for B (0.25 times $290).

Thus, Epstein's "proportionate division of the surplus" rule clearly produces results that are wildly removed from a proportionate tax on income. This particular example produces a tax scheme in which 100 percent of the tax burden falls on the person with the lower amount of earned income. That particular result simply reflects the numbers chosen. If we vary the assumptions to produce a rank reversal for A and B in moving

Table 6.1 *Epstein's Tale of Two Pies*

	Person A: Hunter turned taxi driver	Person B: Gatherer turned TV repairman
SON wealth	$10	$20
Wealth in Lockean state	$230 ($140 income and $90 imputed income)	$260 (all income)
Tax allocation required to get pro rata distribution of surplus	$100	$0
After-tax wealth	$130	$260
Net of rights in SON	–$10	–$20
After-tax share of surplus	$120	$240
Tax allocation under 25 percent proportionate income tax	$35	$65

from the SON to society, we will produce a confiscatory tax on the rich. Imagine, for example, that in place of A, we have A', a wily but puny hunter, whose brains compensate only partially for her absence of brawn, leaving her with $5 of wealth in the SON. In the Lockean minimal state circa 2000, A' becomes a well-paid law professor, with an income 10 times B's income as a taxi driver. A tax designed to return A' and B to their relative SON positions must take from A' enough not only to defray the full costs of running a minimal state, but also to finance the substantial transfer payment necessary to leave B four times better-off than A' (B's relative position in the SON). It must, in short, confiscate almost all of the market return to her labor. The larger point, however, is clear: Only by the most implausible coincidence—that our respective endowments retained the same relative values at every point in time in American society as they would have had in some hypothetical SON—would Epstein's rule *ever* produce something approximating proportionality.[37]

Epstein appears to assume precisely that coincidence, by implicitly assuming that the value of market rights in a hypothetical SON is indeed simply a scaled-down version of the value of each individual's aggregate rights at any given moment in society. Thus, if Brains is earning 100 times more than Brawn in America circa 2000, we can assume that the use value of Brains's human capital in the SON was 100 times the use value of Brawn's. For Epstein's argument, that assumption has two immense virtues: (1) simultaneously solving the otherwise insoluble task of fixing the relative values of people's SON assets (they were exactly what they are now), and (2) meeting the precondition for proportionate tax to achieve a pro rata distribution of the surplus. But it is hard to see what else would recommend it.[38]

In the end, proportionate taxation—whatever else can be said on its behalf—seems such an implausible outcome of Epstein's own premises that it is hard not to conclude that the desired outcome (proportionate taxation) rather than the premises (Lockean division of the pie) is what has gripped the author's imagination. The host of other (benefits-based and vaguely utilitarian) arguments offered by Epstein (1985) to support proportionate taxation reinforces this conclusion. It should be no criticism of an outcome that all roads seem to lead to it. At a certain point, however, the convergence does raise the suspicion that the author of such coincidences is hell-bent on getting to a given result by any means available. While that determination does not make the outcome wrong, it does leave open the question of what makes the outcome so compelling. Why does proportionate taxation seem so irresistible to the (vaguely) libertarian imagination?

Social Welfarist/Consequential Theories of Distributive Justice

The intuition that the distribution of tax burdens should minimize the aggregate burden has long held appeal. For the second part of the 19th century and the first half of the 20th century, that intuition was embodied in the often-expressed views that tax burdens ought to be allocated in accordance with ability to pay or to minimize sacrifice. For reasons thoroughly explained elsewhere, neither ability-to-pay nor minimum-sacrifice theories have moral coherence as free-standing principles of distributive justice.[39] They are incomplete intuitions of a deeper, unarticulated (social welfarist) theory of distributive justice, in which the state has an obligation to use its fiscal powers to further the aggregate welfare of society, aggregated in accordance with some implicit or explicit social welfare function.

Viewed in that larger context, the social welfarist case for *any* tax structure judged in isolation from other fiscal tools is inherently unsatisfactory, for reasons long recognized by liberal and conservative critics of ability-to-pay and equal-sacrifice theories. Once we recognize the redistribution of income for social welfarist ends as a legitimate role for the government, isolating the tax side from the transfer/expenditure side of the fiscal ledger becomes a morally incoherent stance. As Wicksell commented more than a century ago, there is no point in achieving "a just part in an unjust whole" (quoted in translation in Musgrave 1959, 72).[40] It is also operationally incoherent to isolate the tax side of fiscal affairs, for the simple reason that we can undo any tax distribution on the transfer side. Take the following simple example. Suppose we have a two-person society in which Poor earns $1,000 and Rich earns $10,000 and a flat-rate tax of 45 percent. The tax reduces Poor's after-tax income to $550 and Rich's to $5,500. Suppose we then take the resulting $4,950 in tax revenues and distribute them in-kind and in-cash entirely to Poor. One would be hard-put to disagree if Rich complains that the net result of all this fiscal legerdemain is a confiscatory tax on Rich for the purpose of achieving absolute income equality between Rich and Poor.[41]

What an optimal tax-and-transfer scheme would look like under a plausible range of social welfare functions that gives priority to the needs of the worst off has been much debated. The central problem, of course, is how to balance welfare gains from redistributing income to the poor (assuming a declining marginal utility of income) against welfare losses from the distortionary effects of taxes required to finance the redistribution. Some researchers have suggested that a degressive tax, or even a tax rate structure that declines slightly at the top, may well be optimal *if combined with* substantial lump-sum transfers to the less well-off.[42] The intuition behind flattening rates at the top is that the rate on the last dollar earned, or the taxpayer's marginal rate, is what determines a taxpayer's decision to work or save more or less, at the margin. In a world with perfect information, each person would have his or her own optimal tax schedule—with rates highest for inframarginal earnings, then declining, ultimately to zero, on the last (marginal) dollar earned. In our actual world, where people's true preferences are not observable, a degressive tax structure might best approximate that ideal result. More recent work has cast doubt on the conventional efficiency arguments for a degressive tax in at least some markets.[43] The larger point, however, remains clear. The case for any tax structure on social welfarist grounds derives purely from moral commitments to a particular social welfare function and empirical hunches about the combination of tax and transfer scheme that will best bring about the desired result.

Notwithstanding the foregoing, many thoughtful people, operating under essentially social welfarist premises, have found assessing the desirability of a given tax arrangement in isolation from the transfer side of fiscal affairs irresistible. This approach may be an inevitable occupational hazard for professional tax types, whose habitual frame of reference and claims to expertise push toward that partial view. It may also, in some cases, sensibly reflect political exigencies. If a decisionmaker is limited politically to making changes in the distribution of tax burdens, then it makes sense for him or her to take all other policy instruments as given. The tendency for social welfarists to assess the fairness of tax burdens in isolation from the government's other fiscal functions extends far beyond the situations described here, however. It includes those scholars who are trying to work out a just scheme of income distribution de novo. One of the most striking recent examples is that of Rawls.

In *A Theory of Justice*, Rawls (1971) suggests that the fairest tax scheme for raising funds to "provide for the public goods and make the transfer payments necessary to satisfy the difference principle" would be a proportional consumption tax (278–79). Rawls offers the suggestion in passing, as a part of a hodgepodge of proposed fiscal arrangements to effect a just state, but he does not seem to have thought through the implications of any of these institutional arrangements very clearly.[44] At any rate, one suspects he would think better of many of them on further reflection.

In defense of a proportional rate structure—the element of the scheme of relevance here—Rawls notes only that "it treats everyone in a uniform way (. . . assuming that income is fairly earned)" (278–79). At the outset, Rawls's argument runs smack into the same difficulty faced by most libertarian defenders of a flat-rate tax: The tax rate structure Rawls supports is not a proportionate one but a degressive one, since Rawls, like most other proponents of proportionality, would permit the "usual exemptions for dependents" (278). Whatever the merits of such a scheme, it surely lacks the virtue of "uniformity" as the word is used here. Setting aside that difficulty, the form of uniformity or equality that Rawls implicitly champions, taking equal percentages of income, is hardly an obvious solution to the question, "Equality of what?"—a matter to be returned to later. Indeed, the difference principle Rawls himself would use to set transfers adopts quite a different notion of uniformity: uniformity of absolute income levels after tax and transfer, subject to the exception for inequalities that help the least well-off.

That last observation points to what is surely the greatest oddity of Rawls's championing of a flat-rate tax. In the context of the overall Rawlsian scheme, the right not to have one's income taxed at a higher marginal rate than one's neighbor stands as an island of deontological rights swamped by a sea of redistribution. As illustrated by the example of Rich and Poor, if the proceeds of a Rawlsian tax are used to finance the transfers to the least well-off required by the difference principle, that the rich are treated "uniformly" with the poor on the tax side should be cold comfort to them and should be a matter of total moral indifference to a Rawlsian.

Indeed, the same attack Rawls rightly makes on "traditional criteria" for fair taxation—that taxes should be levied in accordance with benefits received or ability-to-pay—can rightly be made on Rawls's proposed tax scheme: It does not "take a sufficiently comprehensive point of view" of the government's role in securing a just distribution of income (Rawls 1971, 280).

As a final oddity in Rawls's defense of proportionality, Rawls suggests that flat rates are obviously fair only in an already just world. Given the injustice of existing institutions, Rawls argues, there may be a role for "even steeply progressive income taxes" (279). By "injustice," Rawls appears to mean here a world in which not all income is "fairly earned."[45] It is hard to figure out what this essentially Nozickean principle of recti- fication is doing in a Rawlsian world. Given Rawls's view that talents, including a taste for hard work, are undeserved, and hence that the income derived from those talents is undeserved, what could it mean to Rawls for a person to earn income fairly, such that it was *not* up for grabs under a steeply progressive income tax?

In the end, the impossibility of making any logical sense of Rawls's positions on tax policy in general, and rate structures in particular, in the context of his larger aims, makes those positions of great interest in appreciating the breadth and strength of the irrational pull they exert. If Rawls, of all people, could think a flat tax is a just tax because "it treats everyone in a uniform way," surely there is some powerful instinct at work here that resists logic. What is it?

Equality of Tax Burdens As a Percentage of Income As a Default Position

Rawls may be the most surprising expositor of the view that a flat tax is the fairest tax of all, but he is hardly alone. Many people believe that (1) it is possible to assess the fairness of a tax system in isolation from government expenditures or any other government policies affecting the distribution of wealth, and (2) if we view our tax system from such a perspective, a proportionate scheme evidently is the fairest one because, in the words of Rawls, "it treats everyone in a uniform [that is, equal] way" (278–79). Indeed, to many, flat rates, or more precisely, a degressive rate structure, appears to be the *only* feature of the tax system that is mandated on fairness grounds.[46]

Everyone is in favor of equality. The question, of course, is, equality of what? Why the version of equality embodied in the flat tax—that we should take an equal percentage of everyone's income—has had such widespread and persistent appeal is something of a mystery. Of course, it has history on its side, in the religious tradition of tithing, but that argument merely pushes the mystery one step back.

To take the case for proportionality at its most sympathetic, let us assume that the beneficiaries of public expenditures are absolutely impossible to trace, thereby precluding any benefits-theory-based defense for any tax rate. Here we can invoke Blum and Kalven's (1952) helpful suggestion that we treat the collection of taxes "as though it were only a common disaster—as though the tax money once collected were thrown into the sea" (517). Also assume that the state has no legitimate, social welfarist interest in redistribution—that is, that the background distribution of pretax incomes is just. In this limited context—in which the fairness of tax burdens is judged completely in isolation—can we say anything at all about their just distribution?

For most people, the default assumption in such a case, where taxes are, in the words of Blum and Kalven, "a necessary evil falling upon a distribution of money . . . which is otherwise acceptable," is that the tax burden ought to be shared equally by all taxpayers (460). This view is obviously reflected in the long-standing argument, going back at least to Mill, for equal sacrifice in taxation.[47] But that argument once again raises the question, equality of what?

This thread leads into a long-running dispute, well-documented elsewhere, that is not rehashed at length here.[48] In brief, commentators have disagreed about the proper meaning of both equality and sacrifice in interpreting "equality of sacrifice." Two principal measures of equality have been proposed: equal absolute sacrifice and equal proportionate sacrifice (in proportion, that is, either to income or any substitute tax base).[49] In addition, two principal measures of sacrifice have been proposed: that sacrifice should be measured by the *utility of dollars* relinquished and by *dollars* relinquished.

The resulting four-cell matrix obviously yields four different interpretations of "equality of sacrifice." Of the four, only one—equal *proportionate* sacrifice measured by *dollars* relinquished—leads unambiguously (indeed, by definition) to a flat-rate tax. Equal *proportionate* sacrifice measured by the *utility of dollars* relinquished, under most plausible utility schedules for money, would yield a progressive rate structure. Equal *absolute* sacrifice measured by *dollars* relinquished obviously yields a highly regressive head tax. Equal *absolute* sacrifice measured by the *utility of dollars* relinquished is the most ambiguous: Under differing but plausible assumptions about the declining marginal utility of income, it could imply a regressive, proportionate, or progressive rate structure.[50]

What, then, explains the apparently widely shared intuition that the equality principle should be interpreted to require equal proportionate sacrifice, measured by dollars relinquished? The choice to use dollars, rather than the utility of dollars, as a measure of sacrifice, does not seem hard to understand or defend. Indeed, the contrary choice, adopted by numerous tax theorists over the last century, is much harder to understand.[51] We customarily measure the price exacted for goods or services by nominal dollars paid, not by the subjective disutility to the payor of relinquishing those dollars. Opting for the latter measure here, a measure that is, under conventional assumptions of the diminishing marginal utility of wealth, inversely correlated with initial wealth, is hard to explain except as an indirect way to smuggle in the very redistributive objectives that we ruled out of bounds at the start of this inquiry, when we took the background pretax distribution of incomes as just.

The former choice, however—the choice of *proportionate* over *equal absolute* sacrifice—seems much harder to defend. Probably the most famous, albeit indirect, brief for proportionate taxation, Blum and Kalven's "Uneasy Case," has only two things to say on behalf of the fairness of flat rates in the course of its 100-page assault on graduated rates. The first is that "as a principle of justice [proportionate sacrifice] is intuitively attractive" (1952, 460). The second is that the "virtue of the proportionate sacrifice formula is that it remains neutral as to the relative distribution of satisfactions among taxpayers" (460). Virtually all defenses of proportionality ultimately boil down to some variant of the former "I know fairness when I see it" claim, or the latter tautology. In the tautological vein, for example, consider Hall and Rabushka's (1995) argument that "the principle of equity embodied in the flat tax is that every taxpayer pays taxes in direct proportion to his income" (27). Or consider Hayek's: While progression represents "discrimination against the wealthy," proportionality "raises no problem of a separate rule applying only to a minority" (1960, 313, 314–15).

Can we do no better than this? The usual starting point for implementing equality-based norms is that people who are identical in relevant respects should be treated identically. The case for *any* tax rate structure tied to income level, be it progressive, proportionate, or even regressive, thus depends on showing that income levels are morally relevant in setting differential tax burdens. In the case of benefits theory or social welfarist approaches, the claim for moral relevance of income levels is obvious. In the case of benefits theory, income is taken as a proxy for benefit levels. In the case of social welfarist approaches—whether embodied in inchoate form in ability-to-pay arguments or in full-blown optimal tax analyses—income, or the capacity to generate income as reflected in actual income, is taken as the prime measure of welfare.

If the justice of tax burdens were really judged in isolation from either the distribution of government benefits or the desired end-state distribution of income, it is difficult to see how income levels would ever be relevant in measuring equal treatment. Rather, the far more plausible measure of equality under those conditions would be equal treatment of individuals, a premise that would seem to lead to a head tax. Indeed, Blum and Kalven argue as much in another context, when they attack Mill's "equimarginal sacrifice" as a plausible interpretation of equality. If we really confine the discussion to how we should allocate a burden and ignore benefits and distributive concerns, Blum and Kalven argue, the principle of equimarginal equality "seems not a little absurd. . . . It is strange indeed to have [two men] share a common burden by putting all of it on the wealthier man" (1952, 470–71). No less absurd in principle, although less extreme in degree, is to put more of the burden on the wealthier person than on the poorer one just because he or she is wealthier. At least, it is hard to see how the absurdity could be removed, except by reference either to benefits theory or to social welfarist concerns.

Taxes Should Be Levied So As to Leave People's Choices Undistorted

A number of commentators with libertarian sympathies have argued for proportionality on the ground that it would leave people's choices undistorted from what they would have been in a no-tax world.[52] Minimizing tax-induced distortion in behavior is, of course, one of the prime goals of public economics, on efficiency grounds. For Epstein, Gauthier, and others, that aspiration appears to have libertarian roots of a Randian/personalist sort. As Epstein (1987) put it:

> The creation of a system of government should strive not to reduce the scope of permissible individual choice from what it was before. Accordingly, no person or group should be able to use the tax system to change the pattern of preferences of other individuals. If A ranks a set of (noncoercive) alternatives 1 to n before taxation, then A's ranking of those alternatives should remain 1 to n, without alteration, after the tax is imposed (55).[53]

This statement is hardly a universally shared interpretation of the requirements of libertarianism. It treats individual liberty as residing in undistorted individual choice among actions, rather than, for example, the utility that any particular choice generates. Thus, nothing in Epstein's example would preclude a near-confiscatory tax on earnings from any source, provided only that it did not reverse rank orderings of choices. Be that as it may, contrary to Epstein's assumption, the requirement that we preserve the rank orderings of choices does not lead in the first instance to either proportionate taxation or—what Epstein erroneously takes to be same thing—a tax system that leaves the relative wealth of taxpayers constant.[54] It leads to a highly regressive head tax, endowments tax, or some other form of pure lump-sum taxation. As a second-best alternative, where lump-sum taxation is politically infeasible or distributionally undesirable, it leads to a Ramsey-type optimal tax on labor or capital, in which tax rates are set in inverse proportion to the elasticity of supply, in order to have the tax burden fall, as far as possible, on suppliers' rents.

What precisely such an optimal tax scheme implies about the rate structure in a broad-based income tax has been much debated, without any definitive conclusion. A case can be made on efficiency grounds for a degressive, or even a regressive, rate structure at the top of the income scale (see Bankman and Griffith 1987). But the choice to opt for any broad-based income tax in preference to lump-sum taxation in the first instance must be driven by distributional concerns that are hard to reconcile with the Randian libertarianism driving Epstein's argument here, or with the more conventional, property rights–based libertarianism reflected in benefits theory.

Political Economy Arguments for a Flat Tax

Proponents of proportionate taxation have offered a variety of political economy arguments on behalf of flat rates. Perhaps the most prominent argument, chiefly associated with Hayek but also espoused by many others, is that proportionality, as a rule of general application, precludes the possibility of the majority's imposing upon "a minority a rule which it does not apply to itself" (Hayek 1960, 314).[55] Such an imposition, Hayek argues, "is an infringement of a principle much more fundamental than democracy itself, a principle on which the justification of democracy rests" (314).[56]

Hayek's argument for proportionality here, of course, depends on the fact that in raising rates on the minority rich, the majority also raises rates on itself. Whatever merits the argument might have as an empirical or normative matter, however, the property Hayek seizes on is hardly unique to proportionate taxation. It is even more true of a head tax, under which any rate increase imposed on the minority rich will fall on the majority even more heavily than under a proportionate scheme, a fact Epstein inadvertently surfaces in mistakenly defending a flat tax on the grounds that "a rule that says you must pay a dollar for the dollar that you wish to exact from your neighbor" is an important constraint on political intrigue (1987, 70). Indeed, the same property holds for *any* rate structure, including a highly progressive one, in which the rates of each income group are a positively correlated arithmetical function of the rates imposed on others. With little ingenuity, one could accommodate virtually any level of progression within that constraint.

There is, however, a further problem with Hayek's argument. It presumes that, as Epstein argues, "the flat tax gives the government only one degree of freedom: what is the level of the revenues and, hence, of [the tax rate]?" (70). That conclusion is true, however, only if a flat tax, once enacted, cannot be repealed. If it can be repealed—and unless constitutionalized, it formally can be as easily as the progressive rate structure it has hypothetically replaced—then at any time after a flat-rate structure has been enacted, the government has not one degree of freedom, but as many as it ever had, since such enactment does not itself preclude the bottom 51 percent of the population from "sticking it" to the top 49 percent at any time, simply by voting to abandon flat rates in favor of progressive ones. Thus, to make sense, the Hayekian argument must depend upon a further assumption: If the majority can be convinced to go for a flat-rate structure to begin with, it is, as a positive matter, unlikely to abandon it. What could such an assumption be based upon?

Flat Rates As a Schelling-Like Focal Point

One possible answer is that the broad appeal of proportionate taxation is attributable less to any easily explicable moral theory than to its role as a Schelling-like focal point for people—that is, a solution that is psychologically prominent because of its apparent mathematical certainty, along with its apparent properties of equality.[57]

I say "apparent" mathematical certainty and simplicity because one can achieve equal or greater simplicity through other schemes (for example, a head tax) and equal mathematical certainty through *any* determinate function that correlates the tax rates of different income groups. That logical quibble, however, is, in a sense, beside the point here—the point being that, for *whatever* psychological or historical reasons, this particular relationship among tax burdens has a strong pull on the popular imagination.

Much in the literature, particularly in Hayek's writings, supports the focal-point explanation. It may explain why people as divergent in their political commitments as Rawls and Hayek might fix on the flat-tax in good faith to begin with, as unselfconscious participants in a Schelling-like convergence. It also explains why proponents of less progressivity than now exists would fix on it as a strategic matter, as a political solution that is both obtainable and sustainable. Hayek himself seems to concede as much when he acknowledges that he is seeking a principle "which has [a] prospect of being accepted and which would effectively prevent those temptations inherent in progressive taxation from getting out of hand," and rejects as an alternative solution "setting an upper limit which progression is not to exceed" (1960, 323). The problem with such a solution, notes Hayek, is that "such a percentage figure would be as arbitrary as the principle of progression and would be as readily altered when the need for additional revenue seemed to require it" (323). Of course, a flat-rate scheme could also be altered at will to revert back to a progressive rate structure, and it is arguably as arbitrary as any progressive rate structure as an expression of distributive justice (or so this chapter has argued). These cavils, however, are, in a certain sense, beside the point. Hayek has, perhaps, captured a psychological truth: A flat-rate structure has a psychological prominence that might make it easier to sell to voters than other possible rate structures that are less progressive than the existing one and make it more likely, once enacted, to resist fundamental change.

Political Framing

Finally, the convergence of opinion on proportionate taxation also seems to be a product of political framing. Benefits theory—at least under the strict construction of "benefits" that seems most congenial to libertarian premises—would almost certainly lead to a highly regressive tax structure. Most writers who oppose progressivity on fairness grounds resist that outcome as politically unpalatable and hence infeasible. Blum and Kalven, for example, take a regressive tax off the table, as they take off the table a tax that does not exempt basic income, not because it is unpersuasive, but because "it is so clear no one today favors any tax because it is regressive . . . [that] a regressive tax on income is not a serious [policy] alternative" (1952, 419). Epstein takes a head tax off the table without any justification whatsoever.[58]

That decision permits opponents of a graduated-rate structure to narrow and restate their position as follows: "On what grounds is a progressive tax on income to be preferred to a proportionate tax on income?" (Blum and Kalven 1952, 419)—or more precisely, for the overwhelming majority of flat-rate proponents who also support an exemption for basic income, "On what grounds is a progressive tax on all incomes over a minimum subsistence exemption to be preferred to a proportionate tax on all incomes over a minimum subsistence exemption?" (420). Once regressivity is off the table as a viable alternative, along with a true proportionate tax, a degressive tax becomes the best available alternative to those who are hostile to the degree of income redistribution effected at the top of the income scale by a graduated-rate structure. Indeed, the whole structure of Blum and Kalven's implicit argument for proportionality depends on getting regressive taxes off the table, because almost all of the arguments they make against progressivity, to the extent they are persuasive, would more naturally lead to a highly regressive tax structure than to a degressive one. (It might also be noted that once a regressive tax and a true flat tax are off the table, proponents of a degressive, rather than graduated, rate structure have narrowed the choice to two alternatives that are so close to each other in so many respects that it seems implausible that the differences between them will be dispositive under most theories of distributive justice.)

We have lived with a progressive tax-rate structure for so long that we are all accustomed to think regressivity unthinkable. As Thatcherite England taught us, however, the unthinkable can become thinkable. If that happened in the United States—that is, if the political landscape changed enough to make a regressive tax-rate structure or, at the extreme, a head tax, a politically plausible alternative—then there is every reason to expect that the odd convergence on a flat tax as "the fairest tax of all" would dissipate. Whatever Rawls and other social welfarist participants might make of their inexplicable enthusiasm on second thought, one would surely expect defection within the libertarian ranks. For libertarians, a regressive tax seems the more likely logical outcome of their philosophical precommitments.

NOTES

1. The corresponding works are Hayek (1960), von Mises (1949), Friedman (1962), Rawls (1971), Epstein (1985, 1987), and Blum and Kalven (1952).

2. Examples include Epstein (1987) and Hall and Rabushka (1995).

3. For other, recent expositions of a libertarian, social contractarian justification for a flat tax, see Dorn (1985) and Wagner (1985). A number of other libertarians, while not explicitly defending proportionate taxation, limit their attacks on redistributive ("discriminatory") taxation to progressivity, thereby, at least by implication, treating proportionate taxation as nondiscriminatory, and hence fair. See von Mises (1949, 803–05, 851–54) and Lutz (1945, 73–82).

4. For a summary of the proponents of proportionate taxation through the early part of the twentieth century, see Seligman (1908, 148–84). Notable early proponents included Hobbes, Locke, and (somewhat more ambiguously) Adam Smith. For Smith's famous support of proportionate taxation on fairness grounds, see Smith (1937).

5. For similar statements, see Epstein (1985, 74), Friedman (1962, 175), and Smith (1937, 777).

6. Under the Hall/Rabushka version of a flat tax, for example, exemption amounts range from $9,500 for a single person to $25,500 for a family of four; amounts in excess of that are taxed at a 19 percent rate (Hall and Rabushka 1995, 144).

7. Blum and Kalven's astonishingly bare concession to exemptions reads as follows: "It is almost unanimously agreed that some exemption keyed to at least a minimum subsistence standard of living is desirable. Since such an exemption will necessarily result in some degree of progression among taxpayers above the exemption level, and since this degree of progression appears inescapable, the real issue is whether any added degree of progression can be justified" (1952, 420). See also Hayek (1973), endorsing in a slightly different context a uniform minimum income "to all those who, for any reason, are unable to earn in the market an adequate maintenance" (87); and Smith (1937, 815–18 [opposing taxes on the wages of laborers], and 821–24 [opposing taxes on "necessaries"]).

8. For a proposal along these lines, see Bankman and Griffith (1987, 1905, 1950–55). Those who oppose progressivity via graduated rates, but support progressivity of a degressive sort, have long seen the potential for the latter to approach the former if exemption levels get high enough (see Blum and Kalven 1952, 513). Such opponents have erroneously assumed, however, that the two could not converge, because they have ignored the government's redistributive arsenals on the transfer side.

9. See Epstein (1985, 297) and Schoenblum (1995).

10. See Epstein (1987, 53). Both Nozick's (1974) "liability rule" compensation scheme for private protective agencies banished by the ultraminimal state, and his justification of private appropriation out of the commons whenever nonowners are better-off with a private property regime than they would be in a state of nature, rely on strict pareto compensation for rights lost in the creation of the Lockean state. For a similar argument justifying private appropriation of the commons with a liability rule of compensation, see Gauthier (1986, 291–92).

11. See Epstein (1985, 20). For the contrary view from Epstein and Gauthier, suggesting that strict paretianism is required for *every* government program, see Epstein

(1987, 55–56) and Gauthier (1986, 258). Given that no government expenditure could pass this test, it seems unlikely that either author really means what he says.

12. See Fried (1995, 226, 233, n. 20).

13. For a discussion of John Bates Clark, a prime expositor of this view, and his critics, see Fried (1998, 131–31). For a contemporary version of the argument, see Gauthier (1986, 92–93, 97).

14. Gauthier's position on rents is confusing, if not confused, but at least at points in *Morals by Agreement* he appears to equate rents with any payment in excess of the supplier's reservation price (1986, 97–98). For discussion of the meaning of "rent" in *Morals by Agreement,* see Fried (forthcoming [b]).

15. For a classic statement of the problem, see Samuelson (1954). See also Mueller (1989, 123).

16. For an overview of Lindahl's solution and the variants on it proposed by Bowen and others, see Mueller (1989, 43–50), Atkinson and Stiglitz (1980, 487–89), and Musgrave (1959, 74–80). For Samuelson's general equilibrium version of the Lindahl solution, see Samuelson (1954).

17. The marginal price at any given quantity represents the marginal utility of the last unit of that good at that quantity. In Lindahl's formulation, the bids reflect the percentage of the cost at any specified quantity that each individual is willing to pay. In Bowen's formulation, the bids reflect the absolute dollars at a specified quantity that each individual is willing to pay.

18. Thus, while in private goods contexts we add up demand horizontally to ascertain the total quantity demanded at a given price, in public goods contexts we add up demand vertically to ascertain the total amount that all individuals are willing to pay for a given quantity of public goods. This difference simply reflects the difference in what we take as given in the two contexts—price versus quantity.

19. See Atkinson and Stiglitz (1980, 509–12). The solution parallels the optimal solution for pricing jointly produced products, where the shared fixed costs of production are allocated between the products in proportion *not* to respective variable costs, but to respective demand. In the public goods context, rather than facing two products with shared fixed costs, we face one product with shared benefits. The solution, however, is the same: The costs of the product are allocated among consumers who share the benefits in proportion to their demand schedule for the product.

20. See Musgrave (1959, 80) and Samuelson (1954).

21. Most of these demand-revealing solutions are traceable to Groves (1973). Groves's argument was anticipated two years earlier in Clarke (1971, 17–33). William Vickrey laid the foundation for the literature on demand-revealing price structures with his famous work on auctions (1961, 1962).

22. In some models, the supplementary tax is not paid in dollars at all, but instead in scarce voting points; in others, it is paid in dollars, but the dollars are wasted, or at least not returned in any systematic fashion to the individual voters (if they were, that would undermine motives for honest revelation).

23. See Mueller (1989, 145).

24. For such a suggestion, see Tideman (1977, 71, 74). The logic here is that, while taxpayers might still have a mild incentive to depress their income levels to avoid Lindahl taxes, they have no incentive to lie about their true preferences, since their individual,

truthful revelations have virtually no effect on aggregate output, and hence on the absolute amount of the Lindahl share borne by their income class.

25. Epstein's arguments in *Takings* (1985) prefigure his position in *Taxation in a Lockean World* (1987).

26. More precisely, it comes into existence owned in common by the society that has produced it, with each member of society having a call on it, in accordance with Epstein's and Gauthier's respective formulas for dividing the social surplus. From the Nozickean perspective, however, that difference is hardly material.

27. I ignore here the government's powers, under Nozick's principle of rectification, to undo the effects of past unjust acquisitions. As others have noted, in the real world, that power may well imply extensive redistribution.

28. The work done by each of these radically divergent notions of justice is not always clear—a confusion shared by Rawls's and other social contractarian arguments on the left, as well as Harsanyi's derivation of utilitarianism from a rational choice perspective (Harsanyi 1953). While justice as impartiality appears to dominate Epstein's argument, certain aspects of his argument are probably best understood as implicit ideal bargaining theory—that is, endorsing an arrangement because it is the likely theoretical outcome of rational bargaining under certain idealized conditions. Justice as ideal bargaining outcome clearly dominates Gauthier's argument. Indeed, Gauthier's *Morals by Agreement* (1986) is probably the most famous recent exposition of that view from the liberal/libertarian camps.

29. Epstein also states: "The implicit normative limit upon the use of political power is that it should preserve the relative entitlements among the members of the group, both in the formation of the social order and in its ongoing operation. . . . Each gain from public action therefore is uniquely assigned to some individual, so that none is left to the state, transcending its citizens" (1985, 3, 5). Returning to the question of just division of surplus in *Bargaining with the State,* he reaches the same answer, this time on largely utilitarian grounds (1993, 90–97). Epstein does, however, reiterate in passing the largely tautological fairness justification for proration urged in *Takings*: Proration is desirable because it "advances the welfare of [cooperators] in equal proportions that speak of formal equality and equality of impact" (98).

30. Epstein's (1985) invocation of the partnership analogy reads: "The principle of proration requires that those who make the largest investment in the state receive from it the largest return" (163). For his appeal to the partnership metaphor as a guide to dividing the surplus from cooperation, see Gauthier (1986, 140–41, 152, 154).

31. See Nozick (1974, 192–96). For a similar argument implicit in his parable of the greens and the purples, see Gauthier (1986, 284–86).

32. For a recognition that surplus sharing and cost sharing present structurally parallel issues, see Moulin (1988, chap. 6). The relevant game theory literature is inconsistent in how it distinguishes "cost-sharing" from "surplus-sharing" games. For example, at one point, Moulin appears to distinguish them based on whether the cooperative venture was profitable (that is, generated a return in excess of the partners' opportunity costs in joining it), with "surplus-sharing" solutions dealing with cases in which it is profitable and "cost-sharing" solutions dealing with cases in which it is not (145–46). Even this distinction is ambiguous, however, depending on how one defines the bonds of the cooperative venture. Moulin, for example, treats settlement of a bankruptcy as a problem of cost shar-

ing, because the total value of the creditors' shares exceed the value of the debtors' estate, and it is therefore the task of the agreed-on division of the estate to assign each creditor a share of that aggregate loss (145). But while the underlying investment proved a losing one for the individual creditors, their joint venture—pursuing a cooperative strategy in bankruptcy rather than an independent one—by hypothesis generates value (that is, reduces expected losses). As a consequence, settlement of a bankruptcy can as readily be seen as a problem of surplus sharing—of sharing, that is, the increase in the aggregate value of creditors' claims created by a joint solution within bankruptcy.

At other times, Moulin appears to distinguish between them based on what constraints are taken as given. Where the distribution of the gross benefits of a venture are taken as given and nontransferable and only the allocation of costs (e.g., of providing pure public goods, or of litigation) is treated as up for grabs, the problem is thought to be one of cost sharing. Where the distribution of costs is taken as given and nontransferable and only the allocation of benefits is up for grabs (e.g., dividing the proceeds of an orchestral performance among the players), the problem is thought to be one of surplus sharing (145).

The important (functional) question for our purposes is simply what constraints exist on the solution. If we take civilization to be a single, indivisible good that offers increasing returns to scale, and assume that the aggregate benefits of civilization are transferable between individual members through a tax-and-transfer system, the game-theoretic problem is best understood as a problem of allocating surplus (benefits of the state minus the out-of-pocket costs of running it), with the allocation of such out-of-pocket costs through the tax system merely one device to achieve the desired distribution of surplus.

33. For a discussion of this "stand alone property," see Kornhauser (1998, 1561, 1568–72) and Moulin (1988, 89–95). The "core" is the set of solutions in a coalitional game, such that no subset of players in the game can break away from the solution and pursue a joint strategy that leaves them all better-off. The concept is thus analogous to the Nash equilibrium for noncooperative games: a solution is stable, and hence in the core, if no deviation (by an individual or subgroup) is profitable. For a discussion of the core, see Osborne and Rubenstein (1994, ch. 13) and Moulin (1988, 87).

34. Given the inherent administrative limitations of an income tax, which does not tax leisure, the rich do, of course, have a less costly means of exit available to them, if tax rates get high enough: They can trade off productive labor for (untaxed) leisure. As a practical matter, that form of exit is likely to constrain political choice far more than the more extreme sort of exit contemplated here.

35. For the thoughtful argument that there *are*, in a deep sense, such increasing returns to scale from organized society, see Arrow (1983, 188).

36. For a proof of the latter proposition in the context of joint litigation costs, see Kornhauser (1983, 145).

37. In fairness to Epstein, it should be noted that the problems created by imputed income in the above example are hardly unique to his version of tax fairness; they plague any fairness-based tax scheme. The same cannot be said of the assumption, necessary to his argument but not to most other versions of tax equity, that people's marketable assets retain roughly the same relative values in the Lockean world that they had in the SON.

38. In a pre-*Morals* work, Gauthier (1974) makes the identical assumption that the values of people's assets in the SON must be a scaled-down version of the values of

those assets in a full-blown, stable, market economy. In Gauthier's version, however, the assumption may be even stronger and less plausible than in Epstein's. Gauthier's SON is clearly the Crusoeian island. What precisely Epstein's SON is meant to be is unclear, but (as noted in the text) it seems to be some social organization in which at least minimal cooperation exists, albeit hampered by the Hobbesian war of all against all. However weak the correspondence may be between the value of our assets in America circa 2000 and the value they would have in a Hobbesian world, the correspondence is surely weaker between those assets and the value they would have had in a Crusoeian SON.

39. See Musgrave (1959, 90–115).

40. See also Edgeworth's and Pigou's observations to the same end, both cited in Musgrave (1959, 111); see also discussion in Fried (1998, 155).

41. The potential for undoing any tax distribution on the transfer side has not been lost on the right, although proponents of proportionality on libertarian grounds have probably underestimated the extent to which it undercuts any fairness arguments for proportional tax rates judged in isolation. See Hayek (1960, 307), recognizing the potential for effecting radical redistribution through use of proportionate tax and differential transfers to the lower classes, but assuming that potential is limited in practice by the inflexibility of in-kind transfers as a tool for income redistribution. Of course, once one admits the possibility of straight cash transfers, that problem goes away.

42. See Bankman and Griffith (1987, 1955–58).

43. For a very suggestive treatment of these issues, see Frank (1998), who suggests that in winner-take-all markets and contexts where work and savings decisions are driven by a desire for relative status, steeply graduated rates may well be *more* efficient than flat rates. For a much earlier treatment of the relative status problem along the same lines in a slightly different context, see Pigou (1947).

44. Following Musgrave, Rawls divides the government into four functions: the allocative, stabilization, transfer, and distribution branches. For our purposes, only the latter two are relevant. The transfer branch Rawls defines as concerned with guaranteeing a social minimum, provided either piecemeal by family allowances, special payments for sickness, and employment, or more systematically by a negative income tax (1971, 275). He subdivides the distribution branch into two functions: (1) regulating intergenerational transfers, through gift and estate taxes and restrictions on rights of bequests, in order to "prevent concentrations of power detrimental to the fair value of political liberty and fair equality of opportunity" (277); and (2) raising tax revenues necessary to "provide for the public goods and make the transfer payments necessary to satisfy the difference principle" (278).

There are a number of peculiarities here. First, it would seem that the guaranteed minimum income that is the focus of the transfer branch should be subsumed under transfers necessary to satisfy the difference principle, the task of the second leg of the distribution branch. Rawls himself seems to concede as much, in stating that "once the difference principle is accepted, however, it follows that the minimum is to be set at that point which, taking wages into account, maximizes the expectations of the least advantaged group" (285).

Second, it is not clear why the first and second legs of the distribution branch should be treated as distinct. Why single out intergenerational transfers as a unique violation of the just state that need to be dealt with through their own institutions, rather than simply treat them as one of many possible sources of inequality that all require governmental correction in accordance with the difference principle? One customary reason for distinguishing intergenerational gratuitous transfers from other sources of wealth, such as labor income and returns to one's own lifetime savings, is because the former is regarded as uniquely "unearned" and hence undeserved. See Fried (1998, 97–99) and Rakowski (1991, 158–62). Whatever the problems with this view—and they have been much debated over the centuries—the view is clearly not one congenial to Rawls. Rawls (1971), consistent with his broad view of undeserved privilege, explicitly states that "the unequal inheritance of wealth is no more inherently unjust than the unequal inheritance of intelligence," and that "as far as possible inequalities founded on either should satisfy the difference principle" (278). This statement suggests that wealth from inheritance should be treated like wealth from any other source, presumably all under the second distribution branch. The second danger that Rawls suggests is posed by inherited wealth—that when it creates inequalities in wealth that exceed a certain limit, it threatens "the fair value of political liberty and fair equality of opportunity" (277) in society—likewise suggests no ground for separating inherited wealth from all other sources. If the concentration of wealth is what matters, the source should not.

Finally, Rawls's hostility to intergenerational transfers is hard to reconcile with the solicitude he shows to savers in supporting a consumption tax in place of an income tax. The salient difference between a consumption tax and an income tax is the treatment of savings: A consumption tax exempts from taxation at least some forms of capital income currently taxed under our income tax. See Bankman and Fried (1998, 539, 540–42). In defense of a consumption tax base, Rawls (1971) appeals to the "common sense precepts of justice," precisely the ones that appealed to Hobbes some three hundred years ago, that "it imposes a levy according to how much a person takes out of the common store of goods and not according to how much he contributes (assuming here that income is fairly earned)" (278). Whatever the merits of this position, the statement is hard to reconcile with Rawls's position on intergenerational transfers. Given that a significant portion of lifetime savings, at least among the wealthy, is destined for intergenerational transfer through *inter vivos* gifts and bequests, the choice to protect the return to savings during a taxpayer's lifetime, through a consumption tax, while burdening the same decision heavily upon death, seems to require some justification.

45. Or so I infer from his repeated insistence on this qualification on his support for a flat-rate consumption tax in the preceding passage (Rawls 1971, 278–79). Rawls doesn't state explicitly what injustices he has in mind here.

46. Epstein, for example, treats all other fundamental choices in the tax system, including the choice of a taxable base, whether income or consumption, double taxation at the corporate level, the realization requirement, the home mortgage interest deduction, and the preferential treatment of capital gains, as normatively discretionary calls, on the empirical assumption that the resolution of each of these questions will have little systematic impact on the distribution of surplus (1985, 300–302). That assumption is almost certainly wrong with respect to many of these items, given the highly skewed distribution of capital income in this country. The only other tax policy choice attracting constitutional scrutiny from Epstein is industry-specific tax breaks like percentage depletion for oil and gas.

Others, of course, including Rawls, have argued that the choice between an income and consumption tax base raises fundamental issues of fairness. That argument is conspicuously absent, however, from most contemporary defenses of the so-called Hall/ Rabushka flat tax adopted as the model for the Armey/Shelby plan now pending before Congress. The Hall/Rabushka plan, along with most so-called flat tax schemes, adopts a consumption tax base in place of an income tax base, in addition to shifting from a graduated to a degressive rate structure. Notwithstanding that fact, most proponents of the plans on fairness grounds are conspicuously silent about the former change. Hall and Rabushka (1995, 23–51), for example, completely ignore the consumption tax feature of their proposal in their 30-page defense of the fairness of their flat tax.

47. For typical expressions of that view, see Epstein (1985, 73–74) (where the benefits and other costs of government are hard to assess, "a test of equal treatment across taxpayers becomes the next best alternative"), and Blum and Kalven (1952, 460) (if taxes are a necessary evil falling on a distribution of income otherwise just, the object is "to leave all taxpayers equally 'worse-off' after taxes.")

48. See Blum and Kalven (1952, 455–65), Musgrave (1959, 90–98), and Fried (1998, 153–54).

49. The third measure proposed by Mill, equimarginal sacrifice, was rightly dismissed by friends and foes alike as nothing more than a stand-in for utilitarian concerns. See Fried (1998, 154–55).

50. See Musgrave (1959, 99–100) and Blum and Kalven (1952, 458–59). Gauthier (1986, 272), to take one recent example, assumes that the measure, which he mistakenly conflates with his own measure of sacrifice—minimax relative concession—would result in a flat-rate tax. There is clearly no more empirical, or even strong intuitive, support for that conclusion, however, than for the alternative Friedman-esque (1962) assumption, which Gauthier rejects, that the *quantity* of public goods people consume is proportionate to their income (1986, 271).

51. See Antonio de Viti de Marco, cited in Musgrave (1959, 73), and Fried (1998, 154–55, 301 nn. 261–62). For a more recent defense of utility as a measure of sacrifice, see Gauthier (1986, 271–72).

52. See Epstein (1987, 74) and Gauthier (1986, 272–73).

53. For similar comments from Gauthier, see *Morals* (1986, 272–76).

54. "If tax neutrality [in this sense] could be perfectly achieved, the laws would act as a prism which magnified equally all preexisting endowments. The nature of private activities would not change, nor would the relative endowments of private persons" Epstein (1987, 56). The former conclusion is true; the latter is decidedly not.

55. For similar sentiments, see sources cited in Blum and Kalven (1952, 435 n. 60) and Epstein (1987, 70).

56. Epstein, wearing for the moment his utilitarian hat, trumpets the same property of proportionality for a different reason, arguing that by reducing the available choices to the choice of one tax rate to apply to all, proportionality reduces the opportunities for, and hence transactions costs of, factional fighting (1987, 53, 57).

57. See Bankman and Griffith (1987, 1914). The certainty of a proportionate rate structure is a recurrent argument offered in its favor. See Hayek (1960, 313–14), Blum and Kalven (1952, 430–35, 511), and Lutz (1945, 70, 73–76).

58. "(I ignore here capitation taxes that call for all persons to pay a fixed amount of taxes, regardless of income)" (Epstein 1987, 68).

REFERENCES

Arrow, Kenneth J. 1983. *Social Choice and Justice.* Cambridge: Harvard University Press, Belknap Press.

Arrow, Kenneth J., and F. H. Hahn. 1971. *General Competitive Analysis.* San Francisco: Holden-Day.

Atkinson, Anthony B., and Joseph E. Stiglitz. 1980. *Lectures on Public Economics.* New York: McGraw-Hill.

Bankman, Joseph, and Barbara H. Fried. 1998. "Winners and Losers in the Shift to a Consumption Tax." *Georgetown Law Journal* 86: 539–68.

Bankman, Joseph, and Thomas Griffith. 1987. "Social Welfare and the Rate Structure: A New Look at Progressive Taxation." *California Law Review* 75 (6): 1905–67.

Blum, Walter J., and Harry Kalven Jr. 1952. "The Uneasy Case for Progressive Taxation." *University of Chicago Law Review* 19: 417–520.

Clarke, Edward. 1971. "Multipart Pricing of Public Goods." *Public Choice* (Fall) 11: 17–33.

Dorn, James A. 1985. "Introduction: The Principles and Politics of Tax Reform." *Cato Journal* 5: 361–83.

Epstein, Richard A. 1985. *Takings: Private Property and the Power of Eminent Domain.* Cambridge: Harvard University Press.

———. 1987. "Taxation in a Lockean World." In *Philosophy and Law,* edited by Jules Coleman and Ellen Frankel Paul (49–74). New York: B. Blackwell for the Social Philosophy and Policy Center, Bowling Green State University.

———. 1993. *Bargaining with the State.* Princeton, N.J.: Princeton University Press.

Frank, Robert H. 1998. "Progressive Taxation and the Incentive Problem." Working Paper 98-4. Office of Tax Policy Research. University of Michigan Business School.

Fried, Barbara H. 1995. "Wilt Chamberlain Revisited: Nozick's 'Justice in Transfer' and the Problem of Market-Based Distribution." *Philosophy and Public Affairs* 24 (3): 266–45.

———. 1998. *The Progressive Assault on Laissez Faire: Robert Hale and the First Law and Economics Movement.* Cambridge: Harvard University Press.

———. Forthcoming (a). "If You Don't Like It, Leave It: The Problem of Exit in Social Contractarian Arguments." Draft manuscript.

———. Forthcoming (b). "Proportionate Taxation as a Fair Division of the Social Surplus: The Strange Career of an Idea." *Economics and Philosophy.*

Friedman, Milton. 1962. *Capitalism and Freedom.* Chicago: University of Chicago Press.

Gauthier, David. 1974. "Justice and Natural Environment: Toward a Critique of Rawls' Ideological Framework." *Social Theory and Practice* 3: 3–26.

———. 1986. *Morals by Agreement.* New York: Oxford University Press.

Groves, Theodore. 1973. "Incentives in Teams." *Econometrica* 41 (4): 617–31.

Hall, Robert E., and Alvin Rabushka. 1995. *The Flat Tax,* 2d ed. Stanford, Calif.: Hoover Institution Press, Stanford University.

Harsanyi, John C. 1953. "Cardinal Utility in Welfare Economics and in the Theory of Risk-Taking." *Journal of Political Economy* 61 (5): 434–35.

Hayek, Friedrich A. von. 1960. *The Constitution of Liberty.* Chicago: University of Chicago Press.

———. 1973. *Law, Legislation and Liberty.* London: Routledge and Kegan Paul.

Kornhauser, Lewis. 1983. "Control of Conflicts of Interest in Class-Action Suits." *Public Choice* 41: 145–75.

———. 1998. "Fair Division of Settlements: A Comment on Silver and Baker." *Virginia Law Review* 84: 1561–72.

Lutz, Harley. 1945. *Guideposts to a Free Economy.* New York: McGraw-Hill.

Moulin, Hervé. 1988. *Axioms of Cooperative Decision Making.* New York: Cambridge University Press.

Mueller, Dennis C. 1989. *Public Choice II.* New York: Cambridge University Press.

Musgrave, Richard A. 1959. *The Theory of Public Finance.* New York: McGraw-Hill.

Nozick, Robert. 1974. *Anarchy, State, and Utopia.* New York: Basic Books.

Osborne, Martin J., and Ariel Rubinstein. 1994. *A Course in Game Theory.* Cambridge: MIT Press.

Pigou, Arthur C. 1947. *A Study in Public Finance,* 3d (rev.) ed. London: Macmillan.

Rakowski, Eric. 1991. *Equal Justice.* New York: Oxford University Press.

Rawls, John. 1971. *A Theory of Justice.* Cambridge: Harvard University Press, Belknap Press.

Samuelson, Paul A. 1954. "The Pure Theory of Public Expenditure." *Review of Economics and Statistics* 36 (4): 387–89. (Reprinted in 1969 in *Readings in Welfare Economics,* edited by Kenneth J. Arrow and Tibor Scitovsky. Homewood, Ill.: Published for the American Economic Association by R. D. Irwin.)

Schoenblum, Jeffrey A. 1995. "Tax Fairness or Unfairness? A Consideration of the Philosophical Bases for Unequal Taxation of Individuals." *American Journal of Tax Policy* 12: 221–71.

Seligman, Edwin R. 1908. *Progressive Taxation in Theory and Practice,* 2d ed. Princeton, N.J.: American Economic Association.

Smith, Adam. 1937. *An Inquiry into the Nature and Causes of the Wealth of Nations.* 1789. Reprint, New York: The Modern Library.

Taussig, Frank W. 1911. *Principles of Economics.* New York: Macmillan.

Tideman, T. Nicolaus. 1977. "Ethical Foundations of the Demand-Revealing Process." *Public Choice* 29: 71–77.

Vickrey, William. 1961. "Counterspeculation, Auctions, and Competitive Sealed Tenders." *Journal of Finance* 16 (1): 8–37.

———. 1962. "Auctions and Bidding Games." In *Recent Advances in Game Theory.* Papers delivered at a meeting of the Princeton University Conference, Princeton, N.J., October 4–6.

Von Mises, Ludwig. 1949. *Human Action: A Treatise on Economics.* New Haven, Conn.: Yale University Press.

Wagner, Richard E. 1985. "Normative and Positive Foundations of Tax Reform." *Cato Journal* 5: 385–99.

7

The Limits of Justice

The Struggle for Tax Justice in the States

David Brunori

I f at least some level of progressivity is the measure of tax justice, then state tax systems are decidedly unjust. In fact, state revenue systems, without significant exception, are regressive. For most of the last half century, states have asked their poorest citizens to spend a greater percentage of their income than their wealthier citizens to finance the state-level government. And therein lies the paradox: People prefer a mildly progressive tax system, yet state tax structures are generally regressive. State governments are limited in their ability to impose even mildly progressive taxes (Musgrave 1959; Oates 1972). These limits arise from a unique set of economic and political circumstances that keep taxes on wealthy individuals and businesses in check while forcing the costs of government downward to lower-income taxpayers.

The most powerful limitation on the ability of states to tax progressively is the widespread perception that businesses and household mobility make progressive tax structures unworkable. That perception, widely accepted in public finance circles, affects state tax policy in two ways. First, it encourages policies that consciously influence where people live and where firms conduct business. That is, tax policies are implemented solely to encourage people and firms to move to or to remain in the state. Second, it provides another way for powerful economic interests to influence tax policy outcomes.

These conditions have created the impression that states cannot impose progressive taxes. But that impression is merely that—an impression. It is a powerful one, however, because it has remained virtually unchallenged for decades. Moreover, in recent years it has been reinforced by a political atmosphere charged with populist, antitax rhetoric.

This unchallenged but misguided thinking has resulted in a favorable tax environment for the wealthy—one that prevents those currently bearing the tax burden from significantly improving their situations. Using progressivity as the measure of justice, the relative burdens on rich and poor in state-level taxation are manifestly unjust. The real injustice, however, may be state political systems that ensure poor citizens will pay disproportionately more than their wealthy neighbors. This chapter discusses the limits on progressivity and challenges the traditional view that state tax systems are inevitably unjust.

Limits on Progressivity: The Conventional View

It is almost beyond debate that regressive tax systems are unfair. The generally accepted view, shared by both liberals and conservatives, has long been that the poor should be relieved from tax burdens to the greatest extent possible.[1] Yet, state tax systems are still regressive, taking a proportionately greater percentage of income from the poor than from the wealthy (Ettlinger et al. 1996; Pechman 1985; Phares 1980).

The reason for this inconsistency between the goals and reality of fairness is the widely held belief that states cannot impose progressive taxes. The theory that subnational governments cannot impose progressive taxes or otherwise redistribute wealth has long been taken for granted by public finance experts (Musgrave 1959; Oates 1972). Moreover, this view holds that only the federal government can effectively redistribute wealth (Musgrave 1959). What restricts progressivity under this theory is the federal system, since it allows mobility across state lines.

The underlying premise of this theory is that any attempt at redistribution by the states will be self-defeating. If State A imposes progressive taxes, high-income citizens will move to a jurisdiction that imposes a lower tax burden. At the same time, low-income citizens will move into State A to take advantage of its progressive system. State A's tax base will shrink, and policymakers will be forced either to raise taxes on the remaining (lower-income) citizens or cut services. Either way, the state will end up economically worse off and burdened by a more regressive tax system. (For an in-depth explanation of this view, see Reschovsky [1998]).

The conventional view on the limits of progressivity has had a profound effect on state government policy in general and tax policy in particular. The notion that taxes influence where people live and conduct business has fueled the sense that states should—indeed, must—compete with one another. The "war" between the states is a direct result of adherence to the conventional view (Noto 1991).

Interstate competition is now considered not only good politics, but also good policy. Fear of tax-base mobility has given rise to the widespread practice of providing tax breaks to specific companies as an incentive for them to relocate to or remain in a particular jurisdiction. It has led to the creation of tax systems under which business entities in general and corporations in particular escape paying for the benefits they receive from the state. The conventional view has also opened the door for wealthy individuals and business interests to exert undue influence on state tax policymakers. All of these consequences have led to policy choices that limit progressivity.

Interstate Competition

The idea that states should compete is premised on the belief that government policy significantly influences where people live and work. Interstate competition, in its most broadly accepted form, involves the use of a variety of means, including tax policy, to develop an attractive mix of public services at a reasonable cost to taxpayers. Under this model, states attract people and business by providing quality transportation, public safety, and education systems, while keeping their tax burdens in line with other states. Fearing migration, states cannot increase tax burdens substantially beyond those imposed by their neighbors (Musgrave 1959; Oates 1972).

Shannon (1991) has noted that states act like ships in a wartime convoy: They cannot risk getting too far out in front of their comrades by raising tax burdens; nor can they afford to fall too far behind in providing public services. Individuals and firms evaluate the costs (taxes) and benefits (services) of living or doing business in a jurisdiction. If costs outweigh benefits, then the individual or firm will opt to live or conduct business in a more favorable environment. This form of inter-state competition is generally accepted, even endorsed, by many public finance experts (Duncan 1992) and political theorists (Kincaid 1991) as promoting innovation and efficiency.

While seemingly benign, this notion of interstate competition reduces the progressivity of state tax systems. If the premise is true, firms and households will locate in states in which public benefits outweigh costs. However, only wealthy individuals and firms have the means to relocate—and most policymakers know this. To attract (or retain) those wealthy firms and households, states adjust their taxes and services accordingly. Tax liabilities for those at the top of the economic spectrum are thus held in check. At the same time, demand for quality public services must be met. Thus, such competition forces the tax burden downward toward firms and households perceived to be less likely to leave the jurisdiction.

States also engage in a more pernicious form of interstate competition when they attempt to spur economic development by granting tax incentives to specific companies. Typically, state governments offer a package of tax deductions, exemptions, and credits to lure corporations considering relocation or expansion. Moreover, state governments increasingly offer these "targeted" tax incentives to companies considering a move to another state.

Targeted tax incentives have proliferated over the last quarter century as states have stepped up efforts to spur economic development and create jobs. There are literally hundreds of such incentives granted each year, costing hundreds of millions of dollars. (For a discussion of the proliferation, see Brunori 1997.) Despite a legion of scholarly articles and reports criticizing their use, targeted tax incentives remain a favorite weapon in the battle for economic development. Companies need only hint at the possibility of relocation or expansion, and state governments quickly descend with offers to pay for infrastructure improvements, help with job training, and numerous offers of tax breaks.

Indeed, the use of targeted tax incentives is so widespread that an entire industry has developed around finding and negotiating incentives. Large accounting and law firms and numerous consulting groups turn a tidy profit by finding states and local governments willing to provide incentives to their clients.[2]

The proliferation of targeted tax incentives has several causes, the most dominant being the perceived need to create jobs and foster economic development. Job creation has always been a top priority for politicians, especially those in state and local government. With patronage ended and the advent of civil service reforms, political leaders have lost many direct means for creating jobs for loyal supporters. Targeted tax incentives provide a new and expedient way to create jobs (see Spindler and Forrester 1993; Walker 1989; Wolman 1988).

While job creation is the motive, targeted tax incentives would not be possible without a belief that tax policy influences location decisions. The adherence to the conventional view shapes the policies of economic development and leads directly to the use of targeted tax incentives. In practical terms, political leaders will not take the chance of losing jobs—extant or potential—by not competing.

Unfortunately, there is no empirical work on the distributional effects of targeted tax incentives. Nonetheless, it seems reasonable to conclude that targeted tax incentives for industries and specific companies have a regressive effect on state tax systems. Removing these businesses from the tax rolls (while often spending state money on infrastructure to support these businesses) shrinks the tax base and increases government costs. With businesses paying less taxes, the burden of paying for government is further shifted to individuals, with the wealthiest paying a proportionately smaller share of the costs.

Failure to Adequately Tax Corporations

The influence of the conventional view and the quest for economic development have reduced the tax burdens on American corporations. The notion that tax policy affects location decisions has led to the failure of state governments to adequately tax all business entities and, in particular, corporations. Taxation of corporations has long been a controversial issue in America. The idea that high taxes can spur businesses to close or relocate, thus thwarting economic development and worsening unemployment, has provided powerful arguments against taxing business interests.

As a result, the state tax burden placed on corporations has continued to decline, steadily eroding as a percentage of total state tax revenue. In 1977, state corporate income taxes accounted for about 10 percent of total state tax revenue (U.S. Census Bureau 1977). By 1998, however, that proportion fell to less than 6 percent (U.S. Census Bureau 1999). Even in states with a long tradition of progressive taxation, the corporate income tax has fallen to almost irrelevant levels. In Oregon, for example, the corporate income tax produces less revenue than the state lottery.

More significantly, the decline in the relative importance of the corporate tax over the last two decades has coincided with a nearly 200 percent increase in corporate income (Dubin 1999).

Much of the decline in corporate tax revenues is the result of interstate competition. It is corporations, after all, that benefit from most public policies designed to make a state more competitive. The idea that business taxes in general and corporate taxes in particular should be kept low is woven in the fabric of state tax policymaking. Tax incentives offered to corporations in return for relocating to or staying in a state amount to hundreds of millions of dollars in lost tax revenue.

In addition to directly offering low rates, exemptions, credits, and other tax breaks to corporations, states have for years been shifting the tax burden away from in-state companies through the redesign of their corporate tax systems. Specifically, states have systematically moved away from the traditional three-factor apportionment formula as a means of dividing corporate income. Instead, states have been adopting double-weighted and single-sales-factor apportionment formulas that greatly reduce the tax burden on corporations manufacturing products in one state and selling those products in other states. The theory behind apportionment formulas weighted toward sales is that they will make the state more attractive to companies seeking to build manufacturing facilities. By 1998, 27 states had adopted single- or double-weighted sales factors, collectively costing the states nearly a half-billion dollars a year (Pomp 1998).

There are other causes for the decline of state tax burdens placed on corporations in the United States. But all stem, at least in part, from the notion that tax policies influence where companies do business. State corporate tax scholar Richard Pomp argues that some of the decline of corporate taxes is attributable to aggressive tax planning on the part of multistate businesses (Pomp 1998). Implementing policies to make state tax systems more competitive often provides corporations the opportunity to reduce their tax burdens without fundamentally changing their operations. For example, state laws regarding pass-through entities and holding companies are designed to improve a state's business climate. In many instances, however, they allow corporations and businesses, through clever planning, to reap tax benefits without more investment, new jobs, or any additional economic development. In that regard, state corporate tax planners have devised ways to shift income to states with lower or no tax burdens, or to create nonbusiness income that is not subject to apportionment. They also take advantage of congressionally created loopholes such as Public Law 85-272, the federal law that prohibits states from imposing income taxes on companies that merely solicit sales for tangible goods. Since the early 1980s, state corporate taxation has taken on new significance with the reduction in federal corporate tax burdens. Corporations now spend more money and time trying to reduce their state tax burdens.

While little quantitative analysis is available on the effects of the decline of state corporate income taxes, it is reasonable to believe that they have had a regressive impact on state tax systems. As corporations pay fewer taxes, the burden of paying for government shifts to individual taxpayers. And if states are mindful of the tax burdens placed on wealthy individuals—and much evidence suggests that they are—then those costs are inevitably shifted to the poorer segments of society.

Political Consequences of Adhering to the Conventional View

The conventional view has held the tax burdens on the wealthy in check. But to blame limited progressivity on the fear of mobility alone is too simplistic. Arguments that progressivity will lead to flight have provided political cover for more pragmatic efforts to take care of a state's wealthiest citizens and business interests. Economic interests wield extensive clout in virtually every society and at every level of government. All states, for example, support their dominant industries, whether it is tourism in Florida, financial services in New York, or mining in West Virginia. Some dominant industries are very old (e.g., auto manufacturing in Michigan), while others are relatively new (e.g., high technology in Virginia).

State political leaders have long tried to protect and foster such industries, recognizing the jobs and economic wealth these industries create. These industries also exert tremendous political influence through campaign contributions, intense lobbying efforts, and networks of voters interested in keeping the industry strong. Accordingly, such industries receive hundreds of exemptions, deductions, and credits every year, many of which are not generally available to other industries.

From the perspective of state policymakers, adherence to the conventional view is a politically convenient device for deflecting the true aim of legislative behavior. Granting tax favors to political allies or powerful economic interests can lead to harsh criticism from tax policy experts and politicians opposing such measures. Exchanging favorable tax treatment for campaign contributions or other political support is universally frowned upon. But the granting of favorable tax treatment to prevent corporations from leaving the jurisdiction is broadly accepted and endorsed by a broad cross-section of policy specialists—the very experts that make the conventional view so conventional. It has become routine to characterize favors for politically powerful allies as more high-minded measures to stay competitive with other states. Indeed, virtually every tax break offered to an in-state industry is couched in terms of keeping the state competitive, saving or creating jobs, or encouraging economic development.

If the conventional view provides a measure of cover to political leaders, it also empowers the wealthiest citizens and business interests when dealing with state tax policymakers. Increasingly, economic interests use the threat of relocation or the promise of new jobs to extract favorable tax treatment from the government (see Brunori 1997). In-state business interests also raise the possibility that without additional tax benefits, industries in other states will gain a competitive advantage, forcing in-state companies to reduce their workforce or curtail expansion plans.

Many political leaders use the possibility of capital flight to justify favorable tax treatment for allies (Brunori 1999a). There are even more examples of economic interests using threats or promises of relocation to extract tax benefit expenditures.[3]

Other Limitations on State Tax Progressivity

In addition to the real and perceived limitations produced by the mobility of firms and households, several other causes explain the bias against progressivity in the states.

Diversity in Tax Sources

One constraint on state tax progressivity is the widespread practice of using a diverse mix of tax sources, most of which have the effect of making state revenue systems more regressive. It is generally believed by economists and accepted by policymakers that state government should generate revenue from a variety of different sources. The National Conference of State Legislatures (NCSL) (1992) in its seminal work *Princi-*

ples of a High-Quality State Revenue System calls for a tax system that relies on a broad mix of revenue sources. Using such a mix, it argues, helps offset the negative aspects of any single type of tax.

Using a variety of taxes to fund government services, however, can also create a more regressive revenue system. Personal income taxes account for about a third of total state tax revenue. Other taxes generally considered progressive (e.g., corporate income and estate levies) account for less than 7 percent of total state tax revenue, and that percentage has continued to fall. Sales and excise taxes, the most regressive sources of revenue, account for nearly half of total state tax revenue. User fees, another regressive source of revenue, account for about 10 percent of total state revenue (U.S. Census Bureau 1999).

Virtually all state lawmakers believe that diversity is beneficial and impose multiple types of taxes. Forty-one states levy a combination of broad-based personal and corporate income taxes, sales taxes, and a variety of excise taxes. Only nine states do not assess a broad-based personal income tax, and most of these generate revenue from unique sources such as severance taxes and gambling.[4] Five states impose no broad-based sales tax at all.[5]

The perception that states need to raise revenue from diverse sources has led to a heavy reliance on sales and excise taxes. This reliance, in turn, has led to generally regressive tax systems. As long as states continue to rely on consumption taxes as a major source of revenue, state tax systems will remain regressive.

Politics of Antitaxation

The political environment that has shaped American government for the past quarter century has also reinforced the limits on state-tax progressivity. In recent decades, antitax sentiment has dominated politics at all levels of government. The politics of antitaxation arose from a variety of sources, including frustration with government, the reality of unfair taxes, and a general conservative shift in the political preferences of voters. In recent decades, tax policy issues have been at the core of both electoral and legislative politics. Since the mid-1970s, opposing taxes has been good politics. It should be noted, however, that antitax politics have had little to do with the fair allocation of tax burdens; support for tax cuts has not involved people thinking that they pay too much or too little in relation to others. Rather, the focus of antitax politics has been the opposition to taxation in general.

In 1978, California's Proposition 13 set off a countrywide chain reaction against state and local taxes. Proposition 13 was followed by property tax limitations in 32 other states. At the same time, taxes began to play an increasingly important role in gubernatorial and legislative elections and, indeed, became the central focus of many state elections. The gubernatorial election campaigns conducted by Christine Todd Whitman (New Jersey) in 1992 and Jim Gilmore (Virginia) in 1997 are two of the most notable examples. By 1999, the politics of antitaxation helped Republicans take control of the executive and legislative branches in more than half the states.

Ironically, the politics of antitaxation, while often viewed as an antigovernment, populist, grassroots movement, has led to a more regressive tax system. Given the choice of reducing progressive taxes (e.g., personal and corporate income tax) and regressive taxes (e.g., sales and excise tax), antitax champions typically chose the former. That choice in itself should not be surprising since the movement has been led, financed, and supported by those who have the most to gain from reducing taxes on income.[6]

The antitax atmosphere in electoral and legislative politics has influenced and pervaded tax policymaking. In turn, those policies have negatively affected tax progressivity. During the economic boom of the mid and late 1990s, states routinely reduced tax burdens. At least 28 states significantly reduced taxes each year between 1995 and 1998 (NCSL 2000). Cutting taxes during good economic times is hardly unusual. However, state legislatures in the 1990s were much more likely to cut personal income taxes than more regressive sales and excise taxes. While the conservative political strategy was purportedly based on reducing tax burdens in general, wealthy individuals benefited far more than the lower-income and middle-class individuals. Conversely, during the recession of the early 1990s—when states desperately needed revenue to preserve existing funding levels—considerable political debate ensued. In the end, legislatures were more likely to raise sales and excise taxes than more progressive personal income taxes (Johnson and Lav 1997).

Direct Democracy

In addition to influencing legislators and candidates, the politics of antitaxation have resulted in new government processes and structures intended to limit spending and taxing power. Conservative political leaders have championed a variety of purportedly democratic means to limit state taxation and government spending.

Perhaps the most important development in the politics of state taxation during the past 25 years has been direct democracy, the process by which the voting public determines policy issues in statewide elections. Issues are brought before the voting public through initiatives or referenda. In the initiative process, citizens vote on statutory or constitutional amendments, while the referendum process allows voters to reject laws or constitutional amendments proposed by the legislature. Twenty-seven states have some form of direct democracy.[7] In the 1990s, more than 150 statewide tax issues were determined through the initiative and referendum process (Brunori 1999b).

Over the past 40 years, conservatives have used direct democracy to limit government, especially its taxing power. Between 1960 and 1990, initiatives reduced spending and taxes, decentralized spending from state to local governments, and shifted revenue from broad-based taxes to user fees for services (Matsusaka 1995). While no studies have measured the effects of direct democracy on tax incidence, it has likely reduced.[8]

Supermajority Requirements

Many states have adopted "supermajority" voting requirements for raising taxes, further limiting the capacity for progressive tax structures: In 14 states, more than a majority of legislators must approve a tax increase, while in 2 states, more than a majority of citizens voting in a referendum must approve a tax hike.[9]

Supermajority requirements are an outgrowth of the antitax politics that have dominated American public policy. In 13 of the 14 states requiring supermajority approval, the requirements were adopted after 1978, and 12 adopted them through the initiative process. Conservatives such as Peter Sepp, of the National Taxpayers Union, and Grover Norquist, of Americans for Tax Reform, have long championed supermajorities as a means of limiting taxes and spending (Brunori 1999b).

Supermajorities inevitably lead to more regressive tax systems because such states favor public service cuts over tax increases. When states face budget deficits, they must either raise revenue or cut spending. Wealthy individuals likely to be hurt by progressive tax measures, including personal income and corporate tax increases, need only muster the support of a minority of legislators to thwart such measures. On the other hand, a simple majority vote can cut public services.

Supermajority voting requirements also restrict a state's ability to reduce or eliminate tax expenditures. In every state with supermajority requirements, reforms that eliminate special tax breaks are treated as tax increases. Thus, legislators looking to balance state budgets tend to favor public service cuts over tax reform. Indeed, the evidence suggests that supermajority states are more likely to grant tax expenditures than non-supermajority states (Johnson and Lav 1998). Meanwhile, their ability to reduce taxes is not affected and legislative coalitions in support of tax cuts can be fashioned more easily.

Again, there is no quantitative evidence on the effects of supermajority requirements on progressivity. But since such requirements make tax increases more difficult to enact, they likely restrict states' ability to craft progressive tax systems.

Tax and Expenditure Limitations

Another political development intended to limit the ability of states to impose progressive taxes is the growth of tax and expenditure limitations (TELs). TELs exists in various forms and are used in 27 states.[10] Statutory and constitutional rate limitations such as California's Proposition 13 are one type, limiting the maximum rate for a particular tax by statute or constitutional amendment. Another type of TEL involves expenditure limitations, which prohibit increases in state spending beyond predetermined levels. Still other TELs involve revenue growth limitations, which prevent tax collections from increasing above established levels; these TELs often require rate rollbacks or refunds if revenue growth exceeds statutory or constitutional limits.

TELs are designed to limit government spending and lower tax burdens, and advocates argue that legislatures are unwilling or incapable of limiting the growth of state government. Contrary to the desires of their supporters, however, some evidence suggests that TELs do not necessarily restrict state taxing or spending (Kenyon and Benker 1984). State legislators, it seems, will somehow find the necessary revenue to support services demanded by the public.

The question is not whether a TEL-encumbered state can raise the revenue, but who bears the burden of paying. States constitutionally limiting tax rates, for example, are likely to force the burden downward to lower- and middle-class taxpayers by broadening the tax base. At the same time, states trying to operate within spending limitations are more likely to decrease services for the poor than limit economic development initiatives.

The Need for Money

Within the structural, economic, and political constraints on tax capacity and tax progressivity, states must raise adequate revenue to pay for the services that the public demands. In 1998, state governments spent more than $826 billion (NASBO 1999), mostly on traditional state services such as transportation, public safety, and higher education. In this regard, state spending reflects public desires, and most of that spending is within the control of the state legislature.

More recently, however, developments outside the traditional political/ budgetary framework have influenced state spending. First, the shifting of responsibilities from the federal government to the states, ongoing since the Nixon administration, has increased pressure on state budgets. Unfortunately, adequate federal funding has not always accompanied this devolution. Today, states administer many programs that were traditionally the responsibility of the federal government, and the costs of those programs continue to increase. Between 1980 and 1997, for example, Medicaid spending rose from 8 to 16 percent of total state budgets, while public welfare spending increased 136 percent (NASBO 1999). Although unfunded mandate protections have lessened the negative effects on state budgets, states have nonetheless experienced the direct and indirect financial pressure of dealing with new responsibilities.

Second, state governments are shouldering a greater share of public education costs, once the domain of local government and paid for through taxes on real property. Since the mid-1970s, states have encountered political and legal pressure to assume a greater share of public education funding, a burden that has threatened the financial stability of many states. In fact, states spent $182 billion on elementary and secondary education in 1998 (NASBO 1999).

To finance increased education spending, states have been forced to find new revenue sources. Michigan, for example, adopted a significant sales tax increase in 1994. New Hampshire, facing a $1 billion budget shortfall, opted for a statewide real property tax, and Vermont implemented a controversial property-tax-base-sharing arrangement in 1999.

Finally, constitutionally mandated balanced-budget requirements also increase the pressure on states confronting increased service demands. In 46 states, governors must submit a balanced budget to their legislatures, and in 41 states, the legislature must enact a balanced budget. Balanced-budget requirements emphasize paying for government services through tax revenue; they effectively preclude most states from borrowing to pay for operating expenses. Combined with the real and perceived limitations on taxing the wealthy and business, heightened emphasis on relying on tax revenue rather than on borrowing further shifts the burden of paying for government toward the lower end of the economic spectrum.

The Struggle for Justice

Nearly everyone recognizes the injustices of state tax structures. Political leaders from both parties have tried to alleviate tax burdens, at least for the poorest Americans. While determining appropriate levels of progressivity necessarily involves comparing the tax treatment of wealthy citizens with that of their poorer neighbors, the politics of state taxation have generally focused on the absolute burdens placed on the poor. This focus reflects a widespread conviction that justice requires sheltering the poor from taxation as much as possible. However, alleviating tax burdens on the poor within the framework of the real and perceived limitations on progressivity is difficult. The states' two primary sources of revenue, the personal income tax and the retail sales taxes, best illustrate the struggle.

Personal Income Tax

The income tax has become an important part of the state revenue system, accounting for about 34 percent of total state tax revenue (U.S. Census Bureau 1999). In fact, only nine states do not impose a general tax on personal income (see note 4). That most states levy an income tax testifies to its widespread public acceptance. The public considers it generally fair and efficient, and the tax has not spurred the political protests engendered by the sales and property taxes (Brunori 1998). Yet, even within this progressive form of taxation, there remains a long-standing debate about burdens placed on the poorest citizens. Imposing an income tax on the poorest citizens deprives them of money for their most basic needs.

Recognizing the need to shelter the working poor from taxation, states have adopted various income tax relief policies. As noted, the personal income tax is the only major state tax that can be considered progressive. But all 43 states that assess a broad-based income tax allow for some sort of exemption. Thus, even high-income taxpayers in states with flat rates pay a progressively greater percentage of their income in taxes. States have devised several methods for providing relief. As of 1998, 33 states provided standard deductions, 41 states offered personal exemptions, and 18 states extended targeted tax credits. As of December 1999, 11 states provided state-level earned income tax credits (EITCs).[11] Moreover, in 8 of the 11 states, the credits are refundable. Eighteen states have established thresholds below which no tax is due. Each of these measures is intended to reduce the tax burdens of low-income workers and lessen the overall regressivity of state tax systems.

The cost of this tax relief is substantial, however. The lost tax on exempt income alone adds up to hundreds of millions of dollars. And unlike the federal income tax, most states do not phase out relief as income increases. States working under balanced budget requirements must balance the high cost of lower-income tax relief with their need to pay for government services.

Recognizing those costs, states hesitate to provide too much tax relief for less fortunate citizens. Indeed, much more can still be done. Nineteen states impose income taxes on taxpayers at or below the federal poverty level; six states require families of four with income at one-half of the federal poverty level to pay income tax (Johnson, Fitzpatrick, and McNichol 1999). Moreover, only 14 states index their deductions and exemptions to inflation. In those 29 states without indexing, inflation erodes the value of the deductions and exemptions intended to help the poor erode.

Thus, the states struggle to find ways to bring relief to the working poor and middle class and, at the same time, to pay for publicly demanded services. That struggle would be eased if the states could shift the burden of paying for government to those economically better-off. However, states have been unable, or unwilling, to do so. The top rates in most states that impose a personal income tax is in the 4 to 5 percent range. As of January 2000, only three states (Montana, North Dakota, and Oregon) imposed rates over 9 percent. In the end, state tax policymakers simply believe that they cannot raise adequate revenue by taxing upper-income citizens to provide additional tax relief for the poor.

Sales Tax

The sales tax has been an important part of state revenue systems for more than a half-century. The sales tax accounts for about one-third of total state tax revenue, and in 1998 it raised more than $225 billion (U.S. Census Bureau 1999). As noted earlier, only five states (New Hampshire, Delaware, Montana, Oregon, and Alaska) do not impose a statewide sales tax. These states make up less than 3 percent of the nation's population.

State sales taxes have sparked even more debates over tax justice than personal income taxes. The sales tax is the most regressive of all state taxes, with the poor spending a larger percentage of their annual income on taxable goods and therefore paying a greater share in sales taxes. Wealthy individuals, on the other hand, spend more of their income on services typically exempt from sales taxation—such as financial, accounting, legal, and medical services.

Multiple exemptions from the tax, all of which are designed to ease the burden on the poor, testify to its inequity. As of 1998, 27 states exempted groceries, and 9 states that tax food provided an income tax credit or sales tax rebate. Forty-four states exempt prescription medicine, and 9 exempt nonprescription drugs. Twenty-six states exempt utilities, and 6 states exempt all or part of clothing purchases. These items are all deemed necessities, for which the poor, of course, pay a greater percentage of their income. The very existence of necessity exemptions is evidence that the sales tax is unfair. These exemptions, moreover, have support from both political parties and widespread approval from voters.

Despite their popularity, many exemptions detract from state tax policy. Exemptions defeat the logic of the sales tax, for example, which was designed to be levied on all final consumption (Mikesell 1998). Moreover, exemptions force tax rates on other nonexempt products higher. Bahl and Hawkins (1998) found that the sales tax exemption for food resulted in higher sales tax rates for all other taxable items and did not, in fact, reduce regressivity. Exemptions also draw distinctions between exempt and taxable goods, leading to distortions in the market and greatly complicating tax compliance and enforcement.

Most important for purposes of tax justice, exemptions do not necessarily alter the relative tax burdens borne by rich and poor. They provide considerable relief not just to poor families, but also to high-income households. In fact, at least one study has found that tax reductions for people in the highest income quintile were more than twice those for people in the lowest quintile (Mikesell 1996).

How the states levy sales taxes reflects the ongoing struggle to achieve some level of fairness. As the numerous exemptions suggest, the sales tax is considered unfair by both the public and political leaders. However, states cannot eliminate the levy altogether since they rely on the billions in revenue it produces. States that wish to make up for lost sales tax revenue would have to raise personal and/or corporate income tax burdens to unreasonable heights.

At the same time, states do all they can to minimize the unfairness by exempting as many necessities as possible. These exemptions lead to higher tax rates, however, and generally leave the allocation of burdens unchanged. Moreover, exemptions do not necessarily increase progressivity since they apply to the wealthy as well as to the poor and thereby greatly increase the costs of such relief measures. Food exemptions alone cut the sales tax base by over 20 percent (Mikesell 1998).

As political leaders periodically discover, easing tax burdens on the poor in a system that limits progressivity is difficult. State governments with balanced-budget requirements must find ways to pay for public services without incurring debt. The cost of those services has risen consistently for most of the past 50 years. When policy reflects the perception that the burdens of paying for government cannot be placed on the wealthy or business, heavier burdens inevitably fall on middle- and lower-income taxpayers.

Opportunities for Reform

This chapter has been premised on the belief that tax justice requires at least some measure of progressivity. Yet, the limitations on progressivity are embedded in state public policy, and reversing the bias is a daunting task. However, the restrictions on progressivity are neither inherent nor inviolate—they are instead the consequences of political decisions. They can be changed, albeit not easily. Discrete changes to particular sections of the tax law will not work. Additional exemptions and credits may alleviate some regressivity, but such tinkering, characteristic of the last several decades, has not solved the problem. Rather, the underlying assumptions that dominate state tax policy must be challenged.

Challenging the Conventional View

The primary impediment to progressivity is the belief that progressive taxation leads to wealth migration. This view assumes that states cannot impose progressive taxes and has dominated public finance for most of the last half-century. To some extent, this view is correct. At some level of taxation, firms and households will migrate to states with more attractive tax climates. Evidence indicates, however, that states can adopt more progressive tax systems that both shelter the poor and ensure adequate public services. Most Americans would feel that where they live and work is determined by variables and considerations that have little to do with taxation. Within that framework, a case for a mildly progressive system can be built. (The term *mildly* is used here because there is clearly no political support for an aggressively progressive system.)

The conventional view is based on several assumptions that, while logical in the abstract, do not reflect how people come to decide where to live and work. First, it assumes that firms and people are freely mobile, and that the costs of relocating from one state or another are minimal or nil. This assumption is simply incorrect. Moreover, it assumes that people have all the information needed to calculate the relative tax burdens in various locations; given the complexities of the modern state tax system, this task is difficult enough for trained professionals.

The conventional view is also based on the assumption that people are detached from their communities in such a way that tax burdens play a dominant role in location decisions. It assumes that people and firms make location decisions without considering the emotional and psychological attachments to where they live and work. The conventional view does not consider that family, friends, or a particular way of life may be the reason—at times the only reason—for living in a particular state. Many of these factors cannot be quantified and are thus difficult to measure. These admittedly subtle factors do exist, however, as everyone who has ever considered leaving a loved one, a cherished hometown, or another familiar part of their lives knows. The truth is that most people choose where to live and work on factors that do not fit into an algebraic expression of costs/benefits or quantifiable tax burdens.

Perhaps it is not surprising, then, that the conventional view that states cannot impose progressive taxes is increasingly being called into question. For example, there are often stark differences in the relative progressivity between states (Ettlinger et al. 1996). While states impose regressive tax systems overall, there are still differences in how they allocate the costs of government among their citizens. As an example, the nine states without personal income taxes tend to have more regressive tax systems, while the five states without general sales taxes tend to have more progressive tax systems. Under the conventional view, higher-income people and businesses will move from states with greater progressivity to states with lower progressivity. Yet, there has never been a mass exodus from states with slightly higher tax burdens to states with lower burdens. That is not to say that a mass exodus is not possible. However, it would require a degree of confiscatory taxation that has never occurred in the United States.

Reschovsky (1998) notes an absence of convincing evidence that the locational decisions of individuals and business are sensitive to inter-state tax rate differentials. Actually, data show that levels of progressivity have little effect on economic development. Chernick (1997) finds that the progressivity of state tax systems does not negatively impact their rate of economic growth. If the conventional view were true, then economic growth would decline as progressivity increased since wealthy individuals and firms would leave the jurisdiction.

Recent scholarship indicates that since 1980, states with higher income tax burdens have experienced greater economic growth than states with relatively lower or no income tax burdens (Institute for Taxation and Economic Policy 1999). Again, if the conventional view were accurate, states with progressive tax policies would experience slower economic growth than states with more regressive systems.[12]

The evidence suggests that states have some latitude in their ability to impose progressive taxes. Those who question the assumptions and premises that underlie the conventional view should encourage more research on the effects of progressivity on economic growth. Evidence that progressivity does not hamper growth should be used to further the argument that regressive taxes are not a foregone conclusion for the states.

Ending the Use of Targeted Tax Incentives

Targeted tax incentives are the scourge of modern state tax policy. Virtually every economist and public finance expert has decried their use (Duncan 1992). And there is little question that targeted tax incentives violate the principles of sound tax policy (Brunori 1997). Despite the widespread condemnation, targeted tax incentives have proliferated for decades. They have increased the difficulty of providing relief for the poor in a system that already has limitations on progressivity.

Those who believe that targeted tax incentives are unjust must change the political culture that gives rise to their use.[13] This change will be difficult since the perceived benefits of using targeted tax incentives are firmly established in the minds of those who set state tax policy. Convincing lawmakers that targeted tax incentives constitute unsound tax policy has never worked. Arguments that incentives are inefficient or inequitable (both horizontally and vertically) have never swayed policymakers, who often believe in the power of incentives to create jobs and foster economic development. To end the use of tax incentives, lawmakers will have to be convinced that they do not work.

As a start, opponents of incentives should challenge the underlying premise that tax policy significantly influences business location decisions. There are numerous economic studies on the subject, and most find little or no correlation between tax burdens and where a company chooses to do business. The lack of correlation is understandable, since state taxes make up a very small percentage of the cost of doing business—as low as 2 percent according to one recent study (Lynch 1996). The factors that influence location decisions are investments in infrastructure, transportation systems, and education (Brunori 1997).

The lack of correlation between tax burdens and location decisions suggests that targeted tax incentives are unnecessary. Indeed, the abundance of anecdotal evidence suggests that most companies receiving incentives would have made the same business decisions without the incentive (Brunori 1997). Some corporations actually ask for incentives after they have already relocated or expanded—further evidence that tax incentives are not as necessary as the conventional view indicates (Brunori 2000).

Ultimately, ending tax incentives requires convincing lawmakers that public policy should not be made this way. Lawmakers should be held accountable when they give in to what is essentially bribery and blackmail. A corporation demanding favorable tax treatment before it takes or refrains from taking action is actually setting tax policy. That function should be reserved for the state's elected officials.

Regaining Control of Business Taxation

For too long, American business has garnered tax benefits as a result of both traditional political pressure (such as lobbying and campaign contributions) and the belief that without such favorable tax treatment, business will migrate or be placed at a competitive disadvantage. Yet, there is a compelling reason for taxing corporations and other business entities. Businesses use many public services—roads, police, fire, and schools—either directly or indirectly—and taxpayers pay for these services. The question is whether the businesses that benefit from these services should pay some portion of the costs. The answer, under any theory of taxation, must be yes.

When business is left untaxed, the costs of providing public services are shifted to individuals who may or may not benefit from those services. Moreover, as Pogue (1998) has argued, business taxes that reflect nonmarket costs of production are necessary for a market economy to allocate resources efficiently.

To be sure, people ultimately pay business taxes as the economic burden is shifted to owners, employees, or customers. But it is often difficult, if not impossible, to identify and charge those who ultimately benefit from public services provided to corporations. A corporation's shareholders may—and in the case of large multinational companies probably do—reside outside the state in which the corporation does business. This may also be the case for the customers, and even for some employees. Many owners and customers may themselves be corporations. Those who benefit from the services provided by the public will likely not share the costs unless the corporate entity is taxed.

Challenging the Reliance on Consumption Taxes

The assumption that states need to impose consumption taxes to "balance" their revenue systems needs to be reevaluated if states will ever attain a more progressive system. A primary justification for the sales tax is that it brings stability to the revenue system (NCSL 1992). This stability is consistent with the goal of obtaining a reliable source of funds to pay for government services (NCSL 1992). Personal income taxes yield revenue that grows faster than personal income during prosperous economic times. Personal income tax revenue, however, declines faster than personal income during times of recession. Consumption and excise taxes, on the other hand, are thought to yield more consistent revenue through times of economic change (NCSL 1992).

The idea that the sales tax is more stable than other sources of revenue is premised on the belief that all consumption will be taxed. Since people will consume in good times as well as bad, there will be a more or less steady stream of revenue. However, the widespread use of exemptions for necessities, states' inability or unwillingness to tax services, and the continuous growth of remote sales have resulted in less than half of total consumption being subject to sales tax. The decimation of the tax base should raise serious questions about the level of stability the sales tax brings to state revenue systems.

It is also believed that diversity minimizes market distortions by allowing the states to impose lower rates on all types of taxes (NCSL 1992). Lower rates, in turn, lessen the impact on individual and firm behavior and reduce the likelihood of migration. But the goal of minimizing market distortions, while a laudable goal of tax policy, does not really justify the sales tax. Once again, because of numerous exemptions and exclusions, an abundance of real and potential market distortions arise from the use of sales taxation.

There are, however, some benefits to levying consumption taxes. The sales tax has proven an efficient and effective means of collecting revenue. But the positive aspects of the sales tax must be balanced against its inherently regressive nature.

Currently, policymakers confront a unique opportunity to lessen the country's dependence on the sales tax. The sales tax faces many challenges in the new millennium. The changing economy has shifted consumption patterns toward services, which generally are exempt from sales taxation. Electronic commerce and constitutional limitations have hampered the ability to administer the tax, and the tax base continues to shrink as states exempt consumer purchases on equity grounds and business purchases for economic development reasons. While no one is predicting its complete demise, the sales tax will likely continue to decline in importance (Fox 1998). Indeed, in 1999, for the first time ever, personal income taxes raised more revenue than state sales taxes.

This situation allows lawmakers to reevaluate heavy dependence on consumption taxes. The solutions to the problems facing the sales tax are difficult and costly, and states have spent and will continue to spend much time and energy searching for these elusive solutions. If the sales tax no longer promotes stability and neutrality, perhaps there should be less emphasis on "saving" the sales tax from the 21st century.

Using the Political Process to Promote Progressivity

The regressive character of state tax systems is a political phenomenon. Furthermore, the decisions as to who should bear the burden of paying for government are political. They are made by elected officials account-able to the public. One must believe, therefore, in the possibility of reversing the current political trend and creating at least a mildly pro-gressive tax system.

Those who believe that justice requires a more progressive state tax system must use the political process more effectively. State legislators must be convinced that the existing regressive tax system is unfair. Orga-nizations that represent lower- and middle-income taxpayers must con-front lawmakers on the issue of who should bear the tax burden. Labor, religious, and civic groups should not hesitate to decry tax policies that require their members to pay proportionately more than wealthier citi-zens in support of government. And while economic interests have greater monetary resources, the majority of Americans who would ben-efit from a fairer tax system can exert considerable electoral strength. Advocates of a more progressive tax system must work to elect leaders who share their view.

Changing the legislative bias in favor of regressivity requires infor-mation, and lawmakers need to understand the consequences of their tax policy choices. State legislators often have little idea of who will ben-efit and who will be burdened when specific taxes are raised or lowered. Unfortunately, information for lawmakers is scarce because few states conduct distributional analyses of proposed tax changes. The Joint Committee on Taxation and the Department of Treasury routinely perform such studies at the federal level. But only Minnesota conducts incidence studies of all major tax proposals, while six more states occa-sionally study some tax proposals (Johnson and Lav 1997). The effect is clear. Most legislators have no real knowledge about whether the mea-sure on which they are voting will make the system more or less regres-sive. Lawmakers cannot effectively consider or debate the merits of a tax proposal if they cannot identify with some certainty who benefits and who suffers. While this chapter is not written to make specific policy recommendations, requiring every state legislature to conduct an inci-dence analysis of pending tax legislation would go far toward fostering the debate over fair and just tax policy.

If legislators are largely blind to the effects of tax policy, the public is more so. Only a minority of citizens, one suspects, understand that low-income individuals bear a disproportionate share of the tax burden. Most citizens do not realize that a person making $1 million a year will pay a smaller percentage of his or her income in state taxes than a person earning $30,000 a year. Most people do not voice their concerns about the incidence of taxes because most people have little information about the effects of tax policy.

Knowing the concepts of progressivity and regressivity is not enough. What the public needs to know, or at least have access to, is who wins and loses from the tax policy choices made by their elected leaders. When legislators propose a bill that would grant a tax incentive, raise the sales tax rate, or lower income tax rates, the public should be aware of the winners and losers associated with the change. Tax justice is not attainable unless the public is fully aware of the consequences of tax policy.

As America rethinks the way it raises revenue for state government in light of the immense political, economic, and technological changes taking place, those who believe that justice requires a more progressive tax system should try to shape the debate. State tax systems will change, and they could change in a progressive direction.

NOTES

1. The various national tax reform efforts proposed by conservative leaders in the past 10 years all contain generous tax relief for the nation's poorest citizens (Sullivan 1996).

2. The growing importance of incentives is illustrated by the fact the *Journal of Multistate Taxation*, a leading publication in the tax field, changed its name to the *Journal of Multistate Taxation and Incentives*.

3. In 1999 alone, I identified over 40 examples reported in *State Tax Notes* magazine of businesses coercing states to extend tax incentives. The most egregious instance may have been the Marriott Corporation's threat to leave Maryland, for which it received over $40 million in tax breaks (Brunori 1999a). No doubt many more examples go unreported.

4. Washington, Texas, Florida, Wyoming, Nevada, South Dakota, and Alaska impose no personal income taxes of any kind. New Hampshire and Tennessee do not impose broad-based personal income tax but tax some dividend and interest income.

5. New Hampshire, Alaska, Oregon, Delaware, and Montana do not impose a broad-based sales tax.

6. Several works assert that the grassroots nature of the tax-revolt era is an illusion. That is, the revolts have been led by and ultimately benefit the upper classes (Kuttner 1980; Smith 1998).

7. States with initiatives and referenda include Alaska, Arizona, Arkansas, California, Colorado, Florida, Idaho, Illinois, Kentucky, Maine, Maryland, Massachusetts, Michigan, Mississippi, Missouri, Montana, Nebraska, Nevada, New Mexico, North Dakota, Ohio, Oklahoma, Oregon, South Dakota, Utah, Washington, and Wyoming. In addition, every state except Delaware requires constitutional amendments to be put to a popular vote.

8. Direct democracy is not an inherent limitation on progressivity (Brunori 1999b). After all, the initiative and referendum process can be just as easily used to promote progressivity as to restrict it. Indeed, the 1995 Matsusaka study found that between 1902 and 1942, initiatives were used to increase spending and taxes. Thus, it is likely that the initiative process had a positive effect on progressivity in the state tax systems during the early part of the 20th century.

9. Arizona, Arkansas, California, Colorado, Delaware, Florida, Louisiana, Mississippi, Missouri, Nevada, Oklahoma, Oregon, South Dakota, and Washington.

10. Alaska, Arizona, California, Colorado, Connecticut, Delaware, Florida, Hawaii, Idaho, Iowa, Louisiana, Massachusetts, Michigan, Mississippi, Missouri, Montana, Nevada, New Jersey, North Carolina, Oklahoma, Oregon, Rhode Island, South Carolina, Tennessee, Texas, Utah, and Washington.

11. Colorado, Iowa, Kansas, Maryland, Massachusetts, Minnesota, New York, Oregon, Rhode Island, Wisconsin, and Vermont.

12. Another study in Oregon found that for companies deciding where to locate their headquarters, taxes had little effect. Indeed, California and New York states, with higher tax burdens than average, managed to lure the most corporate headquarters (Suo 2000).

13. Some organizations, such as the Institute for Tax and Economic Policy and the Center for Economic Development, advocate strict accountability laws and even litigation to control tax incentives. While these measures effectively combat abuse, this chapter offers suggestions to end their use.

REFERENCES

Bahl, Roy, and Richard Hawkins. 1998. "Does a Food Exemption Lead to a Higher State Sales Tax Rate?" *State Tax Notes* (January 5): 29–35.
Brunori, David. 1997. "Principles of Tax Policy and Targeted Tax Incentives." *State and Local Government Review* 29 (1, winter): 50–61.
———. 1998. "State Personal Income Taxation in the 21st Century." In *The Future of State Taxation,* edited by David Brunori (191–206). Washington, D.C.: Urban Institute Press.
———. 1999a. "Targeted Incentives: An Unstable Staple." *State Tax Notes* (March 1): 649–51.
———. 1999b. "Initiatives, Referendums Are Here to Stay." *State Tax Notes* (May 17): 1635–37.
———. 2000. "Is There a Silver Bullet for Targeted Tax Incentives?" *State Tax Notes* (January 10): 125–26.
Chernick, Howard. 1997. "Tax Progressivity and State Economic Performance: Is Progressivity Self-Defeating?" *Economic Development Quarterly* 11 (August): 572–85.
Dubin, Elliot. 1999. "Corporate Tax Revenue Trends." Paper presented to the Multistate Tax Commission Annual Conference, Traverse City, Mich., July 29.
Duncan, Harley. 1992. "Interstate Tax Competition: The Good, the Bad, and the Ugly." *State Tax Notes* (August 24): 266.
Ettlinger, Michael P., John F. O'Hare, Robert S. McIntyre, Julie King, Neil Miransky, and Elizabeth A. Fray. 1996. *Who Pays? A Distributional Analysis of the Tax Systems of All*

50 States. Washington, D.C.: Citizens for Tax Justice and the Institute on Taxation and Economic Policy (June).

Fox, William. 1998. "Can the State Sales Tax Survive a Future Like Its Past?" In *The Future of State Taxation,* edited by David Brunori (33–48). Washington, D.C.: Urban Institute Press.

Institute for Taxation and Economic Policy. 1999. "An Analysis of the Cato Institute's special report 'The Case against a Tennessee Income Tax.'" *State Tax Notes* (December 20): 1673–80.

Johnson, Nicholas, Christina Smith Fitzpatrick, and Elizabeth C. McNichol. 1999. "State Income Tax Burdens on Low-Income Taxpayers in 1998." *State Tax Notes* (April 5): 1143–63.

Johnson, Nicholas, and Iris J. Lav. 1997. "Are State Taxes Becoming More Regressive?" *State Tax Notes* (October 6): 893.

———. 1998. "Requiring Legislative Supermajorities to Raise Taxes Undermines Sound Fiscal Policy." *State Tax Notes* (May 11): 1575.

Kenyon, Daphne, and Karen Benker. 1984. "Fiscal Discipline: Lessons from the State Experience." *National Tax Journal* 37 (3, September): 438.

Kincaid, John. 1991. "The Competitive Challenge to Cooperative Federalism." In *Competition among States and Local Governments,* edited by Daphne Kenyon and John Kincaid (87–114). Washington, D.C.: Urban Institute Press.

Kuttner, Robert. 1980. *The Revolt of the Haves.* New York: Simon and Schuster.

Lynch, Robert. 1996. *Do State and Local Tax Incentives Work?* Washington, D.C.: Economic Policy Institute.

Matsusaka, John. 1995. "Fiscal Effects of the Voter Initiative: Evidence from the Last 30 Years." *Journal of Political Economy* 103 (3): 587–623.

Mikesell, John. 1996. "Should Grocery Food Purchases Bear a Sales Tax Burden?" *State Tax Notes* 11 (September 9): 251–54.

———. 1998. "The Future of American Sales and Use Taxation." In *The Future of State Taxation,* edited by David Brunori (15–32). Washington, D.C.: Urban Institute Press.

Musgrave, Richard A. 1959. *The Theory of Public Finance.* New York: McGraw-Hill.

NASBO. See National Association of State Budget Officers.

National Association of State Budget Officers. 1999. "Fiscal Survey." Washington, D.C.: NASBO. June.

National Conference of State Legislatures. 1992. *Principles of a High-Quality State Revenue System,* 2nd ed. Washington, D.C.: NCSL.

———. 2000. *State Tax Actions 1999: Special Fiscal Report.* Washington, D.C.: NCSL.

NCSL. See National Conference of State Legislatures.

Noto, Nonna. 1991. "Trying to Understand the Economic Development Official's Dilemma." In *Competition among States and Local Governments,* edited by Daphne Kenyon and John Kincaid (251–58). Washington, D.C.: Urban Institute Press.

Oates, Wallace E. 1972. *Fiscal Federalism.* New York: Harcourt Brace Jovanovich.

Pechman, Joseph A. 1985. *Who Paid the Taxes, 1966–1985?* Washington, D.C.: Brookings Institution.

Phares, Donald. 1980. *Who Pays State and Local Taxes?* Cambridge, Mass.: Oegeschaler, Gunn, and Hain.

Pogue, Thomas F. 1998. "State and Local Business Taxation: Principles and Prospects." In *The Future of State Taxation*, edited by David Brunori (89–110). Washington, D.C.: Urban Institute Press.

Pomp, Richard. 1998. "The Future of the State Corporate Income Tax: Reflections (and Confessions) of a State Tax Lawyer." In *The Future of State Taxation*, edited by David Brunori (49–72). Washington, D.C.: Urban Institute Press.

Reschovsky, Andrew. 1998. "The Progressivity of State Tax Systems." In *The Future of State Taxation*, edited by David Brunori (161–89). Washington, D.C.: Urban Institute Press.

Shannon, John. 1991. "Federalism's 'Invisible Regulator'—Interjurisdictional Competition." In *Competition among the States and Local Government*, edited by Daphne A. Kenyon and John Kincaid (117–25). Washington, D.C.: Urban Institute Press.

Smith, Daniel. 1998. *Tax Crusaders and the Politics of Direct Democracy.* New York: Routledge.

Spindler, Charles, and John Forrester. 1993. "Economic Development: Preferences among Models." *Urban Affairs Quarterly* 29: 28.

Sullivan, Martin. 1996. *Changing America's Tax System.* New York: John Wiley & Sons.

Suo, Steve. 2000. "Tax Cuts Aren't Sure-Fire Way to Bring Corporate Headquarters, Study Says." *Oregonian,* 26 January, 1.

U.S. Census Bureau. 1977. "State Tax Collection Data by State." Washington, D.C.: U.S. Government Printing Office.

———. 1999. "State Tax Collection Data by State." http://www.census.gov/govs/www/statetax99.html.

Walker, Lee. 1989. *Economic Development in the States: The Changing Arena.* Washington, D.C.: Council of State Governments.

Wolman, Harold. 1988. "Local Economic Development Policy: What Explains the Divergence between Policy Analysis and Political Behavior?" *Journal of Urban Affairs* (10): 19–33.

8

Property Taxation

Fairness and Popularity, Perceptions and Reality

Joan M. Youngman

Public views of the fairness or unfairness of the property tax are of intense practical and political concern because the tax is both a mainstay of local government and the subject of ceaseless controversy. Long portrayed as a particularly unfair and resented levy, it has stimulated many popular tax limitation movements and provoked decades of legal actions portraying its use in education finance as fundamentally inequitable.

At the same time, this centuries-old fiscal instrument continues to function as America's primary source of autonomous local revenue. Most economists now reject the traditional charge of its regressivity, particularly when housing expenditures are matched with long-term income. The property tax, in fact, balances some of the extremely favorable income tax benefits afforded to real property ownership. If inequalities in the tax are capitalized into asset value, the taxpayer effectively pays a lower purchase price. Furthermore, owner-occupied residences, farmland, open space, and property owned by senior citizens receive generous preferential property tax treatment. The property tax is an established form of asset, or wealth, taxation in an era relying increasingly on relatively invisible, and often regressive, consumption taxes. Perhaps most significantly, this tax imports a public element into the basic structure of private property rights.

The passionate nature of this debate surpasses its intellectual clarity, however. The fairness of the property tax can be analyzed from many, sometimes contradictory, perspectives. In particular, property tax discussions often treat fairness and popularity as equivalents. Indeed, the two features can be closely related, and in many cases, public perceptions of a tax will provide inductive evidence of widely held criteria for fairness. However, factors unrelated to fairness also affect the popularity of fiscal measures. A tax that can be exported from the jurisdiction, such as a levy that targets tourists or owners of vacation property, will likely be popular with residents, whatever its fairness.

Rather than introduce a theory of fairness against which to evaluate the property tax, this chapter will attempt to clarify the points of controversy. In particular, it will distinguish questions of the tax's structure and administrative fairness from those that address property rights issues.

A public claim on a portion of private property value can spark contentious disputes about the fairness of any given division between public and private property rights. Moreover, certain types of property pose special fairness questions, such as the protection afforded an owner's personal residence, the public benefit of preserving farmland and undeveloped open space, and the appropriate treatment of the increase in land value due to community development and public investment.

Economic issues, such as incidence and regressivity, are critical but not central to this debate. For example, the tax's impact cannot be understood without considering capitalization. To the extent that tax capitalization reduces the price paid for property, economic analysis considers the current owner free of the burden of the tax. Even stating this proposition, however, emphasizes the gulf that often separates economic analysis and public perception. Scientific and mathematical measures generally fail to arouse deep feelings about the tax's fairness, though observers hold profoundly divergent views on the appropriate public element within the bundle of private real property rights.

Positive Features of the Tax

Because criticism of the tax is so unstinting and praise so rare, it is important to understand both its strengths and its alternatives. The tax often receives only faint praise for its long history as an efficient mechanism for raising revenue. According to Jensen, "The justification of the American property tax is largely one of status. The tax is established; all parties interested have become adjusted to it" (1931, 75). A few decades later, Netzer took a similar position, acknowledging the tax's virtues as "pragmatic rather than philosophical ones. The tax exists; it produces very large revenues; and our society and economy have adjusted to and worked through many of the baleful effects of the tax, at least at present levels of property taxation" (1968, 29).

In addition to longevity, the tax has four important advantages: a transparent and visible structure, unique suitability to independent local finance, a fixed base, and a contribution to an established system of property rights.

Transparency

Transparency may seem a perverse virtue in the case of the property tax, since its visibility often accounts for a great deal of the rancor it excites. But taxpayer awareness promotes accountability and public responsibility. This high visibility—a rare attribute in an era of relatively invisible (and therefore more popular) consumption and withholding taxes— is even more valuable because it would be unusual to find it in any substitute tax.

Two forms of transparency, not always found together, are at issue here. The actual tax bill and the requirement for a substantial lump-sum payment focus taxpayer attention on the absolute amount of the collection or levy. Relative tax burdens on different properties, however, have been extremely difficult to identify under some fractional assessment systems. These systems present taxpayers with valuations below (sometimes far below) market levels, and so discourage complaints. However, some taxpayers—unaware of how much more below market levels other taxpayers' properties are assessed—may actually bear a disproportionate share of the jurisdiction's tax burden. In other words, their property may be absolutely underassessed but relatively overassessed. This problem has greatly diminished in recent years, however, as the property tax has become more fully transparent, often after judicial intervention and sometimes with mixed political results.

Autonomous Local Revenue

Property taxes may be levied in support of local, state, or national governments, special districts, school districts, or a variety of other political jurisdictions. The fairness of the tax is distinct from its assignment to a specific level of government. However, to the extent the public values autonomous local government, the fact that property taxes are well suited to its support will affect public views of the tax itself. Small governmental units' ability to set sales or income tax rates different from those of neighboring jurisdictions is greatly restricted. In fact, the problem of taxing catalog sales and electronic commerce has encouraged efforts to harmonize all sales taxes within a given state to facilitate collection from remote vendors. In this respect, immovable property has an obvious and unique advantage as a local tax base.

A Fixed Tax Base

Land is fixed not only with regard to location but also with regard to supply. This inelastic supply means that a tax on land's value will not change the amount produced and consumed. By avoiding this inefficiency, the property tax can raise revenue with fewer economic burdens than those accompanying other types of taxes. The fixed supply of land also affects capitalization of taxes on its value, for the burden of a tax on a durable good in fixed supply will fall on the owner at the time the tax is imposed. To the extent anticipated future tax liabilities affect a purchaser's bid for the property, he or she has escaped their economic impact. As Jensen wrote, "The taxpayer, by virtue of the process of capitalization, has bought himself free from any calculable, unequal part of the tax, and as for the general or equal or uniform part of it, he bears that in common with others" (1931, 75).

This phenomenon is obviously central to debates over the fairness of the tax—perhaps not fairness over all time, for the owner who suffered the loss in value when the tax was first levied may have been treated unfairly. However, the property owner who purchased land knowing about the tax, and who paid a lower price because of it, has no such complaint.

Public and Private Rights

That the property tax reserves a portion of private real estate value for the public is both one of its unique strengths and the source of many charges of unfairness. A tax set at 1 percent of market value annually at a time when property yields rental income of 5 percent effectively makes the public a 20 percent limited partner in the property-owning enterprise, sharing in the proceeds, but not in managerial decisions. A judgment about the fairness of this situation should be informed by many considerations, including the sources of property value, the property-related benefits afforded by the taxing jurisdiction, the reliability of property wealth as an index of ability to pay, and the other advantages (such as preferential income-tax treatment) afforded property ownership.

This reasoning distinguishes between taxing land and taxing buildings because the value of buildings and other improvements may be the result of private effort, but the value of bare land reflects community growth and investment—and the purchasers' expectations of gain under the governing system of property rights (Brown 1997; Netzer 1998). That bare land value is not the result of individual investment has implications both for equity and efficiency. The owner, whose efforts and improvements have increased the value of property, has an equitable claim to that property wealth not available to the owner of an unimproved site. A tax on a value not the result of individual effort also has efficiency benefits, for it will not distort economic decisionmaking by discouraging or redirecting productive activity.

Three Charges of Unfairness

The property tax's unpopularity stems from problems of asset taxation, nonuniformity, and administration. These include a complex array of issues, the most basic representing objections to the very concept of a tax on property value. Some objections identify practical difficulties that can be remedied, while others reflect misperceptions that may be refutable but are nonetheless deeply rooted and difficult to combat.

Problems of Asset Taxation

Much taxpayer dissatisfaction stems from the substantial annual payment required by the property tax, a payment not necessarily related to cash income or realized gains. This problem is the essence of an asset tax, and it is extremely and understandably unpopular. Whether or not it is unfair is a different question, however.

Other taxes unrelated to net income include wealth taxes, excises, and estate taxes. Each is unpopular—for example, automobile excise taxes are currently a target of many tax protests.[1] Yet the the sources of this dissatisfaction are not always easy to formulate as principles of fairness.

One complaint concerns the taking of property, rather than withholding a portion before it is received, as in the taxation of wages. Another concerns the unpredictability of levies based on fluctuating market values, particularly in times of rapid inflation. Yet another deals with the taxpayer's ability to choose whether or not to incur the tax in the first place. For example, a sales tax is not related to income and can rise in times of inflation, but consumers know the full tax cost at the time of the transaction. Perhaps the most powerful emotional response associated with unpredictability accompanies the specter of dispossession—the loss of a home because of the taxpayer's inability to pay unanticipated property taxes. Again, the roots of unpopularity may be evident, but the charge of unfairness remains to be clarified.

Consider estate and inheritance taxes, similarly unpopular and subject to constant legislative repeal efforts. Yet, the estate tax is similar to the withholding tax since it is a onetime levy imposed before the transmission of assets. Furthermore, estate taxes are not subject to annual fluctuations in market value. In addition, they serve to balance the potentially regressive effects of increasing reliance on sales and consumption taxes, which favor the more affluent households whose disposable income exceeds their spending needs. However, none of these considerations mitigates the unpopularity of estate and gift taxes or diminishes calls for their repeal.[2]

The problems presented by large, annual lump-sum payments can be addressed to some extent by administrative measures, such as quarterly or even monthly billing. Direct debit options, under which tax payments are charged to credit cards or withdrawn from bank accounts, further reduce the tax's visibility. In fact, the tax escrow portion of monthly mortgage payments amounts to a type of withholding of this asset tax. In Sweden, property taxes are withheld from wages (Youngman and Malme 1994), and in the Netherlands, direct debit procedures are common (Verbrugge 1997). These practices pose interesting questions about the relative importance of convenience, popularity, accountability, and fairness. The invisibility of sales taxes, collected in numerous small transactions and never totaled for the taxpayer, enhances their popularity but diminishes accountability. To politicians and tax administrators seeking revenue mechanisms acceptable to the public, it might seem facetious to suggest that a more visible and hence less popular tax could be preferable to a hidden one. Yet, it is legitimate to judge a visible tax more fair even if it is less popular.

Unforeseen shifts in annual assessments resulting from changes in market prices are less responsive to administrative remedies, but there are ways to greatly reduce the scope and impact of these fluctuations. It does not go without saying that lowering the tax rate can help offset an increasing tax base in times of rising inflation. In some cases, rising property values have offered an all-too-convenient source of tax revenues, most notably in pre–Proposition 13 California (Schrag 1998). A different problem arises, however, when separate areas in a single taxing district experience differing levels of price changes. If prices have not risen uniformly, a uniform reduction in the tax rate will not maintain both level revenue and level tax bills. In this situation, new valuations may be phased in over a period of years, and annual assessment increases may be limited to a percentage or dollar ceiling. Not infrequently, situations of this type lead to legislative or constitutional changes modifying or eliminating the requirement for uniform tax rates on all types of property.

Most states offer homestead exemptions, which reduce the valuation of qualified owner-occupied residences by a given amount, and "circuit breaker" programs, which offer rebates for property taxes that exceed a set percentage of income (Mackey 1992). The specific elements of these plans vary across states—for example, in many states these benefits are available only to senior citizens. While the fairness of subsidies limited to homeowners may be debatable, these provisions offer taxpayers of modest income some protection against loss of their residences.

Although these measures reduce the burden of *ad valorem* taxation, the essential question remains, Is it fair if, after tallying all phasing-in and differential assessments, an owner still faces the loss of property because of an inability to pay the property tax? Another administrative relief measure might sharpen the question even further. Many states allow senior citizens to defer payment of tax on their residences, in effect receiving low-interest loans from their jurisdictions (Mackey 1992; Mackey and Carter 1995). These loans are secured by the taxable property, to be repaid when it is sold or bequeathed. If this option were available to all taxpayers (eliminating the threat of dispossession), to what extent would charges of unfairness be resolved? Note that this situation might be approximated without public action by secured loans from private financial institutions.

Again, questions of fairness and popularity must be distinguished. Existing programs for tax deferral are enormously underutilized, mostly because of taxpayer resistance to any encumbrance on family property (Baer 1998;

Ebel and Ortbal 1989). Yet once the catastrophic possibility of eviction is removed, the question of fairness becomes less an issue of unfeeling brutality and more a problem of property rights. Is it unfair to diminish a property owner's bundle of rights, the asset available for transmission to heirs, by imposing a tax lien? Or, again contrasting the property tax to sales and estate taxes, the question may be, Is it less fair to encumber property in possession than it is to withhold a portion of the property at transmission (recognizing that the technical status of the estate tax as a tax on transmission does not impede its political perception as a tax on possession)?[3]

The element of forewarning (or surprise) is clearly important, as in the case of a buyer who knows the full amount of sales tax at the time of the transaction and can use that information in deciding whether to make the purchase. This is the strongest argument for the acquisition-value tax base used by Proposition 13—a kind of sales tax paid in installments over the term of property ownership. In the worst case under a market-value property tax, a prudent purchase of a home appropriate to the buyer's income and wealth could turn into an unsupportable financial burden if rising home prices caused property taxes to increase out of proportion to income.

As always in the case of this intensely practical tax, the factual setting is critical to considerations of fairness. A wave of widespread foreclosures because of unforeseen tax increases is qualitatively different from unusual instances in which a specific home becomes too costly a burden for its purchaser. There is some political check on the former danger to the extent that the electorate would not tolerate widespread loss of property because of rising taxes. In the latter case, the availability of public or private secured loans could mean that most taxpayers experiencing unanticipated increases in property value would face not the loss of the property, but its encumbrance. The necessity of such an encumbrance—when an increase in property wealth outstrips the cash resources—is the essence of wealth or asset taxes, levies not based on cash income. A similar situation may arise even without any change in the tax if the owner suffers financial reversals that leave the home unaffordable.[4] This issue of fairness is thus a question of property rights and whether the public has a claim on a portion of these privately held assets.

Issues of Uniformity

The property tax is not a wealth tax because it reaches only one specific asset. Ironically, this particular type of nonuniformity was a major goal of 19th century tax reformers who saw that the attempt to tax all property, real and personal, moveable and immovable, was doomed to failure. Widespread evasion of the tax on stocks, bonds, bank accounts, and financial assets left farmers and owners of real estate to bear the burden of a nominally universal levy.

One such reformer was Columbia University Professor E. R. A. Seligman, who almost a century ago drew attention to attacks on the general or universal property tax as "a tax upon ignorance and honesty" and "a premium on perjury and a penalty on integrity." To bolster his arguments, he cited an 1897 New Jersey study: "The only ones who pay honest taxes on personal property are the estates of decedents, widows and orphans, idiots and lunatics" (Seligman 1913, 27–28). He pronounced the general property tax "beyond all doubt one of the worst taxes known in the civilized world," providing the title for a subsequent history of the tax (Fisher 1996). However, Seligman was not referring to the property tax as it exists in the United States today, but rather to a *general* property tax, an attempt to tax personal property, real property, tangibles, and intangibles alike. The real property tax, which discriminates between real property and other assets, represents the triumph of an earlier reform movement that saw the futility of attempting to tax wealth on a local basis.

Within the category of real property itself, questions of fairness stemming from nonuniform treatment are of two distinct types. The first is the result of legislative provisions that mandate differential taxation according to the type of property or the status of the owner. The second stems from administrative favoritism or incompetence that without legal sanction assigns different values to properties of equivalent market price, an issue dealt with in the next section.

As a political matter, explicit, legal instances of nonuniformity are extremely difficult to remedy because they enjoy powerful support. In fact, this consideration bridges the divide between the two types of nonuniformity because widespread illegal (or "extra-legal") classification of property was initiated for the same reason. Typically, state legislative and constitutional provisions requiring uniformity in taxation were ignored by informal systems favoring residences at the expense of industrial and commercial property, and favoring certain types of business property at the expense of others. When courts grew willing in recent decades to overturn such practices, legislatures and voters often responded by changing the legal basis for assessment in order to sanction such nonuniformity.[5] If classification has made the property tax more popular, has it exacted a price in fairness? This question can be considered in the context of three major types of property generally accorded special treatment: property used for charitable purposes, farmland in the urban fringe, and owner-occupied residential property.

Many specific charitable exemptions are the subject of intense political debate (Brody 2002). The exemption of church property has long been attacked as inconsistent with the separation of church and state (Balk 1971; Robertson 1968). The growing commercialization of medical services has prompted similar challenges to hospital exemptions (Hyman 1990), and YMCAs have seen vigorous efforts by private health clubs to limit their exempt status (Cooke 1999). In general, however, the existence of legal challenges and energetic public debate undermines any general conclusion that such exemptions constitute evidence of unfairness *per se*. These exemptions are a public grant, the result of a political process and amenable to change by that process, rather than an inherent part of the property tax itself. The issue of unfairness is better directed to systemic failures in the political process, such as absence of information or lack of protection for minority interests.

The two other examples illustrate the types of procedural questions such an inquiry might pursue. Every state provides some form of preferential tax treatment for farmland in the urban fringe, usually by basing its assessment on value for agricultural use rather than market value. The widespread support this practice enjoys indicates a strong political consensus that farmers should not be forced to sell their land because of rising market values—a variant on the dispossession of the homeowner—and that preservation of farms, forests, and open space in the urban fringe is desirable. Yet, the operation of such programs can be at odds with this rationale. Rather than preserving land for the community, they may subsidize speculation by reducing the cost of holding land off the market for maximum profit. They may actually encourage urban sprawl as development is pushed farther from the urban area served by existing infrastructure.

Changing the assessment basis from market value to current use does not benefit farmers in rural areas where agricultural use remains the most profitable use. The tax reduction will be proportional to the disparity between value for agricultural purposes and value for development. In one Arizona case, valuation on the basis of agricultural and grazing income produced an assessment of $3,455 on property purchased for $4,500,000 by a developer who "candidly testified that the purchase was for investment and that he had taken initial steps toward

developing it" (Glennon 1990, 305). A measure designed to protect agricultural land thus afforded a subsidy for development and speculation.
This situation is not unique or unrepresentative,[6] and it raises obvious
questions as to whether public support for farmland preservation would
extend to explicit provisions of this sort. If not, this underscores the
importance of informed debate on property tax policy—as well as the
fairness implications of the subsidies themselves. Concerns about fairness led Henry Aaron to conclude that "special farmland exemptions are
inequitable and should be repealed. They specifically reduce taxes for
owners of a rapidly appreciating asset and, hence, rapidly growing
wealth" (1975, 86). Debate on the fairness of these measures, and the fit
between their goals and their actual impact, might consider such alternatives as tying them to long-term restrictions on development, imposing substantial financial penalties on changes in use, and specifying the
community benefit required in exchange for this subsidy.

Another type of systemic unfairness arises when exemptions that
unquestionably enjoy broad support penalize minority or unrepresented taxpayers—whether deliberately or as an unintended, but
inevitable, result of favoring others. This bears on the operation of a
"residual tax" that provides general revenue for a jurisdiction or special
district. In these cases, the tax rate is usually set annually, after an
accounting of other revenue sources, budget needs, and the total current
assessed value of taxable property. Subject to rate and levy limitations, a
reduction in the tax base through exemption or preferential assessment
of one type of property increases the tax rate on the remaining base. Far
more directly than income or sales taxes, whose rates are set by legislation
and changed infrequently, a residual tax displaces the benefit enjoyed by
full or partial exemptions into a heavier burden on other parcels.

Provisions for preferential taxation of owner-occupied property are
also extremely common, and enjoy enormous political support. It is
because of such support that judicial efforts to enforce uniformity
requirements have often been met by changes to this legal standard
rather than by changes to assessment practices. Yet, as a result, the tax
burden on apartments—some part of which will be transferred to the
tenants in the form of higher rents—will generally exceed the tax on
houses of equivalent market value occupied by residents able to purchase them.

Similarly, disproportionate taxation of vacation homes and time-
share properties is obviously popular when the affected parties are not

able to vote in the taxing district. This is merely a variant on the use of hotel taxes, car rental taxes, and other means of exporting taxes to non-residents. It is related to the exemption issue because the heavier tax on unrepresented parties reduces the burden on voting residents. Again, an inquiry into the fairness of these measures cannot be foreclosed by their political support because, in this case, the question of fairness concerns the political process itself.[7]

Administrative Issues

The property tax has long been administered in a manner at odds with the literal provisions of its governing legislation, and these administrative issues have been central rather than peripheral to many complaints about its fairness.

Many objections to the property tax stem from uncertain and subjective elements of the valuation process itself. The irreducible element of judgment in that process means that expert opinions about the proper assessment of a specific property will frequently differ, and sometimes differ widely. The keen interest with which most homeowners follow developments affecting their own property values provides another vantage point for this debate—one not necessarily expert in assessment or appraisal *per se*, but expertly familiar with the subject property. Legal challenges to the assessment of large industrial and manufacturing properties, in which qualified experts submit appraisals differing from one another by millions of dollars, only heighten skepticism about the objectivity or fairness of the tax.

This particular charge of unfairness combines at least three distinct components. The first concerns the fairness of any tax whose calculation involves the exercise of judgment concerning points on which reasonable experts could differ. Even if some degree of subjectivity is deemed to be fair, a question of how much uncertainty is compatible with fairness remains. A disagreement about whether one suburban house would command a 10 percent premium over its neighbor has implications for fairness different from a disagreement about whether a massive industrial facility specifically built for the needs of its current owner should be assessed upon its replacement cost or its (perhaps negligible) value to a potential purchaser. Finally, the historical development of the property tax leaves the question of overt administrative malfeasance or misfeasance a legitimate issue in any debate over its fairness.

Subjectivity

The first issue—whether any element of subjectivity is incompatible with fairness in taxation—is the easiest to address, if only by looking at alternative forms of taxation. The income tax provides the most dramatic example of the extent to which the computation of the tax base can rely on judgment and informed opinion. Income taxation requires, of course, some assignment of market value to noncash items received in trade or as compensation, but this constitutes only a small part of the uncertainty inherent in its calculation. From the interpretation of arcane and highly specific legislative provisions to the application of overarching judicial concepts, the income tax in this country provides an endless array of points on which informed opinion can and does disagree. Nonstatutory questions, such as whether a transaction has a legitimate business purpose or was undertaken only for tax reasons, whether its form fits its substance, and whether its intermediate steps should be ignored and only the end result taken into account, are inescapably subjective. Nor are these uncertainties and complexities limited to returns of large corporations and sophisticated investors, as the quadrennial political debate over replacing the federal tax code with a simpler alternative demonstrates.

Consider the relationship between fairness and efficiency in the pursuit of certainty in taxation. Subjective assignments of value that can neither be verified nor disproved are obviously unfair, and suspicion that subjectivity influences property tax assessments contributes to the perception that the property tax is unfair. But certainty in taxation also provides enormous efficiency benefits, because the interpretation, application, and appeal of unclear tax provisions are very costly. The most provocative effort of recent times to replace a property tax with a more certain and efficient levy produced Great Britain's short-lived "Community Charge," or poll tax, in the 1980s. In theory, no tax could be more certain or efficient than a head tax, but, in fact, the popular judgment about its unfairness was a major element in ending Mrs. Thatcher's term of office (Butler, Adonis, and Travers 1994). Just as some elements of ambiguity are not sufficient to render a tax unfair, complete certainty is not sufficient to make one fair.[8]

Too Much Uncertainty?

This leads to a question of whether, even accepting that some ambiguity may be inescapable and acceptable, the quantum of uncertainty in the property tax oversteps the bounds of fairness. Does the fact that experts' estimates of the market value of the same property can differ by enormous sums mean that the tax is too inexact to be fair?

Almost by definition, these situations arise with regard to properties that are unusual, sometimes even unique, and infrequently traded. Experts need not agree on the market value of each parcel. Completely different approaches to the valuation process, however, signal a disagreement on the definition of market value when property lacks a conventional market in terms of competing buyers and sellers of similar goods. In such cases, as Justice Brandeis said, "Value is a word of many meanings" (*Southwestern Bell Telephone Co. v. Public Service Commission* 1923, 310), and it is not easy to identify the precise measure that should form the basis for assessment.

Should the assessment of a specialized manufacturing facility reflect its cost of construction, less depreciation? That figure might approximate the value to the owner of useful property that would be replaced if lost. In fact, one interpretation of "market value" would hypothesize an unrelated willing buyer offering this sum for the property only for the purpose of reselling it to the current owner, to whose specifications it was constructed. Bonbright termed this a "*tour de force* by which to bridge the gap between the realization value of a property and its value to the owner" (1937, 60). True realization value of highly specialized property, the actual amount that could be obtained from a party who is not the current owner, might be quite low. In the extreme case, the value of the building could even be negative, reducing the value of the unimproved site by the cost of demolition (*New York Stock Exchange Building Co. v. Cantor* 1927). Realization value and value to the owner have no necessary relationship to one another. For this reason, these types of cases that challenge the meaning of basic concepts of property and market value may present opposing positions on assessment that vary enormously. By contrast, differences in expert opinion over the value of a standard residence will represent disagreements about detail, not fundamental principles.

Public utility taxation has long raised such questions when the cost to replace useful property differs from the capitalized income attributable to it under a regulated rate structure. Similarly, federally subsidized housing subject to strict limits on permissible rents may offer special income-tax benefits to owners and investors through depreciation, credits, and low-interest mortgage loans. Should assessment of the real property reflect the restricted rents that a future purchaser would collect, or the package of cash and noncash benefits that led the current owners to make a higher investment in the property? What market value should be assigned to a television company's right to lay cable under public ways— occupying a relatively small three-dimensional volume but making possible a multi-million-dollar enterprise?

Cases like this are overrepresented in judicial opinions on property tax issues, both because they identify important ambiguities in the legal foundations of the tax and because the amount at stake for both the tax-payer and the taxing jurisdiction can justify the expenses of trial and appellate proceedings. Moreover, the task of drawing specific solutions for such cases from broad and sometimes abstract statutory and con-stitutional language poses a serious intellectual challenge worthy of extended consideration, particularly when large amounts of revenue depend on the outcome. But this attention to individual disputes does not bear on either the quantum of uncertainty in the remaining vast majority of assessments—which do reflect standard market conditions— or the fairness of those cases that must be resolved by judicial or leg-islative action.

The problem of divergent valuation opinions within the sphere of standard property has sometimes led to suggestions that the property tax utilize a self-assessment system, with owners required to accept the jurisdiction's offer to purchase their property at the amount they assign. This counters the problem of deliberate understatement of value, but faces overwhelming political and administrative difficulties. The taxing jurisdiction should not be required to assume the role of real estate broker in order to administer a tax system; more critically, homeowners should not face the loss of their houses by reason of a mistaken value estimate. Forced sale (even at a price set by the owners) of residences would be no more politically acceptable than widespread dispossession by reason of nonpayment of tax. Thus in Florida, which at one time experimented with a version of this approach, homeowner protection prevented any genuine auction or sale from establishing market value. Because owners could prevent a sale by posting a bond, the court over-turning that statute determined that "there will never be a 'willing buyer' or 'willing seller' as those terms have been historically utilized in case law. . . . Were the taxpayer compelled to relinquish his property . . . he would be more disposed to value the property at a higher price. . ." (*ITT Community Development Corp. v. Seay* 1977, 1028).

A true auction would necessarily take place some time after the assessment date, leaving the owner at risk of a rise in market value in the interim. No taxation mechanism that exposed a homeowner to what the court in this case termed a "quasi-forced" sale as the result of a good faith self-assessment error could be deemed fair or acceptable. At the same time, lesser penalties, such as collection of understated taxes with interest or fines, could not draw on the market data provided by a bona fide auction to enforce the self-assessment standard.

The Past and the Present

Although the increasing professionalization of the assessment process, together with the growth of computerized mass appraisal systems, has greatly reduced the subjectivity of property tax valuation (Eckert 1990), there is no question that inequitable assessment patterns persist. Some are individual instances not representative of national practice. The most extraordinary example is New York City, whose byzantine assessment system has remained resilient in spite of decades of meticulous documentation and vigorous attack (Finder and Levine 1990; Real Property Tax Policy for New York City 1980).

More commonly, a failure to update assessment rolls on a timely basis is due as much to inertia, understaffing, and a reluctance to upset taxpayers as to an intent to favor or disfavor specific groups. In either case, outdated assessments subsidize the (often affluent) residents of areas of increasing value at the expense of the (usually poorer) residents of declining neighborhoods. The relevant question is whether this administration failure can effectively be challenged in political or legal forums. Since it has not proved to be an inherent element of the *ad valorem* system, it is not an indictment of the tax itself.

These considerations do not exhaust the charges of unfairness in property taxation through arbitrary or uncertain assessments. Examples of unprofessional and even corrupt administration abound. In some cases, poorly trained local officials were unable to maintain accurate valuations for all parcels in their jurisdiction. In others, assessments at only a fraction of full market value attempted to understate the jurisdiction's tax base in order to obtain more state aid. Such fractional assessments could deprive taxpayers of the ability to challenge their valuations because even an owner suffering relative overassessment, and thus bearing a disproportionate share of the total tax burden, saw an unrealistically low value estimate on the tax bill. In all cases, efforts were made to shift taxes from homeowners to business and industrial taxpayers.

Acknowledging that these practices are manifestly unfair, what do they suggest about the fairness of the property tax itself? Today, when legislators and voters amend state law to permit classification and avoid court-ordered uniformity in taxation, the problem of unequal assessments is primarily political rather than legal. In fact, the most important alternative to *ad valorem* taxation—the acquisition-value tax base introduced in California by Proposition 13 and utilized in more limited ways by a number of other states—is closely linked to the "extra-legal" practices of the past. The most common of these simply carried outdated values on the tax rolls until a property was sold. That practice eliminated valuation complexities, minimized taxpayer complaints, and shifted the tax burden from longtime residents to newcomers. The Supreme Court's rejection of this approach when it was undertaken without legal sanction in West Virginia seemed to many observers to cast doubt on the constitutionality of Proposition 13 itself (*Allegheny Pittsburgh Coal Co. v. Webster County* 1989). The Court refused to take that step, and upheld Proposition 13 as a rational policy explicitly adopted by the state's voters (*Nordlinger v. Hahn* 1992). Yet these two cases offer many provocative reflections on the fairness of these most venerable and contemporary alternatives to full-market assessment.

Classification and Perceptions of Fairness

The past several decades have seen a large-scale transformation in assessment practices, in part because courts have required greater conformity to statutory and constitutional requirements of accuracy and uniformity. In 1923, the Supreme Court rejected the position of many state courts that a taxpayer whose assessment did not exceed market value, but who still bore a disproportionate share of the tax burden because of relative overassessment, could seek only an increase in the assessments of the jurisdiction's other taxpayers. The Court held that the effect of this approach "is to deny the injured taxpayer any remedy at all because it is utterly impossible for him by any judicial proceeding to secure an increase in the assessment of the great mass of underassessed property in the taxing district" (*Sioux City Bridge Co. v. Dakota County* 1923, 446).

The New York experience is further illustrative of modern judicial attempts to correct "extra-legal" assessment practices. There, the Court of Appeals in 1975 broke with long precedent and rejected fractional assessment as illegal, while recognizing that it was so widespread and had been so consistently followed that it had acquired "an aura of assumed legality" (*Hellerstein v. Assessor of Islip* 1975, 286). This decision was one in a series of state court decisions in the 1960s and 1970s over-turning long-standing fractional assessment systems (Beebe and Sinnott 1979). As in many states, New York homeowners and voters did not con-sider the court's efforts to enforce long-ignored uniformity require-ments acceptable or fair. The legislature delayed implementation of full-value assessment for six years, and then over the governor's veto permitted fractional assessment and classification throughout the state, with a particularly convoluted system in New York City and Nassau County (Dionne 1981). Was this continuation of long-standing favoritism to homeowners fair? Not according to the *New York Times:* "While this is calculated to calm uneasy homeowners, it does not adhere to the principle that taxpayers be treated fairly by some universal system" ("A Long, Wrong Realty Tax Bill" 1981).

The cochairman of the New York Suburban Coalition Against Reassessment also opposed the court, arguing that full-value assessment had "proved to be a disaster . . . the equalization resulted in unfair shifts of the tax burden onto homeowners" (Asselta 1981). This statement touches on many of the political concerns that confront efforts to imple-ment uniform assessment systems: the problem of unsettling taxpayer expectations, both concerning the values assigned to their properties and the share of the total tax burden that their class of property shall bear; the assumption that taxes on business are shifted to other parties or exported from the jurisdiction; and the belief that equalization of assess-ments produces "unfair shifts of the tax burden."

Absolute or Relative Equalization?

The California experience strongly suggests that taxpayers are far more concerned about the absolute tax burden than about inaccuracy in assess-ment. There, legislation requiring uniform valuations followed a highly publicized series of scandals involving bribery of assessors (Beebe and Sinnott 1979, 217). Schrag argues that the resulting loss of assessment discretion helped pave the way for Proposition 13 because homeowners had been the greatest beneficiaries of the discredited system. "The more fully the new law kicked in, the more the tax burden was shifted from commercial to residential property. By the late 1960s, there were bumper stickers in San Francisco: 'Bring back the crooked assessor' " (Schrag 1998, 135). The unpopularity of accurate assessments even led one author to recommend realpolitik over legalism: "Had California's assessors retained some of their pre-1965 authority to set assessments, they could have mediated at least some of the housing inflation. Homeowners would have been less battered. Local governments would have retained most of their powers" (Levy 1979, 66). Of course, the ultimate result was the demise of the California *ad valorem* property tax system altogether, replaced by Proposition 13's tax based on adjusted purchase price.

Acquisition Value and Classification

In 1989, the Supreme Court found a violation of due process in a West Virginia county's failure to update assessments except upon a property sale. Coal companies purchasing land were taxed at effective rates 8 to 35 times as high as owners of comparable property (*Allegheny Pittsburgh Coal Co.* 1989). The International Association of Assessing Officers filed an *amicus curiae* brief in support of the taxpayers, arguing that mass appraisal techniques and computerization now make annual revaluations and full-market assessments feasible, and therefore the unequal effective tax burdens produced by unauthorized classification should not be tolerated (International Association of Assessing Officers 1988).

This case led many to believe that Proposition 13 might be found similarly flawed, but three years later the Supreme Court declined to take that step (*Nordlinger v. Hahn* 1992). In fact, the Court had earlier agreed to hear a different challenge by commercial taxpayers who charged that, by favoring long-standing owners, Proposition 13 impeded the free movement of business and thereby violated the commerce clause. That case was withdrawn by the commercial plaintiffs themselves after California protesters threatened to boycott their stores (Freilich, Vaskov, and Ernst 1992, 738). The simpler West Virginia situation permitted the Supreme Court to find an equal-protection violation in a *de facto* acquisition value tax (one stemming from failure to reassess properties in the absence of a sale), while in the California case, the Court was unwilling to apply that result to an acquisition value system explicitly adopted by the state's voters.

Was the West Virginia case, indeed, simple in terms of fairness? Professor Robert Glennon offers a provocative dissenting view, finding the result to "epitomize judicial interventionism in the service of conservative political ends" similar to 19th century cases in which the Court acted as "a handmaiden to railroads and large corporations" (1990, 261). He points out that because valuing unsold residential property at the same proportion of full value as coal land might threaten the ability of homeowners to pay their taxes, the county instead lowered the valuation of the coal company property to the common level. The valuation of the coal companies' lands fell from $36 million to $2.8 million and the county agreed to refund $1.6 million to the plaintiffs at a time when its annual budget totaled only $800,000. Glennon goes on to charge that "*Allegheny* further retards the ability of one of the poorest counties in one of the poorest states to raise revenues . . . to improve its schools and its social and economic conditions" (1990, 293).

This argument intertwines questions of tax fairness with considerations of the use of the tax proceeds. It also suggests, though it does not raise directly, the question of capitalization and forewarning. If coal companies knew that the purchase of mining property would result in a reassessment at market value, would that knowledge influence the amount paid for the land—and, if so, would they still have cause for complaint on grounds of fairness?

In *Nordlinger v. Hahn,* the Court upheld Proposition 13's *de jure* acquisition value system, finding it rational for a state to choose to reward longer-term property owners, "to discourage rapid turnover in ownership of homes and businesses." The Court also endorsed the fairness of Proposition 13 on grounds of forewarning, finding that a current owner "may be thought to have vested expectations in his property or home that are more deserving of protection than the anticipatory expectations of a new owner" (*Nordlinger v. Hahn* 1992, 12).

This particular fairness argument relies completely on the issue of notice, and not at all on the distribution of the tax burden. It would apply equally to an arbitrary levy unrelated to value at all, so long as the amount was known at the time of purchase (Bogart and Bradford 1990). This heavy emphasis on foreknowledge raises important empirical questions about the capitalization of the property tax into prices paid by new purchasers and current owners alike.

The strongest critique of the majority position on grounds of fairness was made by Justice Stevens who, in his dissenting opinion, termed the long-time property owners who benefited by this arrangement the "Squires." He pointed out that the plaintiff's tax bill was almost five times as large as those of neighbors owning comparable homes, and that this situation was not unusual under Proposition 13. Because Proposition 13 allows a child to inherit a parent's acquisition value tax base for property, these disparities are not necessarily corrected even within a generation. Stevens termed this "a privilege of a medieval character" and found Proposition 13 no more a "rational" means of achieving its goals "than a blanket tax exemption for all taxpayers named Smith would be a rational means to protect a particular taxpayer named Smith" (*Nordlinger v. Hahn* 1992, 30, 36 [dissenting opinion]).

Justice Stevens also pointed out that California voters abolished that state's gift and inheritance tax in 1982, undermining the need for property tax benefits to encourage the transmission of family assets. This is a particularly interesting connection. The logic of the Proposition 13 acquisition-value system, which taxes new owners on their full purchase price, suggests that estate or inheritance taxes, also imposed at the time of transmission, could be considered fair as well. Rejection of the inheritance tax as well as the *ad valorem* property tax represents an expansive concept of property rights free of both types of governmental claims on privately held wealth.

A Note on the School Finance Debate

Although the disbursement of property tax revenues is a separate issue from the fairness of the tax itself, recent decades' debate over the equity and legality of funding local public schools through the property tax deserves special mention because this long and important challenge to past practice has often been linked to questions about tax equity. At the same time, school finance questions quickly subsume issues that are crucial to education but ancillary to fiscal policy, from pedagogical approaches and standardized testing to provisions for special-needs students. A consideration of the implications of school finance cases for the fairness of the property tax will therefore touch only on one part of this extremely complex larger debate.

The school finance issue begins with the bedrock problem of impoverished districts without adequate resources to support schools, even at tax rates far higher than those found in more affluent jurisdictions. This is not a property tax problem, but a *local* tax problem. A needy district restricted to its own income or sales tax revenues would face the same difficulty in maintaining an acceptable school system. Therefore, a district unable locally to fund adequate vital services, such as education, requires a transfer of resources. This may be the farthest reach of consensus in this debate.

By itself, this initial premise establishes only that no local tax can serve as the sole support for basic services when the local tax base is inadequate for that purpose. While this in no way demonstrates the unfairness of property taxation, several unstated intermediate steps have led to that conclusion in popular debate.

First, the property tax functions primarily as a local tax in the United States. This was not always so. Before widespread adoption of state sales and income taxes, property taxes supplied most revenue at the state level. Today, many local jurisdictions impose sales or income taxes, but the overwhelming majority of property tax collections fund local governments, and the property tax remains the primary source of independent revenue for most jurisdictions. Debate, therefore, over reliance on local resources for education finance generally focuses on the appropriateness or fairness of property tax funding.

A second and far more problematic issue concerns the distinction between adequacy and uniformity in local funding. Does the fact that poor districts require additional education resources bear upon the amount that affluent districts may raise and spend independently—funds likely to be raised by property taxes? At this point consensus ends. One perspective sees no need to reduce spending in affluent areas in order to increase support for needy districts. But another views equality of expenditure as an important statewide goal. Years of school finance reform brought California, for example, to the point where 95 percent of its school districts differed from one another in basic per-pupil spending by no more than $200 (*Serrano v. Priest* 1986). Unfortunately, the state also fell from 10th in the nation in per-pupil spending in 1969–70 to 41st in 1995–96 (Schrag 1998, 66). A national study on school quality released by the Pew Charitable Trusts in 1997 gave California a grade of D- for adequacy of resources, school safety, and discipline—*and* for the fairness of its system of school funding (Woo 1997).

The relationship of cause and effect in this example is extremely difficult to discern. The Pew Charitable Trusts' report acknowledged that California schools have faced an enormous change in their demographic makeup, with increasing enrollments and perhaps the nation's most diverse and urbanized school population. This same period also saw great increases in the spending required for special education. Passage of Proposition 13 in 1978 reduced property tax revenues, formerly a major source of school funding, by more than one-half. But property taxation limitation measures are related to school spending equalization efforts in that both shift important finance decisions from the local to the state level.

A move from local to state control over education spending can expose school budgets to new political pressure. No state is likely to fund all schools at the level the wealthiest districts could achieve independently. Therefore, a choice must be made between a system that assures impoverished districts an adequate budget without rising to the highest level in the state, or one that seeks uniform funding and does not allow localities to supplement that amount. Under the first approach, use of the property tax to increase the local school budget would not be objectionable; under the second, it would be rejected.

The second point of view was reflected in remarks by one of the attorneys who filed the original challenge to school finance in California. He complained that it was unfair to permit parents to raise funds privately for local schools: "If we have a lousy education system, then the parents of the rich have to be just as concerned as the parents of the poor. It's a common problem" (Seligman 1988). On the other hand, the very court opinion upholding the equalized system gave a frank assessment of its shortcomings, pointing out that from 1974 to 1982, formerly high-revenue districts suffered revenue decreases averaging 16 percent at the elementary level and 24 percent at the high school level. San Francisco, Oakland, and Berkeley lost 32, 15, and 35 percent of their purchasing power, respectively. San Francisco reduced its teaching staff by 25 percent, and Oakland laid off 205 regular and 142 special-needs teachers. The most disturbing part of the opinion was the court's recognition that "[t]he adverse consequences of years of effective leveling down have been particularly severe in high spending districts with large concentrations of poor and minority students"—for example, San Francisco and Oakland, in which the number of minority students exceeded 80 percent of the total student body (*Serrano v. Priest* 1986, 617–19 [footnotes omitted]).

As this opinion noted, "high wealth" jurisdictions with large amounts of commercial or industrial property often also have many low-income urban residents who may suffer because of strict equalization. And because of the social, economic, and environmental difficulties facing impoverished districts, they may require additional expenditures in order to offer students scholastic resources comparable with those found in wealthier areas. Many large cities with significant numbers of poor students spend more, not less, than the statewide average per student on public education (Minorini and Sugarman 1999a, 38). Recognizing this, recent school-finance cases have sought to provide poor areas with funding sufficient for adequate achievement, rather than funding equivalent to other districts.[9] Yet these spending decisions are made without any consensus about the definition of an adequate education, as shown by the abstract and nonoperational statements that result from judicial attempts to offer guidelines in this area.[10] In addition, shifting educational responsibility from the local to state level by no means achieves a general goal of uniformity, for it does not address differences in spending across states—differences that are far more dramatic than those between districts in individual states. "[R]oughly two-thirds of nationwide inequality in spending is between states and only one-third is within states, and thus school-reform litigation is able to attack only a small part of the inequality" (Murray, Evans, and Schwab 1998, 808).

The fairness of the property tax is an issue in this debate only to the extent that local funding is deemed unfair—and then only when the property tax serves as the local tax. A state property tax would not be judged unfair by these lights. In large part, the debate is not concerned with the operation of the property tax itself, but only with its local character. However, several ancillary points may be made about the tax itself.

First, the tax has long been associated with its use for property-related services, such as police and fire protection. This connection is by no means exact: A newly constructed building with private security guards may require far fewer public services than a deserted structure of very low market value. But the underlying parallel between the property tax and a fee for services has been one of its political strengths. To this extent it is necessary to confront the fairness of linking education and property in order to evaluate this particular challenge to the tax.

Because education is a basic and vital need, an argument can readily be made about the unfairness of rationing it according to property, wealth, or income. Again, however, the distinction must be made between an entitlement to adequate education on the grounds of its vital nature and the removal of education from market mechanisms altogether. Confusion between the two risks unintended consequences, particularly when dissatisfied parents can withdraw their children from public schools.

In some cases, the capitalization process that links property values to local spending may provide a fiscal incentive for effective local schools. If homes in successful local school districts enjoy enhanced property values, owners will have a reason to support those schools—even if they do not themselves have children in public school (Fischel 2001). They may also have reason to oppose wasteful or ineffective spending that does not benefit the schools and therefore the value of their property. The capitalization of the tax itself into housing prices also undercuts a major argument against the fairness of local taxation: Poorer districts require higher tax rates than wealthy districts in order to raise equivalent or even lesser amounts of revenue. This argument is found in many school finance opinions, but it does not take into account the economic perspective that "[t]he taxpayer, by virtue of the process of capitalization, has bought himself free from any calculable, unequal part of the tax."

To the extent the as-yet-unresolved issue of adequate educational resources for poor communities can be separated from the ability of affluent districts to invest higher amounts, the need for the former does not establish the unfairness of the latter. As long as private schools remain an option for affluent individuals, restrictions on district spending risk undermining support for public education generally. Such restrictions need not take the form of absolute prohibitions, however. Vermont school finance reform, for example, permits districts to spend more than the standard state education allowance, but the state then redistributes a portion of its taxes to other districts. The state-set spending level was $5,010 per student in 1999, a figure that 90 percent of the school districts exceeded. Those districts are free to raise funds to supplement the state level, but are required to return a portion of these funds to the state to be redistributed—a portion that increases with district wealth. Dorset, Vermont, which was spending $3,000 per pupil more than the statewide average, raised property taxes by 35 percent but still faced a loss of 20 percent of its school budget (Ehrenhalt 1999).

The critical link between public acceptance of local property taxes and use of those taxes for local benefits is broken most dramatically in this case, with a tax increase accompanying a reduction in school funding. Professor William Fischel (1989) has long argued that the California school finance reform of the 1970s, which similarly eliminated the connection between local taxes and local school spending, may have been a major cause of popular rejection of *ad valorem* taxes in Proposition 13. Professor Steven Sheffrin puts this view in more general terms, arguing that school finance litigation "undercuts the rationale for the property tax as a truly local tax. In my view, homeowners were willing to pay higher property taxes if they were convinced this led to quality schools. The school finance litigation movement essentially breaks this tie" (Brunori 1999, 1722).

Restrictions on local spending also motivate schools to raise money in other ways. In Vermont, for example, a charitable foundation has matched private donations to replace tax revenues lost to local schools.[11] In California, more than 500 educational foundations have been established as a means of supplying voluntary nontax contributions to public schools (Brunner and Sonstelie 1996).

Conclusion

This chapter has considered two distinct categories of questions about the fairness of the property tax: those concerned with technical aspects of its structure and administration, an area in which a great deal of improvement has been achieved and more is required; and those objecting to the concept of an *ad valorem* tax, a tax not based on transactions or earnings.

The first category constitutes a challenge to tax design and administration. Property tax professionals can greatly enhance the fairness of the tax by improving the valuation, collection, and enforcement processes, paying special attention to valuation methodology. Although sophisticated issues in the valuation of unusual business property pose many intellectual challenges, they are less critical to a fair valuation process than the continual revision of general assessment rolls to maintain accurate value estimates. Allowing outdated values to stand unchanged not only compounds existing unfairness, but also makes the more dramatic changes needed at a later time far more difficult and disruptive.

The second category can only be addressed by informed public debate on the merits of alternate concepts of property rights. The property tax's reservation of a continuing public claim on privately owned real property is both its unique strength and the root of its greatest unpopularity. Although familiar, this tax is not unambitious. Annual taxation of market value, even at modest rates, confers on the public a significant share of the benefits of ownership, and it is not surprising that this should prove controversial.

An informed controversy should consider the strengths and benefits of this system as well as its drawbacks. These include the advantages of a highly visible tax and the desirability of independent finance for local government, the effect of capitalization, and the availability of exemption and deferral measures to mitigate the threat of dispossession. Balanced attention to alternatives to *ad valorem* taxes, such as an acquisition-value tax, would consider the drawbacks and unfairness of the alternatives as well as their advantages. A discussion about the fairness of the tax should also place new emphasis on distinguishing the treatment of land and buildings, recognizing land as a unique economic element—immovable, in fixed supply, and drawing value from surrounding community growth and investment.

These challenges are substantial, but they offer the prospect of improving the application and acceptability of a levy with benefits beyond the fiscal realm. A revenue instrument that effectuates a public claim to the enhanced property value produced by community growth and public investment has an important place in a fair tax system.

NOTES

1. In reporting on James Gilmore's successful Virginia gubernatorial campaign, which centered on a pledge of "No Car Tax," the *Washington Post* termed the tax "easily the most derided and scorned levy" ("Car Tax Driving State, Local Races" 1997).

2. "The primary reasons for repealing the estate tax are given in a 1998 Joint Economic Committee Study. The report concludes the estate tax decreases the incentive to work, is punitive, and is the leading cause of dissolution of family-run businesses. Rep. Jennifer Dunn, R.-Wash., of the House Ways and Means Committee, put it more emotionally, stating the current tax treatment of a person's life savings is 'so onerous and so burdensome that children are often forced to turn over half of their inheritance to the Federal Government. It is as wrong as it is tragic, and it dishonors the hard work of those who have passed on' " (Yamamoto 1999).

3. In *New York Trust Co. v. Eisner* (1921), Justice Holmes rejected a challenge to the federal estate tax "as a direct tax not apportioned as the Constitution requires." He ruled "not by an attempt to make some scientific distinction, which would be at least difficult, but on an interpretation of language by its traditional use—on the practical and historical ground that this kind of tax always has been regarded as the antithesis of a direct tax" (349).

4. Even Habitat for Humanity will evict low-income homeowners who take title to its subsidized housing but default on their mortgage obligations (Meredith 1999).

5. In *Burns v. Herberger* (1972), the Arizona court explained the sequence in that state:

> Prior to the *Southern Pacific* case, the taxing statutes required that all real property in the state should be assessed at its "full cash value." . . . The various county assessors of this state had traditionally ignored this legislative mandate and based valuation upon various self-made classifications, the end result of which was a discriminatory and arbitrary taxing system which was rightfully struck down in the *Southern Pacific* case. . . . When the results of this new valuation were made public, the hue and cry, especially from the agricultural, livestock, and small homeowner interests of this state, was loud and vociferous.

As a result, a special session of the Arizona legislature enacted a new tax statute calling for current use to be "included in the formula for reaching a determination of full cash value." A.R.S. sec. 42-123, A(5) (1967).

6. See, for example, *Roden v. K & K Land Management, Inc.* (1978) (agricultural classification upheld for land purchased for amusement park development); *Harbor Ventures, Inc. v. Hutches* (1979) (agricultural classification upheld for land rezoned at owner's request for planned unit development); *Fisher v. Schooley* (1979) (agricultural classification upheld for land purchased for commercial development). See also Hanley (1997a):

> The headquarters of BMW of North America sits on a bluff in this well-to-do suburb, flanked by apple and peach trees. Not only does the orchard offer a pleasant view to BMW workers choosing to eat lunch outdoors on warm days, it also provides a significant tax break for the company. The property tax bill for the 20-acre orchard is just $373.52. The owners of houses across Chestnut Ridge Road from the BMW headquarters don't come out so well at tax time. One neighbor who has 1.2 acres paid $3,446.94 in taxes; another paid $2,651.18 for three-quarters of an acre.

and Hanley (1997b):

> The upper-middle-class residents of Florie Farm Road have nice two-story colonial homes on tidy half-acre yards. Property taxes in the 25-year-old subdivision range from $4,705 to $5,606 a year—moderate for the upscale suburbs of northern New Jersey. Meanwhile, not far away, out on Horseshoe Bend Road, the owners of a 15-acre meadow where eight beef cattle graze get a tax bill of $295.40. A 31-acre wood lot that produces five to six cords of firewood a year is taxed $613.97.

7. The economics of capitalization also affect the distribution of the tax burden itself to the extent the heavier taxation of one type of property has influenced the prices buyers are willing to offer for it.

8. See Doherty (1999, 35–36) on the public acceptance of the council tax that replaced the poll tax—an example of economic measures of progressivity diverging perceptions of fairness: "The system is not related to ability to pay . . . but it gives the appearance of being progressive whilst it is, in practice, regressive in nature. It is, however, accepted by taxpayers and is actually perceived as fair."

9. "In 1989, the Kentucky Supreme Court declared the entire state system of public elementary and secondary education unconstitutional and held that all Kentucky schoolchildren had a constitutional right to an adequate education. The decision resulted in a dramatic overhaul of the state's entire public school system, and sparked what many scholars have called the 'adequacy movement' " (Minorini and Sugarman 1999b, 175, referring to *Rose v. Council for Better Education* [1989]).

10. *Rose v. Council for Better Education* (1989) stated:

> We concur with the trial court that an efficient system of education must have as its goal to provide each and every child with at least the seven following capacities: (i) sufficient oral and written communication skills to enable students to function in a complex and rapidly changing civilization; (ii) sufficient knowledge of economic, social, and political systems to enable the student to make informed choices; (iii) sufficient understanding of governmental processes to enable the student to understand the issues that affect his or her community, state, and nation; (iv) sufficient self-knowledge and knowledge of his or her mental and physical wellness; (v) sufficient grounding in the arts to enable each student to appreciate his or her cultural and historical heritage; (vi) sufficient training or preparation for advanced training in either academic or vocational fields so as to enable each child to choose and pursue life work intelligently; and (vii) sufficient levels of academic or vocational skills to enable public school students to compete favorably with their counterparts in surrounding states, in academics or in the job market [footnotes omitted].

11. See Hanlon (1999):

> Although property-wealthy towns have trimmed their budgets to a degree to avoid the impact of the sharing pool, they have spent a great deal of effort to find other ways around sharing their revenues. Many property-wealthy towns have established private funds to collect donations, rather than taxes, from their townspeople. The Freeman Foundation of Stowe, a private charity, has pledged matching funds to most of the property-wealthy towns (and to a few property-poor towns as well). The result is a shortfall in the projected revenues from the sharing pool.

and "Vermont Towns to Get Education Aid" (1999):

> A Stowe philanthropic organization is set to distribute $14 million to schools in 30 towns to match money raised locally for the public schools. The money distributed by the Freeman Foundation would enable some of the 75 schools in those towns to maintain programs without having to raise local taxes as drastically as would be required under Act 60, Vermont's new education funding law.

REFERENCES

"A Long, Wrong Realty Tax Bill." 1981. *New York Times,* 7 November, editorial.
Aaron, Henry. 1975. *Who Pays the Property Tax: A New View.* Washington, D.C.: The Brookings Institution.

Allegheny Pittsburgh Coal Co. v. Webster County. 1989. 488 U.S. 336.

Asselta, Judi. 1981. "How to Protect the Homeowner." *New York Times,* 2 December.

Baer, David. 1998. "Awareness and Popularity of Property Tax Relief Programs." *Assessment Journal* 5: 47–65.

Balk, Alfred. 1971. *The Free List: Property without Taxes.* New York: Russell Sage Foundation.

Beebe, Robert L., and Richard J. Sinnott. 1979. "In the Wake of *Hellerstein:* Whither New York?" *Albany Law Review* 43: 203–93, 411–86, 777–860.

Bogart, William T., and David F. Bradford. 1990. "Incidence and Allocation Effects of the Property Tax and a Proposal for Reform." *Urban Economics* 8: 59–82.

Bonbright, James. 1937. *The Valuation of Property,* vol. 1. New York: McGraw-Hill.

Brody, Evelyn, ed. 2002. *Property-Tax Exemption for Charities.* Washington, D.C.: Urban Institute Press.

Brown, H. James, ed. 1997. *Land Use and Taxation: Applying the Insights of Henry George.* Cambridge, Mass.: Lincoln Institute of Land Policy.

Brunner, Eric, and Jon Sonstelie. 1996. "Coping with *Serrano:* Voluntary Contributions to California's Local Public Schools." *National Tax Association Proceedings* 89: 372–81.

Brunori, David. 1999. "Interview: Steven M. Sheffrin on the 'Worst Tax,' Local Options, and Proposition 13." *State Tax Notes* 17: 1721–23.

Burns v. Herberger. 1972. 498 P.2d 536 (Ariz. App.).

Butler, David, Andrew Adonis, and Tony Travers. 1994. *Failure in British Government: The Politics of the Poll Tax.* Oxford: Oxford University Press.

"Car Tax Driving State, Local Races." 1997. *Washington Post,* 2 November, Prince William Extra, V1.

Cooke, Sarah. 1999. "Private Fitness Clubs Say YMCAs Receive Unfair Advantage." *Oshkosh Northwestern,* 8 August.

Dionne, E. J., Jr. 1981. "A Loss and a Gain." *New York Times,* 5 December.

Doherty, Patrick. 1999. "Collection of Local Taxes." *Journal of Property Tax Assessment and Administration* 4: 31–41.

Ebel, Robert, and James Ortbal. 1989. "Direct Residential Property Tax Relief." *Intergovernmental Perspective* 15: 9–14.

Eckert, Joseph K., ed. 1990. *Property Appraisal and Assessment Administration.* Chicago: International Association of Assessing Officers.

Ehrenhalt, Alan. 1999. "Schools + Taxes + Politics = Chaos." *Governing* 13: 27–31.

Finder, A., and R. Levine. 1990. "When Wealthy Pay Less Tax than the Other Homeowners." *The New York Times,* 29 May, A1.

Fischel, William A. 1989. "Did *Serrano* Cause Proposition 13?" *National Tax Journal* 42: 465–74.

―――. 2001. *The Homevoter Hypothesis.* Cambridge: Harvard University Press.

Fisher v. Schooley. 1979. 371 So.2d 496 (Fla. Dist. Ct. App.).

Fisher, Glenn W. 1996. *The Worst Tax?* Lawrence: University Press of Kansas.

Freilich, Robert, Laurie L. Vaskov, and Frederick Ernst. 1992. "1991–1992 Supreme Court Review: The Court's New Path—The Middle Ground." *The Urban Lawyer* 24: 669–759.

Glennon, Robert J. 1990. "Taxation and Equal Protection." *George Washington Law Review* 58: 261–307.

Hanley, Robert. 1997a. "Five Acres, and a Tax Break?" *New York Times,* 12 January, sec. 13NJ, 1.

———. 1997b. "How Tax Bills Stack Up against a Flock of Sheep." *New York Times,* 12 January, sec. 13NJ, 10.

Hanlon, Paul. 1999. "Band Aid Proposed for Property Tax Act." *State Tax Notes* 16: 565.

Harbor Ventures, Inc. v. Hutches. 1979. 366 So.2d 1173 (Fla.).

Hellerstein v. Assessor of Islip. 1975. 37 N.Y.2d 1, 332 N.E.2d 279, 371 N.Y.S. 2d 388.

Hyman, David A. 1990. "The Conundrum of Charitability: Reassessing Tax Exemption for Hospitals." *American Journal of Law & Medicine* 16: 327–80.

International Association of Assessing Officers. 1988. Brief *amicus curiae* in support of petitioners in *Allegheny Pittsburgh Coal Co. v. Webster County.* U.S. Supreme Court Nos. 87-1303 & 87-1310.

ITT Community Development Corporation v. Seay 1977. 347 So. 2d 1024 (Fla.).

Jensen, Jens P. 1931. *Property Taxation in the United States.* Chicago: University of Chicago Press.

Levy, Frank. 1979. "On Understanding Proposition 13." *The Public Interest* 56: 66–90.

Mackey, Scott. 1992. "State Property Tax Relief Programs for Homeowners and Renters." *State Tax Notes* 2: 474–79.

Mackey, Scott, and Karen Carter. 1995. "State Tax Policy and Senior Citizens." *State Tax Notes* 8: 1405–25.

Meredith, Robyn. 1999. "Charity Group to Foreclose on 14 Homes." *New York Times,* 28 December, A16.

Minorini, Paul A., and Stephen D. Sugarman. 1999a. "School Finance Litigation in the Name of Educational Equity: Its Evolution, Impact, and Future." In *Equity and Adequacy in Education Finance: Issues and Perspectives,* edited by Helen F. Ladd, Rosemary Chalk, and Janet S. Hansen (34–71). Washington, D.C.: National Academy Press.

———. 1999b. "Educational Adequacy and the Courts: The Promise and Problems of Moving to a New Paradigm." In *Equity and Adequacy in Education Finance: Issues and Perspectives,* edited by Helen F. Ladd, Rosemary Chalk, and Janet S. Hansen (175–208). Washington, D.C.: National Academy Press.

Murray, Sheila E., William N. Evans, and Robert M. Schwab. 1998. "Education-Finance Reform and the Distribution of Education Resources." *American Economic Review* 88: 789–812.

Netzer, Dick, ed. 1968. "The Impact of the Property Tax: Its Economic Implications for Urban Problems." Report of the National Commission on Urban Problems to the Joint Economic Committee of the U.S. Congress. Washington, D.C.: U.S. Government Printing Office.

———, ed. 1998. *Land Value Taxation: Can It and Will It Work Today?* Cambridge, Mass.: Lincoln Institute of Land Policy.

New York Stock Exchange Building Co. v. Cantor. 1927. 221 A.D. 193, 223 NY.S. 64, *aff'd mem.* 1928. 248 N.Y. 533, 162 N.E. 514.

New York Trust Co. v. Eisner. 1921. 256 U.S. 345.

Nordlinger v. Hahn. 1992. 505 U.S. 1.

Real Property Tax Policy for New York City: A Study Conducted under Contract with the Department of Finance, City of New York. 1980. New York University Graduate School of Public Administration.

Robertson, D. B. 1968. *Should Churches Be Taxed?* Philadelphia: Westminster Press.

Roden v. K & K Land Management, Inc. 1978. 368 So. 2d 588 (Fla.).

Rose v. Council for Better Education. 1989. 790 S.W.2d 186 (Ky.).

Schrag, Peter. 1998. *Paradise Lost.* New York: The New Press.

Seligman, Edwin R. A. 1913. *Essays in Taxation,* 8th ed. New York: Macmillan.

Seligman, Katherine. 1988. "Creative Fund-Raisers for Schools Keep Affluent Districts Humming." *San Diego Union-Tribune,* 18 November, B20.

Serrano v. Priest. 1986. 226 Cal. Rptr. 584 (Ct. App.), *transferred and dismissed* 1988. 763 P.2d 852 (Cal.).

Sioux City Bridge Co. v. Dakota County. 1923. 260 U.S. 411.

Southwestern Bell Telephone Co. v. Public Service Commission. 1923. 262 U.S. 276.

Verbrugge, Henk. 1997. "Collection and Enforcement." Paper presented to the Conference on Designing Local Government for South Africa, Pretoria.

"Vermont Towns to Get Education Aid." 1999. *The Boston Globe,* 8 January, B3.

Woo, Elaine. 1997. "Report Gives Low Marks to State Schools." *Los Angeles Times,* 17 January, A3.

Yamamoto, Kevin. 1999. "Power Practice; Effects of an Estate Tax Repeal." *Texas Lawyer,* 13 September, 35.

Youngman, Joan M., and Jane H. Malme. 1994. *An International Survey of Taxes on Land and Buildings.* Deventer and Boston: Kluwer.

9

And Equal (Tax) Justice for All?

C. Eugene Steuerle

Concepts of equity and fairness are at the heart of tax policy. Political leaders pay homage to these ideals in virtually every sphere of lawmaking and regulation. Citizens, moreover, are keenly sensitive to arguments about fairness in almost every policy debate.

Yet, for all its populist appeal, tax equity is loosely understood and inconsistently applied. This concept comprises at least three distinct dimensions: horizontal, vertical, and individual equity. The very real tension among these components complicates efforts to craft "fair" tax policy, prompting political debates that invoke the rhetoric of equity without engaging its substance. The most vociferous arguments have centered on the uneasy relationship between vertical equity—most commonly manifested in progressive tax and expenditure structures—and the demands of individual equity, in which individuals freely engage in transactions of their own choosing. While support for some application of vertical equity seems clear, determining the appropriate degree of progressivity has proved to be difficult.

Various details further complicate efforts to apply tax equity in a rigorous and productive manner. Progressivity remains a touchstone in debates over fiscal policy, yet it often means one thing when applied to tax and something very different in discussions of spending. Moreover, crafting fair tax policy is further confused by discussions about the appropriate tax base—income, expenditure, or something else—as well as the many adjustments that can be made to any of these bases. An adjusted tax base often represents an attempt to define equality and inequality along some measure of net well-being.

In the face of all this controversy and complexity, many theorists have thrown up their hands. Many economists, in particular, have often dismissed fairness as more an issue of aesthetics than of analysis. A large contingent has not merely focused on questions of efficiency but largely abdicated its role in debates over tax equity. In doing so, however, these researchers have ceded the ground once dominated by their predecessors—from Adam Smith in the 18th century to Richard Musgrave in the 20th century. The abandonment of tax equity is misguided, stemming from a misunderstanding of the contributions that economists are uniquely prepared to make. Even assuming that answers to fairness questions are more political than mathematical, economists have a vital role to play. They may not always be able to pinpoint the "right" answer in terms of fairness, but they can frequently identify approaches that more consistently and efficiently accommodate the public's demand for equity—a demand as legitimate as its demand for other public services.

Ultimately, tax equity—for all its complexity and undeniably political nature—remains too important an issue for economists to simply forfeit on or to ignore when creating solutions to difficult public finance issues.

The Universal Demand for Equity

Nothing is more fundamental to the character of a successful democracy than its citizens' trust in judicial and legislative processes that protect basic human rights and provide equal justice under the law. These rights are powerful notions—ones for which people have freely given of their lives and property. From the Magna Carta to the U.S. Constitution to the French Declaration of the Rights of Man, one can trace continual efforts to claim for each citizen—defined in broader and more inclusive terms over time—his or her fair due. Many declarations and conventions, such as the United Nations' 1948 Universal Declaration of Human Rights, assert that certain rights are derived from the human condition; they are not merely temporary, national, or cultural preferences.

Efforts to assert equal justice extend beyond these lofty documents, reaching into the everyday world of politics and policy. Indeed, it is hard to identify any major governmental action—legislative, regulatory, or symbolic—in which fairness is not a dominant concern. Consider, for instance, the names attached to legislation. How often do words like equity, opportunity, and fairness appear? Consider, also, how even regulatory processes are designed to allow anyone claiming unfair treatment access to an almost judicial consideration of their claim. How often are regulations delayed or even reversed because of such considerations? Furthermore, consider the use of symbols in a public setting. What authority can, as a matter of equity, deny a statue to some excluded group—veterans of a forgotten war, women who served in war as well as men, black war heroes as well as white ones—in a park already cluttered with statues?

Equity's status as a political principle is unique, but it is not always the driving force behind action. Other objectives—efficiency, growth, simplicity—often take precedence. Emergencies demand attention and sometimes require equity shortcuts. Still, other objectives are almost never pursued without due attention to the equitable distribution of burdens and benefits. In formulating education policy, for example, government officials may want to subsidize education to promote a strong and growing society. Educational programs, however, will inevitably feature significant redistributive elements. Officials will offer arguments rooted in equality of opportunity—somehow defined—as a standard for designing the program. "Equal access to education" or some other catchphrase will permeate debates over proposed subsidies.

Not every principle receives such homage. For example, compare simplicity with equity. Simplicity routinely falls by the wayside in tax bills designed to make some final outcome more progressive or more evenly distributed among those in similar circumstances. A tax simplification bill, on the other hand, cannot veer too far toward inequity before losing political support. An arbitrarily applied tax might be easy to administer, and, if simplification were the only goal, a random tax might be the most efficient way to achieve the objective, but such taxes cannot be enacted.

That tax and expenditure laws are subject to demands for fairness and justice may sound strange. These laws, after all, are widely considered some of the principal "honey pots" of policymaking. Tax and expenditure systems are vehicles for much of the logrolling endemic to democratic legislatures. Even legislation historically recognized as "fair" often includes questionable riders attached to buy winning votes. Indeed, many such riders fail to meet a standard of equal justice.

Examine, however, the arguments put forward to support even the poorest legislation. Instead of attacking the equity standard, lobbyists frequently try instead to twist it for their own purposes. Rather than arguing for special treatment, they assert that some source of inequity justifies their demand for compensation. Such groups might suggest, for example, that past Congresses intended for them to receive some benefit and therefore that the law should now be recrafted to their benefit. In turn, wherever existing legislation draws a line, these lobbyists seek to secure their place on the side that receives more expenditures or pays less tax. Their arguments usually feature examples in which some individual or group in an almost identical situation receives more favorable treatment.

In arguments over fairness, the ground constantly shifts underfoot; raise one standard of equity and another will be cited in its stead. Equal treatment of those with equal incomes may be fine, but advocates for veterans, members of groups that have traditionally suffered from past discrimination in the tax or spending laws, persons in poor health, and individuals who simply start out with less opportunity to acquire income will reject equal income as an adequate measure of equality. The equity standard itself is not being rejected, but its application.

The demand for equity and equal treatment is so natural we often take it for granted. C. S. Lewis, a theologian known best for his children's tales, once suggested that, as a matter of natural law, we humans always appeal to some standard of behavior. We justify our behavior, whatever it is, so we can live with our consciences. In dealings between individuals, Lewis asserts, "It looks, in fact, very much as if both parties had in mind some kind of Law or Rule of *fair* play." In effect, we justify even our worst behavior as a matter of equity (Lewis 1943, 17).[1] Similarly, individuals reject arbitrarily being treated differently, whether by a family member, stranger, or an elected representative.

Under a rule of law, all government actions must be lawful. Under such a system, however, lawfulness and justice are synonymous. Thus, the individual demand for justice, identified by Lewis, is enhanced by a societal demand in legal matters. Arbitrariness in the law is unacceptable. The most ignoble client must still be represented. Remember the classic legal joke about the defense for stealing a pot: "I never stole it; it was broken, and, besides, it was worthless in the first place." This kind of argument has at its core an equity claim—that "I" should be exonerated or charged with nothing because that would be the only fair outcome, one way or another. Tax and expenditure laws, too, must always appear to meet justice standards.

Equity, then, is the first and most basic set of principles applied to constitutions and laws. While constitutions and courts require "equal justice under the law," they do not require greater efficiency or simplicity. No other standard reaches the lofty status of equal justice in the affairs of government or the souls of humans. While conflicts abound, they are much more likely to arise over how to apply the principle consistently, how to measure who are equals, and the extent to which compensation or special consideration should be applied to those who are different along some scale of fortune, need, or ability.

Horizontal and Vertical Equity

Even if equity were not the highest of principles in both lawmaking and administration, it undoubtedly plays a dominant role in the debate over the allocation of taxes and expenditures. Beyond a broad level of abstraction, however, equity must be defined in practical ways in order to allocate these budgetary obligations and rights. Equity and equal justice do not mean equality in all things. In matters of the state, these concepts refer to the way that government will treat us, not our starting point. Since no two people are exactly alike or equal in all things, the task of maintaining equity under the law is far from dull. Indeed, the complex political undertaking of applying equity principles to practical situations has occupied philosophers and government officials since civilization began. Disagreements abound, generally centering on questions about who should be treated as equals, who should not, and what to do about those differences.

Here the public finance literature, particularly as explained by Richard and Peggy Musgrave, is extraordinarily useful in the way it distinguishes between horizontal and vertical equity.[2] Horizontal equity refers to the treatment of equals, vertical equity to adjustments made among nonequals. If income were the only measure of a person, for example, then horizontal equity demands that two persons with equal incomes be treated as equals. Alternatively, vertical equity is based on the premise that someone with little or no income will have difficulty paying the same amount of income tax as someone who is rich.

The easiest and often most useful way to conceptualize horizontal and vertical equity is to imagine people along a particular scale. A classic scale used in the tax literature (but interestingly enough, less in the expenditure literature) is ability—originally thought of in terms of "faculty" as measured by property, but more recently conceived as being measured by income.[3] Thus, we speak of taxing people according to their ability to pay.

Horizontal equity requires that those with equal status—whether measured by ability or some other appropriate scale—should be treated the same. They should pay the same amount of tax and receive the same amount of benefits. As a consequence, those who start out as equals before any governmental action would end up as equals after the government acted. For example, suppose equals are defined by ability, which, in turn, is defined by income. In that case, those starting with the same before-tax income should end up with the same after-tax income.[4]

Vertical equity, for its part, generally requires that those with less ability be treated favorably relative to those with greater ability. Progressivity is often considered synonymous with vertical equity, but even economists trained in the literature of public finance do not apply the term consistently.

Some theorists have argued that horizontal and vertical equity are different sides of the same coin.[5] In other words, the contention that those who *have* less should therefore *pay* less and *receive* more reflects the same concern that those with equal status be treated equally. This belief derives partly from a concept of equity whereby people are placed on a single scale so that the appropriate tax or expenditure is a simple function of what is measured on that scale. For example, if taxes are a positive function of income and income only, then both horizontal and vertical equity fall out of the same functional form.[6]

Despite this functional relationship under one theoretical (almost mathematical) approach to understanding equity, I assert that horizontal and vertical equity should not be viewed as two corollaries of the same principle. Many people strongly support horizontal equity even though they reject the notion that government must adjust the status of any individual along a particular scale. Such a position is not inconsistent.

Examples abound of the application of horizontal equity to government programs: Those individuals with equal incomes should be made to pay equal income taxes. Consumers who purchase the same items at the same price should pay the same sales tax. People living at equal levels of poverty and having equal need should be entitled—at least within their jurisdiction—to equal amounts of food stamps. Indeed, the importance of horizontal equity reaches beyond the realm of economics. Equal crimes should be made to bear the same punishment. Various chemical companies should all be subject to the same environmental limitations on chemicals they can use for agricultural purposes. Automobile companies should face the same limitations on pollution. Each citizen should have an equal right to vote, and so on.

Note, however, that many of these laws are not intended to redistribute or achieve some vertical equity standard. Some, like pollution controls or sales taxes, might be adopted for different reasons and be regressive in their distributional effect. But the demand for equal justice does not go away. Thus, while it is possible to identify government programs that do not aim at and ever contradict some vertical equity goal, identifying one that does not apply some horizontal equity standard, however imperfectly, is virtually impossible. And when equally situated individuals appear to be treated unequally under one definition, it is often because alternative definitions of equality have cast these individuals as unequal.

From one end of the political spectrum to the other, horizontal equity is a universally accepted principle. There are no sides, no divisions between conservatives or liberals, and no conflicts between advocates of big or small government. If a person can prove that he or she is just like another, then no one will likely challenge his or her case for equal treatment under the law. In some ways, horizontal equity is almost tautological: If people are defined as equals, how can government treat them differently, thereby making them unequal? Horizontal equity is a basic application of the broad societal commitment to equal justice.

When it comes to vertical equity and progressivity, on the other hand, agreement quickly breaks down. Economist Herb Stein made this point during 1959 congressional hearings on tax reform, pointing out that while horizontal equity is the "the first, basic rule of taxation," considerations of vertical equity seem to amount to value judgments, questions of degree, and subjectivity. "If A's income is twice B's," Stein asked rhetorically, "should A's tax be twice B's, or one and one-half times or three times as large? . . . Intuitive standards of equity seem to throw no light on questions of 'How much?' " (1959, 110, 114). Conservative economist Harley Lutz condemned the subjectivity of vertical equity. "There is no just or progressive tax rates scale," he insisted in his *Guideposts to a Free Economy*. "Every such scale is the product of guesswork and of political and fiscal expediency. And where expediency is the basis of policy, it is easy to lapse into injustice" (1945, 70, 82). Every person has a particular notion of how progressive government should be, how much it should be involved in assessing different amounts of tax on individuals with different means, or helping differentially those with different needs. Whatever the degree of subjectivity, at one level or another the debate over progressivity has often dominated public debate and even led to the toppling of governments. It was a major issue in the debate between socialism and capitalism, while progressive treatment of the poor and impaired is used continually to assess the success of governments in developed and developing nations alike.

The attack on vertical equity often goes too far. In the historical debate over vertical equity, almost no one argued that the poor should pay more than the rich. This consistency implies that even those who argued that progressivity was a fluid, subjective standard at some level still accepted it as a requirement. For example, *every* example given by Stein involved a larger tax on the richer person than on the poorer person.

When governments try to rectify some real or perceived vertical inequity, some amount of redistribution is almost inevitable. This redistribution may come as a higher tax on a richer person or result in some sort of transfer to the poorer person—in cash, in-kind services, or access to opportunities, such as education. In distributing taxes and expenditures—and regulatory requirements as well—there are usually those who pay and those who receive. In both cases, government shapes the lives of individuals. No matter how necessary or valid such action may be, therefore, it often sparks controversy and conflict. After all, any interference involves costs that, in turn, demand justification.

Vertical Equity versus Individual Equity

Vertical equity connects the rights and obligations of individuals to their ability and well-being. While often applied formally to government finance and expenditure programs, a similar standard applies in the ordinary affairs of the family and community. Within the family, for example, those who can work are expected to contribute more financially than those who cannot. Dependents often have obligations, but fewer than those of working-age adults with greater maturity and ability. Thus, common sense, not just philosophy, leads us to accept vertical equity as a general principle.

Vertical equity often competes head-on with the principle of individual equity, which emphasizes each individual's freedom to partake in transactions without interference by third parties, including the government. In general, each voluntary transaction involves an exchange between two individuals, each of whom expects to be better-off as a result. Government interference in that transaction diminishes the gains for at least one individual and often the total gains to be shared. Moreover, government intervention can distort the nature of the transaction, perhaps even deter it altogether.

In practice, governmental efforts to promote vertical equity usually involve taking from an individual on the basis of a transaction, such as the sale of labor, the employment of capital, or the purchase of some good or service. Consequently, tax issues (along with regulation) are among the most likely sources of claims that government has violated individual equity.

At times it is possible to tax in a way that either does not violate the principle of individual equity or at least minimizes the extent of the violation. In the former case, the transaction between the individual and the state is voluntary, and the individual would not pay unless he received a benefit worth the price paid. In the latter case, the benefits of government action are designed to be approximately equal to, or closely related to, the taxes or contributions made.

The public finance literature distinguishes between "benefit" taxation and taxation according to "ability to pay." With benefit taxation, the tax paid to the government is roughly equivalent to a price paid in the market—only in this case the good, or service, is furnished by the government rather than the private sector.[7] Highway tolls are a common example. By contrast, applying an "ability-to-pay" standard means individuals pay taxes regardless of their highway use.

Adam Smith, the father of economics, is often accused of confusing benefit and ability-to-pay taxation in his argument that individuals "ought to contribute to the support of the government, as nearly as possible, according to their respective abilities [ability-to-pay taxation]; that is, in proportion to the revenue which they respectively enjoy under the protection of the state [benefit taxation]" (1904, 310). But it is not so clear that he was inconsistent, at least for most government taxes in his day and time. Consider the government's primary activities in the latter part of the 18th century: the defense of the state and its people, the maintenance of order and police protection, the sponsorship of trade and new industry, and the enforcement of contracts. Since the resulting benefits could not be calculated easily on an individual basis, it is easy to argue that the benefits were closely related or even proportional to ability to pay. Hence, for some public goods and services, it is possible for benefit taxation and ability-to-pay taxation to result in the same distribution of the tax burden.[8]

If purely voluntary, benefit taxation would not appear to violate the principle of individual equity—assuming that the government did not run a monopoly that distorted prices or otherwise restricted individuals' purchasing choices. Many governmental transactions, however, are involuntary, and the value of those public goods and services cannot easily be attributed to individuals. Some activities, like defense, require collective support. As a practical matter, taxpayers are compelled to share in these costs simply to eliminate "free riders"—those who avoid paying but get the benefit anyway.[9]

Of course, when government engages more in making transfers than providing other public goods, the benefits to transferors are unlikely to equal the involuntary taxes each pays. If there are benefits to the social order, or if most people in society want to act collectively to prevent poverty, for example, then some form of coercion is still required. Individuals have little incentive to contribute voluntarily to such actions, since their individual contributions make little difference. Democracy tries to limit this coercion by requiring that at least a majority of people favor such enforced action, but majorities can still reduce the freedom of minorities.

Mandated benefit taxation violates individual equity, even if individuals receive a benefit from what they put into a system. If I give up a dollar and get back a dollar in some mandated benefit, then I have less freedom than if I am left with my dollar in the first place. For example, considerable debate arises today over the establishment of mandated individual saving accounts inside or outside a social security system. Interestingly, such accounts designed as a carve-out from existing taxes garner support from many libertarians as a move toward individual equity. On the other hand, these same libertarians oppose individual accounts as another form of government interference when they are recommended to be financed from an add-on tax. The difference seems to be that in the case of the add-on, interference is viewed as increasing because the sum of mandated taxes plus contributions to the individual account are higher than the old social security tax.

The rise of social insurance in the 20th century has necessitated new thinking about how to achieve a balance between vertical equity and individual equity in the presence of substantial moral hazard. Social insurance is as much a problem about who should pay as about who should benefit when society decides to provide a minimum level of well-being.[10] Take the case of preventing poverty in old age. A traditional welfare approach—as opposed to social insurance—would simply grant benefits only to those with low incomes. It is very easy, however, for the old and near-old to drop out of the labor force or give their assets to their children to lower their income and disguise their ability to pay. In addition, two people with equal incomes all their working lives may differ in their saving patterns so that one ends up better-off in old age than the other. Most people would consider it unfair to force the saver to transfer to the nonsaver when both had equal saving ability throughout their working lives. Yet, assistance to the nonsaver would force such a result.

Social insurance attempts to deal with this problem by mandating individual contributions for retirement. At the same time, most social insurance programs try to achieve some redistribution from those with greater lifetime ability to those with lesser lifetime ability. Once government mandates that people partly take care of themselves—for example, by contributing to their own retirement, it is difficult then to come in the back door and phase out benefits entirely when income rises as would a welfare system. A hybrid system—one that involves some redistribution but also mandates that individuals receive some return—is a compromise solution.

Even if a social insurance system gives some insurance back to all contributors, the net transfers it makes to those with lower wages or incomes ensures that some people are not going to get back all the money they paid in taxes.[11] The point is simply that social insurance exemplifies an approach that combines a type of benefit taxation—mandated because of a moral hazard problem—and taxation according to ability to pay within the same overall program structure.

In many public debates, advocates will approach equity issues only from the standpoint of vertical equity or individual equity. Think tanks are set up to argue for either more redistributive or more libertarian government. Redistributional policy is sometimes presented as being always good or always bad. Such views reflect a lack of balance. The tension between the two equity principles is healthy. That government programs reflect ability and need is only natural, but restricting individuals' freedom to act is costly.

How Much Progressivity?

The debate over vertical equity has raged at least since the dawn of public finance as an academic specialty. That debate centers on how much progressivity is appropriate, if any. (At this point, the term "progressivity" will be used synonymously with "vertical equity," suspending a discussion of the inconsistent definition of progressivity in the tax and expenditure literatures.) While there is no clear-cut answer, there *are* standards by which some rational judgment can be made. One standard might try to assess the relative amounts of sacrifice individuals should bear; another might assess efficiency losses from different alternatives. Once again, balance is key.

Throughout most of the relatively short history of economics as a formal discipline, the progressivity debate has centered mainly on taxation, rather than government expenditures. Economists have repeatedly sought to define the optimal amount of progressivity in terms of the sacrifice that individuals should make.[12] The very use of the term "sacrifice" narrowly emphasizes the tax (or cost) rather than expenditure side of the issue. That is, one doesn't usually think of sacrifice in the same breath as accepting a benefit. The basic sacrifice theory is utilitarian and based on the commonsense notion that, at the margin, those who have more resources bear less sacrifice when they give up a dollar—for example, by reducing the amount of caviar for their yacht luncheon—than do those with fewer resources who might be threatened with, say, starvation.

Under utilitarian sacrifice theory, then, well-being is a declining marginal function of ability, income, or wealth. This assumption can be examined along several closely related dimensions. It not only implies that a richer person values a dollar less than a poorer person, but, depending upon the rate of decline in utility, it similarly implies that a person with $100,000 might value an additional $10 only as much as someone with $10,000 would value an additional $1. Such comparisons lead to discussions about equal absolute sacrifice, equal relative sacrifice, and equal marginal sacrifice. Economics students are even taught to toy with various precise mathematical relationships between utility and the consumption made possible by income (for example, that utility or well-being equals the square root of consumption). Under these precise mathematical assumptions, economists can develop formal measures to compare the "utility" sacrificed by different taxpayers.

Although these pedagogical devices are useful, no one can really measure someone else's utility nor assess how much sacrifice anyone else has made, regardless of their starting level of ability, wealth, or income. At the same time, despite its inability to *prove* that some degree or another of progressivity is ideal, the utilitarian approach still enjoys widespread commonsense appeal.

In the middle of the 20th century, a series of scholars, including Henry Simons, Walter Blum, and Harry Kalven, argued that progressive taxation was probably a good thing, but they suggested that the case for it was "uneasy" (Blum and Kalven 1953). In their view, a progressive system seemed desirable, but its justification was essentially aesthetic, not economic. As Henry Simons offered in a famous commentary: "The case for drastic progression in taxation must be rested on the case against inequality—on the ethical or aesthetic judgment that the prevailing distribution of wealth and income reveals a degree (and/or kind) of inequality which is distinctly evil or unlovely" (1938, 18–19). Simons offered this defense during a period in which the worldwide debate between socialism and some sort of refined capitalism or mixed economy was raging far and wide, a historical context that helped tip the scale in favor of substantial progressivity, whatever its shaky intellectual underpinnings.

Again, even the most adamant arguments about the shakiness of the progressivity principle never held that the poor pay more than the rich. Nor can one find any treatise suggesting that the income or wealth distribution should be more unequal than it is. Even the early benefit-tax theorists often suggested that the poor- or moderate-wage earner was not expected to pay tax, following the notion that many or even most of the nonpropertied class earned only "subsistence wages." The modern variation suggests that those with incomes below the poverty level should not be required to pay income tax. Modern flat-tax advocates, for example, usually allow for some amount of wages to be exempt from tax. In effect, this stipulation means that their proposals do not have flat rates, but a progressive rate schedule with two rates—one zero and one positive.

By the 1970s and 1980s, many trained economists were being taught that equity was no longer relevant to their discipline. Economics, they were told, had little to contribute to the debate, thus dismissing 200 years of substantial contributions from Smith to Musgrave. The new view, however, was only a logical extension of the notion that equity was simply a matter of qualitative judgment, more an art than a science. Economists were encouraged, instead, to focus on efficiency. Much of their training centered on how interference in various market transactions among individuals distorts behavior, so it was here, not in qualitative equity judgments, that they had some relative advantage.

By the 1980s, supply-side economists stretched these arguments into the political arena but with very strong emphasis on how progressive rate schedules would reduce aggregate saving and the labor supply. If equity did not matter, and only efficiency mattered, then taxes should be set so as to minimize these very large distortions. The net result, the argument went, might be much higher growth rates for the economy as a whole.

To understand how taxes might distort more when progressivity is increased, a little background is in order. Distortions result mainly from marginal rather than average tax rates. In the case of an income tax, lower tax rates on the first dollars earned by many taxpayers are likely to have inframarginal effects and should not affect their behavior. Correspondingly, rates at the highest income levels are more likely to be marginal, because they are more likely to apply to the last dollars of income. For example, the decisions of someone with income of $50,000 would not be affected much by whatever rate applied to the first $10,000 of income. That individual might, however, decide to either work less or save less depending on whether a 40 percent or 20 percent rate applied to income of more than $50,000.

The supply-side attack on progressive taxes, therefore, scarcely mentioned equity as an issue and argued mainly for lowering the highest marginal tax rates, which often applied at the top of the income distribution.

The logical extension of supply-side theory, in fact, is the old argument that head taxes are the most efficient form of tax. If everybody is taxed the same merely for existing (assuming that such a tax can be assessed and collected and that incentives for having children are not affected), then taxes would not affect any dollar earned or consumed after the tax was paid because there would be a zero tax rate on all marginal decisions. The simple fact that almost no supply-sider, no matter how extreme, proposes a head tax as a substitute for all taxes indicates that vertical equity issues are a concern to supply-siders after all—just as Stein hinted at earlier by never giving examples where the poor paid more than the rich.[13]

The new view of equity has been iconoclastic in its sweeping generalizations. For example, even if progressivity is in the eye of the beholder, horizontal equity, or the equal treatment of equals, or equal justice under the law cannot be brushed aside so easily. Thus, equity concerns are not beyond the pale of economic design. Moreover, it is possible to think rigorously about progressive scales rather than imply that all choices along those lines are merely subjective. And, finally, efficiency standards can determine whether equity or progressivity is being advanced efficiently. For example, if a program is designed to help the poor, then such standards can assess whether money is targeted efficiently to meet that end or is wasted on the nonpoor. The potential distortive effects of different levels of progressivity can also be compared.

An uneasy truce now exists between the iconoclasts and most practitioners of public policy and finance. The latter recognize the power of equity principles in the development of policy, but no longer ignore efficiency issues as some—perhaps many—did in the past. The former, despite their claims of indifference to equity principles, are often the first to fall back on them. For example, supply-siders have argued that an across-the-board or proportional tax cut is "fair" (are they merely playing to the politics of equity or do they believe that fairness does matter?). Likewise, many opponents of progressive taxation argue that expenditure programs should be targeted more at the poor; using extreme assumptions about the inapplicability of equity standard, wouldn't random distribution of benefits be just as fair and distort behavior less?

The Inconsistent Measure of Progressivity in Tax and Expenditure Systems

Roughly speaking, a tax or expenditure system is more progressive if it tends to redistribute more wealth from those who are better-off to those who are less fortunate. Beyond that basic understanding, however, progressivity can mean different things to different people. Inconsistencies permeate not just the general press but the academic literature—often with powerful effects on policy development.

One of the most arbitrary distinctions arises from the separate treatment of progressivity in tax and expenditure systems. Even in the most sophisticated newspapers and magazines, tax policy and expenditure policy are likely to be covered differently. Sometimes whole publications are devoted to only taxes or only expenditures. Legislatures separate their expenditure authorization and appropriations committees from their tax committees. Politicians running for office separate their advocacy for lower taxes from their support of more spending, as if the two didn't have to come into some balance.

Textbooks compartmentalize taxes and expenditures as well. Modern public finance texts usually examine the progressivity, horizontal equity, efficiency, and simplicity of tax systems. Their approach to expenditures, however, is very different—often focusing on cost-benefit analysis and how it might be applied to different programs.

Tax progressivity is normally defined relative to a proportional tax system. Take the case of an income tax. If the tax rate is constant, then the same percentage of income is owed to the government by all individuals, no matter what their income. This system is defined as proportional. If tax rates rise as income increases, the system is progressive; if they fall with income, then it is regressive. (Of course, many systems are progressive in some ranges and regressive in others.) Note, however, that higher taxes (not tax rates) are still paid by those with higher levels of income in proportional systems and in many regressive systems.

A different analysis is usually applied to expenditures. In welfare and other income-tested programs, benefits fall as income rises. A system is often said to be regressive when middle-class or rich individuals get more benefits per person than poor individuals. In effect, progressivity here is defined as the granting of more dollars to those with less ability, or income, or other measure of well-being. If a public education or highway system provided the same level of benefit to everyone, for example, then few would claim it was progressive. When an expenditure system (for example, educational grants) gives more to those with higher levels of income, it is often attacked as being regressive.

In the drafting of legislation, congresses and parliaments often display distributional tables and analyze policy changes in the same divided way. Tax cuts and tax increases are usually compared by the percentage change in tax liability, while expenditures are usually compared by how many dollars go to an individual in each income class.

The two measures of progressivity are inconsistent. The tax measure is defined with respect to rates, the expenditure measure with respect to dollars. This inconsistency means that a regressive tax system and a regressive expenditure system can together be progressive. Indeed, when expenditures and taxes are considered together, most government programs—including those drawing resources from proportional and even regressive taxes—end up redistributing from the more to the less wealthy.

To understand this concept, assume a world with only two taxpayers, one with an income of $10,000 and the other with an income of $50,000 (see table 9.1). Imposing a "regressive" tax system in which rates are 20 percent for the first $10,000 of income and 10 percent for any additional income means that the poorer taxpayer pays an average tax rate of 20 percent, while the richer taxpayer pays an average rate of only 12 percent. Assume under a simultaneous "regressive" expenditure system that the taxpayer with $10,000 of income gets $3,000 in benefits and the taxpayer with $50,000 of income receives $5,000 in benefits. In this case, total taxes paid equal total expenditures received, so it is easy to see the net effect of the combined tax and expenditure system. The net gain for the taxpayer with $10,000 of income is $1,000, while the net loss for the taxpayer with $50,000 in income is $1,000. Calculating net taxes (taxes less benefits) or net benefits (benefits less taxes) proves the system's overall progressivity by almost any definition.

The relationship between taxes and expenditures is easier to understand in these systems, where taxes are dedicated to specific outlays. Most individuals consider social security and Medicare progressive, even though taxes and expenditures in each are regressive (based on the inconsistent definitions discussed previously). The tax rate is constant up to a maximum earnings level, then falls to zero. Therefore, taxes are

Table 9.1 *The Inconsistent Measure of Progressivity*

	Taxpayer A	Taxpayer B	Total
Income	$10,000	$50,000	–
Taxes	$2,000	$6,000	$8,000
Average tax rate under so-called "regressive" tax system	20%	12%	–
Benefits under so-called "regressive" benefits system	$3,000	$5,000	$8,000
Average benefit rate	30%	10%	–
Net taxes (taxes less benefits) in overall progressive structure	-$1,000	+$1,000	$0

Note: In this example, Taxpayer B is richer than Taxpayer A, pays a lower rate of tax, receives more in benefits, and yet the system still redistributes some of B's wealth to A.

slightly less than proportional. Meanwhile, benefits are larger for those with higher levels of earnings and, in most cases, with higher levels of income. Yet, these systems are intended to be redistributive to those with lower levels of earnings and, based on net taxes or net benefits, are usually meant to be progressive.

In sum, it is limiting and often misleading to define the progressivity of a tax system independently of what is done with those taxes, or as a corollary, to measure the progressivity of an expenditure system without considering how the necessary revenues are raised.

Determining the Tax (and Expenditure) Base

The theory of equity powerfully influences policymakers. Its practice, however, raises difficult issues. Whether discussing horizontal or vertical equity, it is necessary to define who are equals and who are unequals. The application of equity to a program requires some scale or base—or multiple scales. And even if a simple scale is used, it must be amenable to practical measurement.

Take the idea that equals will be determined according to ability. With what scalar does one measure ability? For many centuries, ability in the field of taxation was measured by property. Before the rise of the middle class, the propertied classes were largely considered to be those "able" to pay; the rest of the population often lived close to a subsistence level. Property, in turn, was largely defined by land. Along with tariffs, the property tax tended to be the primary source of government revenue even as late as the 19th century. In the United States during that period, local property tax collections normally far exceeded state and local taxes or federal tariffs and other federal revenue sources (Brownlee 2000).

But property was limited as a measure of ability. Although the term "human capital" is relatively modern, it has long been clear that some individuals are capable of earning more than others, and that differences in earning power are as important, if not more important, than differences in property ownership. The hoarder might have more property, but the enterprising worker might enjoy much higher levels of both income and consumption.

The rising middle class, in particular, focused attention on income, a measure of ability based on a flow concept, rather than property, which is a stock concept. As merchants, manufacturers, and their workers expanded in numbers and economic significance, skills and human capital became more recognized as major income sources. Yet it was only with the ascent of the corporation and other large organizations that wage payments, profits, and other income could be accounted for with enough accuracy and thoroughness that the income tax could move to center stage in the evolution of tax systems. While there were previous occasional attempts at income taxation, such as the Civil War income tax in the United States, they were still constrained by inadequate income accounting systems.

Consider the situation even in developed industrial countries in the middle of the 19th century. Most people still lived on farms, their income was often in-kind in the form of crop yields, and markets were still likely to involve significant barter without the exchange of money (for example, crop sharing and the exchange of meat, produce, and services among farmers). Whether the farmer kept good books or not, there seldom was anyone on the other side of the ledger whose books could be cross-checked by a tax agent. Even today, net income reported by farmers and sole proprietors is estimated to be underreported by more than one-third in developed countries.

The corporation, on the other hand, seriously needed good income accounting for payments to workers and returns on its activities, even if this need meant creating records not easily hidden from the tax agent. To assess optimal employment and investment patterns, the large business needed to know which of its many enterprises and branches were profitable (yielded net income). It had to keep track of wages paid to its many employees in its many divisions. A large organization would find it most difficult to keep a hidden set of books for tax purposes when so many people are involved; collusion is also harder. Moreover, the wage earners' records of wages received could now be checked against the large organization's records of wages paid, and vice versa. Thus, the rapid advance of the income tax in the 20th century coincided with the development of accounting systems whose records could be tapped for enforcement purposes.

Income had another advantage as well. It could be applied as a measure of ability not just to those who paid taxes, but to those receiving expenditures. Welfare and other means-tested programs in most countries now rely primarily on income as the measure of well-being and as a primary determinant of the amount of subsidy or expenditure that is provided.

Income, however, has never been fully accepted either as an appropriate measure of who are equals for tax purposes, or as the base on which progressivity, if any, should be assessed. Localities and states still retain real estate taxes, as well as personal property taxes levied against such items as automobiles—indicating some tendency to revert back to property as a measure of ability. Estate and inheritance taxes also are levied against property value passing in an estate.

Moreover, wage taxes are also assessed quite widely. In theory, they represent solely a tax on the returns from human capital and work effort. In practice, however, separating wage from capital income is nearly impossible unless there is a formal mechanism to achieve this purpose, as when a corporation accounts for stock earnings separately from the wages of workers. Within the small business, on the other hand, seldom are returns for the business easily separable into capital and labor components; most noncorporate business owners pay wage taxes, such as social security tax, on their capital income as well as on labor income.

Wage taxes, however, are usually associated with some form of social insurance, which ties the tax directly or indirectly to a particular benefit, such as social security, unemployment compensation, or workers' compensation. In those cases, equity tends to be defined within each program as a whole. If redistribution within those programs beyond that normally associated with private insurance did not exist, the taxes could be considered benefit taxes in the form of mandates to purchase insurance for oneself, and the primary equity issue would be whether the mandate itself was fair. However, those programs also redistribute or determine taxes and benefits according to ability. Yet, the redistributive function is often hidden within the insurance function. That fact tends to complicate analyses of whether the programs are fair in the way they treat households in similar circumstances (horizontal equity), provide a fair insurance policy for the premium or tax paid (individual equity), and redistribute to those with greater needs (progressivity).

A major tax debate revived in recent years has centered on the notion that consumption, not income, should represent the principal base for taxation. Separate states within the United States have often assessed excise taxes on the purchases of goods and, sometimes, services. In most countries around the world, a value-added tax (VAT) is a major source of revenue and is designed to allow deductions for investments in such a way that it can be considered a consumption tax. While the VAT often competes with an income tax, it seldom displaces one, at least in developed countries. Recent consumption tax proposals, on the other hand, have offered progressive rather than proportional consumption taxes as a complete substitute for progressive income taxes—often attempting to focus on the appropriate measure or scalar to use rather than on the degree of progressivity.

Among the many equity issues surrounding the consumption tax debate is the question of whether it is fairer to assess tax on individual consumption or earnings. Also of importance is whether two individuals with equal lifetime earnings and inheritances should be taxed the same on a lifetime basis, or whether the one who saves more—and, hence, generates more capital income—should be taxed more. Interestingly, advocates of consumption taxes over all other tax bases do not carry their equity arguments beyond the direct tax system itself. They have yet to explain fully how ability can be measured consistently between tax and expenditure programs and why, if consumption is the right base for explicit income taxation, it isn't the correct base for the implicit taxes used to phase out expenditure benefits. For instance, if all taxes and transfers are assessed on the basis of consumption, then millionaires with low levels of consumption will receive welfare benefits. If these benefits are phased out based on income, however, then we are partially back in an income tax world.

In practice, most governments have tended to use various measures—property, income, wages, or consumption—as a tax base or a base for determining eligibility for expenditures. This multiplicity of bases does not mean that equity does not matter—in that case, almost any base would qualify without reason or rationale. But it does reflect the difficulty of reaching consensus on just who are equals before the law and who are unequal enough to pay more tax or receive more benefits. In the end, only democratic processes are able to resolve those differences.

Adjustments to the Tax Base

Treating equals equally and unequals progressively are the two basic equity principles applied to tax and expenditure policy. Measuring who are equals involves more than deciding which tax base—income, consumption, property, wages, or any other—is adequate.

Even when a base, such as income, is chosen, further adjustments and refinements are usually considered. Seven types of adjustments or sources of disparity will be examined here: income in-kind, potential income or consumption, need, transfers paid and received, prices, household size, and measurement period. Because income is the most prominent measure by which industrial nations assess taxes and eligibility for expenditures, this discussion will primarily center on disparities relative to an income base, although many of the same adjustment issues arise with other bases.

Income In-Kind

Measurement for tax and expenditure purposes almost always uses recorded market transactions where money is the medium of exchange. Important barter transactions are excluded. Perhaps most important, existing measures ignore home production, even though a great many services are provided from the home, and many goods are produced there. This equity issue has come to the fore in recent years because of the movement away from home production and the rise in two-earner couples. One question, for instance, is how to treat one-earner versus two-earner couples with respect to work-related expenses and child care and whether or not those market-related expenses are appropriate adjustments to the measure of net taxable income (or consumption).

Potential Income

Perhaps the most serious defect in using income and almost all other tax bases to determine equality is that they focus not on potential but on actualization. If people with equal ability should be treated the same, then there is no equity reason—although there may be very practical administrative reasons—to more heavily tax the person who works harder or retires later. The problem is most serious in cases where individuals simply avoid recognizing or using their potential. Thus, when it comes to designing welfare and retirement programs, determining the extent to which subsidies and lower taxes to low-income individuals should be allowed is difficult because differences in actual potential are hard to distinguish from differences in realized potential.

Take two individuals each capable of earning $40,000. One works and pays taxes. The other does not work, pays no taxes, and collects benefits. If they have equal potential, then their benefits and taxes should be the same, not different.

Often the law tries to make distinctions in potential by relying on a separate categorical qualification other than income—such as age (old or young) or physical or mental impairment. Even here, however, measures are crude. In recent years, for instance, with the extraordinary growth in the number of individuals who are retired for one-third or more of their adult lives, many have questioned whether someone really has less ability (and, therefore, is more worthy of transfers and less capable of paying tax) simply because he has reached a 62nd birthday.

Unfortunately, potential—whether in the form of income, property, or anything else—cannot be measured well. Few would suggest that individuals should pay tax according to arbitrary assumptions about ability. If we assume naively that all individuals have the same ability, then the appropriate tax on ability is a head tax—an equal tax on all individuals just for existing. Yet, few believe that mere existence measures ability or that billionaires have no more potential for paying tax than anyone else.

Assessing ability among those who work full-time is easier. Differences in wage rates are related to differences in potential. Even here, however, it is clear that some jobs are easier than others, and some persons are glad to earn less in exchange for more leisure on the job.

Need

While many individuals may possess the same earning potential or realize the same amount of income, they do not necessarily have the same level of need. For example, one person may be in poor health and have large medical expenses. Few would argue that someone with $50,000 of income and $25,000 of annual medical expenses has the same ability to pay tax or the same need for government subsidy as someone who has the same income and is identical in all other respects except that he has no medical expenses.

Adjustments for Interpersonal Transfers and Other Taxes

Tax and expenditure systems also make adjustments, albeit inconsistently, for transfers made and received. The core issue is whether to measure household ability before or after transfers are made. For example, the existence of tax breaks for households with nonworking spouses reflects, in part, a view that some of the earner's income is transferred to the spouse, who should be granted his or her own tax-free level of income.

Charitable deductions are allowed partly on the theory that the transferor should be taxed on net income available for consumption, although a strict but unenforceable adherence to consistency would then require that the beneficiaries be taxed on transfers received.

Federal deductions for state and local taxes follow a similar transfer logic: If the tax does not generate services closely related to the amount of tax paid, then those taxes are less like fees and more like transfer payments to the eventual beneficiaries of the services.

Adjustments for Prices

Still another problem arises when $1 of income is really worth a different amount in different jurisdictions. Suppose it costs $20,000 in New York City to achieve the same standard of living that $10,000 will buy in Lexington, Kentucky. Then a person with $20,000 in New York City would not have an equal ability to pay an extra $1 in tax as a person with $20,000 in Lexington.

Adjusting for prices, however, is not easy. In national income accounting, there is no pure way to compare one set of prices with another. Moreover, where there are multiple differences in price, comparisons of income can be done using multiple scales. For example, suppose that rent, food, and clothing all cost twice as much in New York City, but only New York City offers access to Broadway plays. For a person uninterested in those plays, New York City may look expensive relative to Lexington, but for one whose life is consumed by such plays, New York City is a real bargain. Once differences are established on average for one region versus another, moreover, the intraregional differences are often as important or more important than the interregional differences.

Adjustments for Family Size

A difficult issue in both tax and expenditure theory centers on the "household unit." For example, if the goal is to tax all units in equal circumstances equally, how should one-person families be compared with two-person families?

One attempt to measure equals, according to family size, is through an "equivalence scale." Despite its esoteric name, most people deal with this type of scale all the time. Perhaps the most familiar application is to poverty. When the government reports a certain number individuals in poverty, it is measuring their income against an equivalence scale. That scale might treat a single individual with $8,000 of income as being in poverty, whereas for a married couple the equivalent standard might be $11,500, and for a married couple with two children it might equal $16,000. Here there are two types of adjustments. Each additional individual in the family is generally treated as costing marginally less to support at a given standard of living, and children are usually treated as costing less than an adult.

Equivalence scales are based on the notion that there are economies of scale in living together. Yet, the application is quite arbitrary. For example, adults living together include students in dormitories, the elderly in old-age homes, unmarried couples living together, friends in shared apartments, and married couples sharing a home. Typically, tax and expenditure systems force equivalence scale adjustments on two adults only if they marry, regardless of whether they live together and achieve the economies of scale or not.

On the other hand, tax systems often treat income as if it is shared among married couples in some split, such as 70-30. In a progressive income tax, such as in the United States, this system allows those with more uneven splits—for example, 90-10—to effectively push more income (in this case, 30 percent rather than 10 percent for the low-earning spouse) into the lower tax brackets. Here a "marriage bonus" is created—thus taxing two married adults with very unequal incomes less than two adults with equivalent incomes living separately. On the other hand, those with 50-50 income splits would pay marriage penalties relative to other couples with equal combined income.

Endowment and the Accounting Period

A final and crucial issue often ignored is that a tax system almost inevitably must arbitrarily choose an accounting period over which to tax or determine expenditures. Such arbitrariness is largely a function of practical administration: The tax system usually latches onto the conventions of financial accounting with its annual focus. Nonetheless, a 5- or 10-year period, or even a lifetime, would represent a different way of measuring who are equals and who are not.

Many years ago it was shown how endowment could be considered as equal to the present value of wages and inheritances received and also equal to the present value of consumption and inheritances made.[14] According to this accounting, one might not want to tax capital income during life, since that would penalize a person according to when he or she saved and consumed rather than how much funds were available to consume or transfer over a lifetime. Thus, ignoring transfers, this lifetime perspective provides some justification for a consumption tax over an annual income tax. If one takes transfers into account, however, then this perspective suggests that we could tax those with equal endowments equally if we had either a wage tax backed up by an inheritance tax or a consumption tax backed up by an estate tax. In that last case, however, the tax would be more like an income tax with a lifetime accounting period than a consumption tax.

Conclusion

That equity principles have a powerful influence on policy should not be surprising. Equity is closely associated with justice, and justice is closely aligned with lawmaking.

Many, if not most, public laws represent attempts to improve equity. Even laws that emphasize other concerns, such as efficiency, must pay homage to equity principles. From this lofty ideal, we then turn to details. Different notions of equity compete—for example, vertical equity and redistribution toward the needy compete with individual equity, which asserts people's right to transact freely with others. Equity is not even defined consistently between tax and expenditure systems, so that what is sometimes called regressive tax policy and regressive expenditure policy can still be progressive; this inconsistency is made most apparent when programs with both designated taxes and benefits are considered as a whole.

The base or bases by which to measure who are equals and who are more or less able to pay must be determined; this requirement is no easy matter, and much disagreement persists among those who emphasize income, consumption, or some other measure as the base. Finally, in determining who pays taxes and who receives expenditures, possible adjustments for the potential income of the individual, household size, transfers made, lifetime endowment, and many other items must be taken into account.

In the midst of this complexity, it is tempting to conclude that equity must merely be in the eye of beholder and that there is no reason to pay homage to the standard of justice when developing policy. Some economists imply, and others state, that their profession has nothing to say about equity. From this perspective, equity debates are merely over unmeasurable qualitative matters, similar to competing assessments of a work of art.

In some cases, progressivity is really what is being attacked as unworthy of economic analysis; in other cases, almost all aspects of equity are under siege. Economists are told to focus their efforts on the efficiency aspects of government policy and, it would seem, turn the equity debate over to lawyers and advocates.

This chapter reclaims the equity ground on which policymakers instinctively move, and on which economists from Adam Smith to Richard Musgrave quite naturally walked. The problem of public finance cannot be separated from the development of a just society. Political decisionmakers need the best advice on how to create a just society, which means much more is at stake than simply minimizing the inevitable distortions that accompany all tax and expenditure systems. Equity is not only a legitimate field of inquiry for economists, but also a necessary exercise for any would-be policymaker who must balance the benefits and costs of various public actions. Public finance without consideration of equity is like a body without a soul.

The attempt to apply benign neglect to equity involves two types of errors. The more general error is the idea that since no simple standard of equity can be proclaimed universally and applied simply, no standard exists. The more specific misjudgment is that no "scientific" analytical thinking, or at least economic reasoning, can be applied to making equitable choices.

That one cannot necessarily proceed from the particular to the universal, of course, is well-known; this given exposes the logical weakness of the first, more general attack. The presence of hard choices does not mean the absence of viable choices. Suppose a person finds $100. He or she could, perhaps, think of a million good ways to spend the money. He or she could also find a trillion ways to waste the money.

Tax and expenditure choices are merely the public equivalent of these private decisions. If only one choice were feasible or rational, we would have less need for a democracy to sort out choices in a nonviolent manner. Nonetheless, equity principles can be applied usefully even in the midst of disagreement. One example occurred during the tax reform effort at the Treasury in 1984. At that time, those who favored a consumption tax and those who favored an income tax had reached a stalemate. Not knowing which type of tax would eventually be proposed made it difficult to start the decisionmaking process. The solution was simple: Concentrate the initial discussions on those aspects of tax law that were not dependent on the income/consumption debate, such as many itemized deductions, employee benefits, tax credits, and other preferences. In most cases, the equity choices to be made on those issues were the same for a consumption tax as for an income tax.

Thus, suppose a society is undecided over whether two people with equal consumption or equal income should pay the same amount of tax. We can and should agree that any tax system should not unequally tax individuals with both equal consumption and equal income.

Think of two competing principles as two points in space. An infinite number of points represent a compromise between these two points. But there is a subset of points that make up the line stretching between the two original points. The points on this line represent the minimum total distance from the original points and represent an array of compromises that make more sense than the myriad other points floating about in the space. The points not on the line between the two points of principle can then be rejected as being too far from both the principles. That is, compared with these "rejected" points, it is always possible to find points on the line that are closer to at least one principle without being farther from the other.[15]

The error of the more specific attack, the one more commonly expressed by many economists, proceeds from several sources. Surely economists are trained to understand efficiency. That training, however, no more detracts from their ability to consider equity than does medical training prevent a doctor from examining mind and body. In fact, economists' training prepares them to examine equity issues because their analytical techniques emphasize understanding and quantifying relationships, approaches that can easily be applied to considerations of which individuals are equal and which individuals are not.

Economists' study of efficiency also allows them to spot the inconsistencies in purported theories of equity. For example, one theory espoused in different forms is that government actions must be judged first on what they do for the poor.[16] While this principle sounds idealistic, economists recognize that at times it disregards the value of transactions among people, including the nonpoor, that make the parties to the transactions better-off without making anyone else worse off.

This second attack on equity, of course, is concentrated particularly on vertical equity or progressivity itself, where qualitative judgment is a necessity. However, that people care about equity, including progressivity, should be recognized, in the language of economists, as a "revealed preference." If people want to pay for justice—for example, by preventing the poor from starving—then why should this valued service be downgraded relative to other consumption desires? Why should the demand for steel in cars be considered a higher point of inquiry than the demand for poverty relief? Once equity is recognized as having a value which people are willing to sacrifice resources for, then it becomes an issue of efficiency as well.

Examining how different equity goals can be met efficiently requires considerable effort. For example, governments often attempt to target programs toward the poor and must develop least-cost options. In designing many programs aimed at improving equity, the efficiency aspects of both implicit and explicit tax rates need to be examined. And any government consideration of interfering in imperfect markets requires some understanding of both potential equity and efficiency consequences.

Having gone so far to oppose those iconoclasts who would remove equity as a standard, let's go one step further. There is a notion, sometimes taken from a book by Arthur Okun (1975), that equity and efficiency require a "big trade-off." Yet, the analysis here suggests that such a trade-off often is not required, and equity and efficiency often go hand in hand. Consider, in order, individual equity, horizontal equity, and progressivity. Individual equity emphasizes that we are entitled to the rewards of our efforts and from the trades and transactions that we make and thus is closely related to traditional market notions of efficiency. Horizontal equity and efficiency, however, are also linked. The equal tax treatment of different sources of income, for example, often leads to both equity and efficiency gains by simultaneously taxing those with equal incomes equally and removing tax-induced distortions. Finally, the pursuit of progressivity, adequately balanced against claims of individual equity and efficiency, is nothing more than the pursuit of the good society in the end, and a good society is going to be efficient and richer in the broadest sense of that word.

Can the last point be proven? No. From one perspective, it requires a holistic, rather than individualistic, view of humanity—a view that no part of the societal organism is totally independent from the other parts. Of course, the pursuit of progressivity is fraught with costs and dangers, which is why it must always be balanced against other principles.

The final claim that progressivity and efficiency must at least be considered together derives from the demand for equity already discussed. Equity is a service for which individuals reveal a preference, and like all services, it should be provided efficiently.

In sum, despite many sources of complexity, equity principles are the first standard against which policy is assessed and judged. Put simply, our democratic world cannot be otherwise. True, equity might be ignored at certain times and in certain legislation. Certainly, much bad policy today derives from nothing more than an inadequate consideration of the demand for equal justice. And the tension between vertical and individual equity will always remain. Yet, the standard of equity simply cannot be ignored for long or the bounds of inequity pushed too far. Equity will always reassert its rightful place as the first and most basic set of principles applied to constitutions and laws.

NOTES

1. Lewis is basically arguing for a natural law of morality, but his examples constantly seem to reflect some equity standard. See Lewis (1943, 17).

2. See, for example, Musgrave and Musgrave (1976) and Musgrave (1959, 1985, and 1996).

3. Again, see Musgrave (1959, 60–61, 90–115) for a useful summary.

4. In theory, economists will extend this notion to argue that those who start out with equal "utility" or well-being should end up with the same utility after the imposition of the tax.

5. See Musgrave (1959, 160).

6. For a discussion of the dependent vs. independent nature of vertical equity, see Musgrave (1990). See also Musgrave's earlier argument that horizontal and vertical equity are "different sides of the same coin. If there is no specified reason for discriminating among unequals, how can there be a reason for avoiding discrimination among equals?" (1959, 160). See also Kaplow (1989).

7. For example, in 1919, Erik Lindahl (1958) suggested that political processes substitute for the market economy and determine a price for public goods based on marginal benefits received.

8. Richard Musgrave has suggested that Smith "rather ingeniously combined both benefit and ability-to-pay considerations in one dictum" (1996, 344). In another article, Musgrave tried to clarify the meaning of Smith's statement on benefits and burdens. "Smith might have indeed wanted to have it both ways, or he might have been aware

(if not stating so explicitly) that the ability and benefit doctrines may be linked via the income elasticity of demand for public goods. His ability-to-pay rule could then be viewed as a prescription for benefit taxation" (1990, 114).

9. For a good textbook discussion of both "free riders" and "moral hazards," see Rosen (1999, 69–70, 206–8).

10. See Steuerle and Bakija (1994, chapter 2). Of course, social insurance has also been used politically as a vague term to justify redistributive policies, whether well designed or not.

11. This passage omits many other issues related to social insurance, such as how much rising levels of transfers from future generations can be used to somehow protect earlier generations and whether mandated contributions are really saved.

12. See contributions to this book by Richard Musgrave, Barbara Fried, and Dennis J. Ventry Jr.

13. It is notable, for instance, that Margaret Thatcher finally lost her position as prime minister of Great Britain not long after proposing a type of head tax as a substitute merely for one small part of the British tax system.

14. See Steuerle (1980). See also Daniel Shaviro's contribution to this book.

15. One can go on with this mathematical analogy when three legitimate principles compete. Three points form a plane, but there is even more space in the three-dimensional space outside the interior part of the plane that is formed by connecting the points. By thinking rigorously about the competing principles, one can remove options not lying within the plane.

16. See Rawls (1971, 83), where, among other places, he argues that "social and economic inequalities are to be arranged so that they are . . . to the greatest benefit of the least advantaged." Religions often make claims here as well, as in the case of the "preferential option for the poor" put forward by Roman Catholic bishops. See also Steuerle (2000).

REFERENCES

Blum, Walter J., and Harry Kalven Jr. 1953. *The Uneasy Case for Progressive Taxation.* Chicago: University of Chicago Press.

Brownlee, W. Elliot. 2000. "Historical Perspectives on U.S. Tax Policy toward the Rich." In *Does Atlas Shrug? The Economic Consequences of Taxing the Rich,* edited by Joel B. Slemrod (29–73). New York and Cambridge: Russell Sage Foundation and Harvard University Press.

Kaplow, Louis. 1989. "Horizontal Equity: Measures in Search of a Principle." *National Tax Journal* 42 (2, June): 139–54.

Lewis, C. S. 1943. *Mere Christianity.* New York: Macmillan. (Collier Books paperback edition.)

Lindahl, Erik. 1958. "Just Taxation—A Positive Solution." In *Classics in the Theory of Public Finance,* edited by Richard A. Musgrave and Alan T. Peacock (168–76). London: Macmillan.

Lutz, Harley. 1945. *Guideposts to a Free Economy.* New York: McGraw-Hill

Musgrave, Richard A. 1959. *The Theory of Public Finance.* New York: McGraw-Hill.

————. 1985. "Public Finance and Distributive Justice." *In Public Choice, Public Finance, and Public Policy: Essays in Honour of Alan Peacock,* edited by David Greenaway and G. K. Shaw (1–14). Oxford: Basil Blackwell Ltd.

————. 1990. "Horizontal Equity, Once More." *National Tax Journal* 43 (2 June): 113–22.

————. 1996. "Progressive Taxation, Equity, and Tax Design." In *Tax Progressivity and Income Inequality,* edited by Joel B. Slemrod (341–56). Cambridge: Cambridge University Press.

Musgrave, Richard A., and Peggy B. Musgrave. 1976. *Public Finance in Theory and Practice.* New York: McGraw-Hill.

Okun, Arthur. 1975. *Equality and Efficiency: The Big Tradeoff.* Washington, D.C.: The Brookings Institution Press.

Rawls, John. 1971. *A Theory of Justice.* Cambridge: Harvard University Press, Belknap Press.

Rosen, Harvey S. 1999. *Public Finance,* 5th ed. Boston: McGraw-Hill.

Simons, Henry C. 1938. *Personal Income Taxation: The Definition of Income as a Problem of Fiscal Policy.* Chicago: University of Chicago Press.

Smith, Adam. 1904. *An Inquiry into the Nature and Causes of the Wealth of Nations,* edited by Edwin Cannan. Vol. II. London: Cambridge University Press.

Stein, Herb. 1959. "What's Wrong with the Federal Tax System?" U.S. Congress. House. Committee on Ways and Means. *Tax Revision Compendium: Compendium of Papers on Broadening the Tax Base.* Vol. 1. Washington, D.C.: U.S. Government Printing Office.

Steuerle, C. Eugene. 1980. "Equity and the Taxation of Wealth Transfers." *Tax Notes* (September 8): 459–64.

————. 2000. "Social Security and the Preferential Option for the Poor." *America* (October 23): 8–11.

Steuerle, C. Eugene, and Jon M. Bakija. 1994. *Retooling Social Security for the 21st Century: Right and Wrong Approaches to Reform.* Washington, D.C.: Urban Institute Press.

About the Editors

Joseph J. Thorndike is director of the Tax History Project at Tax Analysts and a contributing editor for *Tax Notes* magazine. His recent publications include articles on the Civil War income tax, the history of Internal Revenue Service reform, and the tax ideology of Franklin Roosevelt. He is currently writing a history of federal taxation during the Great Depression and World War II.

Dennis J. Ventry Jr. is the Lawrence Lederman/Milbank Tweed Fellow in Law and Business at the New York University School of Law and associate director of the Tax History Project at Tax Analysts. He was previously a research fellow at the Brookings Institution and a visiting fellow at Harvard University. He has published and lectured on various tax issues, including the earned income tax credit, negative income taxation, the estate and gift tax, family taxation, and the tax expenditure budget. He is currently completing a study of the treatment of marriage under the U.S. federal income tax.

About the Contributors

W. Elliot Brownlee is professor emeritus in the Department of History at the University of California, Santa Barbara. He is a specialist in economic history and the history of public finance, and is the author of *Federal Taxation in America: A Short History* (Woodrow Wilson Center Press and Cambridge University Press, 1966). He is currently writing a history of the financing of World War I and editing a book on Ronald Reagan's presidency.

David Brunori is a contributing editor for *State Tax Notes* magazine and the author of "The Politics of State Taxation," a weekly column on state tax and budget politics. He is a research professor of public policy at the George Washington University, where he also teaches state and local tax law at the university's law school. His recent books include *State Tax Policy: A Political Perspective* (2001) and *The Future of State Taxation* (1998), both published by the Urban Institute Press.

Barbara H. Fried is professor of law and Deane Johnson Faculty Scholar at Stanford Law School. She has written extensively on tax policy and issues of distributive justice. She is the author of *The Progressive Assault on Laissez Faire* (Harvard University Press, 1998), an intellectual history of the law and economics movement in the early part of the 20th century.

Carolyn C. Jones is a professor of law at the University of Connecticut School of Law. Her research focuses on the legal history of taxation in the United States. She has written articles on such subjects as the development of the joint return, the use of public relations in selling the mass federal income tax, and taxation arguments in the woman suffrage movement.

Richard A. Musgrave worked at the Federal Reserve Board during the 1940s, taught at the University of Michigan during the 1950s, and retired from Harvard University in 1980. He is now an adjunct professor at the University of California, Santa Cruz. His major publications include *The Theory of Public Finance* (McGraw-Hill, 1959), *Public Finance in Theory and Practice,* with P. B. Musgrave (McGraw-Hill, 1973), and *Public Finance in a Democratic Society—Collected Papers* (New York University Press, 1986–2000). Along with academic pursuits, he has been an active participant in public affairs and the conduct of tax missions in developing countries.

Daniel Shaviro is professor of law at New York University Law School. His research interests include tax policy, public economics, social insurance, and budget policy. His recent publications include *Do Deficits Matter?* (1997), *When Rules Change* (2000), and *Making Sense of Social Security Reform* (2000), all published by the University of Chicago Press.

C. Eugene Steuerle is a senior fellow at the Urban Institute, a columnist for *Tax Notes* magazine, president of the National Tax Association (2001–2002), and a former deputy assistant secretary of the Treasury for tax analysis. His books include *Social Security and the Family,* with Melissa Favreault and Frank Sammartino (2002), and *Nonprofits and Government,* with Elizabeth Boris (1999), both published by the Urban Institute Press.

Joan M. Youngman is a senior fellow at the Lincoln Institute of Land Policy, where she chairs the Department of Valuation and Taxation. She is also a research fellow at the Harvard Law School International Tax Program. She has written extensively on property tax issues, and is the author of *Legal Issues in Property Valuation and Taxation* (International Association of Assessing Officers, 1994).

Index

tax incentives, targeted, 196, 197
  ending the use of, 211–212
tax justice. *See also specific topics*
  1860 to 1945, 29–34
  struggle for, 206–209
tax preferences, 38
tax reform, 40, 45. *See also* liberalism;
    progressivity
  current issues in, 17–23
  opportunities for, 209
    challenging the conventional view,
      210–211
Tax Reform Act of 1969, 50
Tax Reform Act of 1986, 50, 81
tax reform movements, 57
tax reformers, 45–46, 59
tax revolts, 57
tax simplification, 19
tax sources, diversity in, 200–201
tax-transfer policy, 136, 142
transfer branch of government,
    188–189n.44
transfers, government's making, 262
"trickle-down" theory of economics, 42
two-bracket system, 18

"Uneasy Case for Progressive Taxation,
    The" (Blum and Kalven 1952), 95
Uneasy Case for Progressive Taxation, The
    (Blum and Kalven 1953), 1, 49
unlimited savings allowance (USA), 18
unlimited savings allowance (USA) tax, 3,
    20
upper-income individuals, taxing, 52, 58,
    77
  mobilization for World War I and,
    78–79
  mobilizing for World War II and, 80
  reductions in early 1980s, 81–86
  rollback of, post-World War I, 79
  slow reduction in, post-World War I,
    80–81
  "soaking the rich," 71, 72, 76, 78, 82, 87
  three waves of, in Great Depression,
    79–80

utilitarian sacrifice theory, 264
utilitarianism, 14–16, 137, 141
utility of dollars, 177

vacation homes, 231
value-added tax (VAT), 272–273
Vermont school finance, 245, 249n.11
vertical equity, 3, 9–10. *See also*
    progressivity
  government efforts to promote, 261
  vs. horizontal equity, 44, 61, 63n.2,
    257–260
  vs. individual equity, 260–263
votes, budget, 13
voting, tax expenditure, 13
  by ballot *vs.* "by foot," 12–13, 22
voting requirements, supermajority,
    203–204

wage-income base, change to, 21–22
wage payments, exclusion of, 21
wage-rate analysis, 131–132
wage taxes, 272
Warren, Alvin C., 123
wealthy persons. *See* upper-income
    individuals
welfarism, 140
  egalitarian, 146n.24
welfarist perspective, 126, 142. *See also*
    under inequality measures; social
    welfare
  taxing "endowment" from, 136–140
  "weighted," 137
West Virginia, 239–240
Williamson, Jeffrey G., 82
Wilson, Woodrow, 31, 32
Wilson administration, 32
Wisconsin income tax of 1911, 84
women. *See also* stay-at-home spouses
  working, 139
World Council of Churches (WCC), 97
World War I, mobilization for, 78–79
World War II, 88, 99
  mobilizing for, 80